TAIWAN'S POLITICS:

The Provincial Assemblyman's World

Arthur J. Lerman
Baruch College
City University of New York

University Press of America

Library of Congress Catalog Card Number: 78-64524

For Charles Griffith Nelson (1940-1978)

> L'homme n'est qu'un roseau,
> le plus faible de la nature;
> mais c'est un roseau pensant.

> —Blaise Pascal

CONTENTS

v

ACKNOWLEDGMENTS

This book could not have been written without intellectual and emotional support from a number of people. Among these, I would especially like to acknowledge support from the members of the third-term Taiwan Provincial Assembly, as well as from the many other people on Taiwan who extended their hospitality to me and taught me so much; from Lawrence W. Crissman, Donald R. DeGlopper, Stephan Feuchtwang, Jerry A. Fowler, Bernard Gallin, J. Bruce Jacobs, David K. Jordan, and Arthur P. Wolf, eight brilliant observers who immersed themselves in Taiwan's society, subsequently teaching me almost as much as the Assembly members did; from my colleagues and students in the Political Science Department of Baruch College, City University of New York, for their patience with a professor who kept slighting his departmental and classroom responsibilities in order to complete his book; and from J. Bruce Jacobs (again) and Richard W. Wilson for reading and carefully criticizing earlier versions of the manuscript.

The most meticulous reader of the manuscript was Susan M. Cohen, who deserves acknowledgment for editing and proofreading, forcing my prose into grammatical, logical, and readable bounds. Acknowledgment must also be given to my mother and sister for their support, and to my father for his support as well as for his proofreading. Regarding my wife, Sabrina Siang-chün Lee, in addition to a great appreciation for her willingness and ability to endure the emotional stress that writing a book places upon a family, there is acknowledgment for reading, criticizing, typing, repeatedly retyping, and proofreading the entire manuscript.

Finally, a special acknowledgment to the professor who taught the interviewing skills that enabled me to go into another country and learn about its politics. Following his advice I did my best to be cordial, frank, courteous, temperate, and deferential, thus obtaining the information that fills the following pages.

*   *   *

INTRODUCTION

For one hardened to the sight of Taiwan's gray skies and gray buildings, overlooking the noisy chaotic struggle of bicycles, motorcycles, taxis, and private cars, all kicking up enormous amounts of gray dust from gray streets, the parklike grounds of the Taiwan Provincial Assembly are a sumptuous feast for the eyes. On the Assembly grounds, the gray chaos of Taiwan's urban centers fades from the mind, as one strolls in the peace and quiet of shade-giving palm trees, past the fragrance of techni-colored flower gardens, coming to rest beside the silence of a secluded pond.

At the end of a road lined with palm trees, behind a circle of green grass, upon which stand the flags of the Republic of China, Taiwan Province, and the flags of each of Taiwan's counties and provincial cities, is the Assembly meeting hall. Under its dome sit the seventy-odd members of the Taiwan Provincial Assembly.

Linguistically most of the members speak the Minnan dialect of Amoy, the language their ancestors took with them during their prenineteenth-century emigration from the Chinese mainland. A smaller group speaks the Hakka dialect, reflecting their particular mainland origins. A few of the members speak Mandarin, emphasizing an identification with the mainlanders who retreated to the island in the wake of the Communist victory. Even lan-guages related to Malay are spoken in the Assembly by the members who represent Taiwan's non-Chinese aborigines.

Geographically members can be described as mainland-ers, those who have just come to Taiwan; half-mainlanders, Minnan or Hakka members whose families left Taiwan to live on the mainland during the 1895-1945 period of Japanese rule; and those of Japanese background, members who grew up on Taiwan under the Japanese and received their education in Taiwan or Japan.

Studies of legislatures usually stress the impor-tance of the relationship of individual members to po-litical parties. In Taiwan's Provincial Assembly, almost all the assemblymen are members of the Nationalist (Kuomin) Party (tang). Still, as with other legislatures with one dominant party, the following categories are useful for description: members belonging to mutually opposed

1

factions internal to the dominant party, party members
neutral in the party's factional struggles, and members
unaffiliated with the dominant party. Also useful are
categories not tied to legislatures with one dominant
party--namely, party leaders, regular party members, and
independent party members.

Categories for the description of other types of behavior are also helpful. Through them the Taiwan Provincial Assembly's subject experts, conscientious members,
bored members, good bargainers, clever compromisers,
friendly colleagues, members distinguished by their ability
to take the lead in and channel debate at crucial junctures,
"big cannons" who specialize in scolding the government
for its shortcomings, and the one or two members who would
rather physically beat up their opponents than rely on
scolding are revealed.

Just as descriptive, but less a matter of behavior
than a reflection of other characteristics, the categories of women members, members who are terribly busy
with their enterprises outside the Assembly (enterprises
that probably have made them very rich), members who have
little to do besides fulfilling their role as provincial
assemblymen (and perhaps, because of lack of enterprises
outside the Assembly to be busy with, are relatively poor),
and all those members who hold medical degrees, taken
together, round out the categorization of the Taiwan
provincial assemblymen.

As with any legislature, the assemblymen do not meet
in a vacuum. This is made evident in Taiwan by the physical setting immediately surrounding the members' seats.
Directly in front of the assemblymen is a long curved table,
where staff members sit busily recording the debates and
arranging material relevant to matters soon to be brought
to the floor. Immediately behind the staff is a raised
platform, where those reporting to the Assembly stand.
Behind this platform, raised to even greater heights,
is the speaker's chair. On his right hand, at a slightly
lower level, is the chair of the deputy speaker. On the
left, level with the deputy speaker's chair, sits the
secretary general, the official in charge of all the
secretarial operations of the Assembly.

To the right and to the left of the staff desk the
government benches are arranged facing the assemblymen.

2

To these benches come the officials of the various provincial government departments and bureaus. There they use the Mandarin dialect to argue for the passing of the resolutions and budget items they support and to defend their policies from the criticisms of the Amoy-speaking assemblymen. On the left the government bench continues to curve until it reaches halfway around the meeting hall. But on the right it ends abruptly and is continued on a lower level by a press table, where reporters from Taiwan's many newspapers gather news for the next edition.

If physical level of seats means something, then one might guess that most legislatures are the ultimate in democratic institutions--this because the galleries where ordinary people come in to watch their representatives debate and vote are almost always physically at a higher level than the floor of the legislature itself. In Taiwan the galleries are set above, though to the rear, of the floor. Here, as with the members on the floor, it is worthwhile to find categories with which to describe some of the types of people who fill these galleries.

For present purposes, the most important category is the assemblyman's constituents. This category is further divisible into such groups of constituents as those from the assemblyman's home town; those from his local political faction; those from his family, relatives, and friendship groups; those from interest groups, such as the Farmers' Association and the Fishermen's Association; and those from the firm that the assemblyman owns or in which he is employed.

Although the government officials are assigned seats at the government benches, the members of the press at the press table, each assemblyman at his desk, and constituents in the galleries, relationships need not be so formalized. An assemblyman motioning to a constituent in the gallery to meet him outside the chamber or an assemblyman and a government official walking to the exit together are common sights. And once outside the chamber, the halls are lined with numerous sitting rooms where men and women fitting into all of the above categories mix together in discussion.

A covered walk takes one to the library, which contains committee meeting rooms. As in many legislatures, the members of the Assembly spend much of their time not in the main chamber but in these rooms, preparing bills and reports for action on the floor. Meaningful categories with which to describe the committees follow the formal organization chart of the Assembly. A well-made chart would emphasize the role of some committees--such as the Committes on Transportation, Civil Affairs, Agriculture and Forestry, and Budget Coordination--but would not emphasize others--such as the Committee on Rules or the Committee on Discipline.

If one continues walking, the library is soon left behind, and one enters directly into the dormitory where the assemblymen stay while the Assembly is in session. The dormitory rooms, along with the dining room and additional sitting rooms, not only serve as a place of rest and work for the individual assemblymen but also, as with the sitting rooms that line the halls of the legislative chamber, are places where the various actors connected with the Assembly can get together for informal discussions.

At night, when many of the actors in the Provincial Assembly system leave, either to go home or to entertain and be entertained in Taichung City, some of these rooms become the center of games of Mah-jongg--young assemblymen in one room, the Hakka Mah-jongg circle in a second, old-age and women's Mah-jongg in a third, a fourth room for some core members of the Transportation Committee, and a few other rooms where nonmembers who have business before the Assembly are said to be invited in to lose money to the assemblymen.

After one walks out of the dormitory toward the bus stop near the flower garden, the tour of the Assembly buildings now finished, the environment of the assemblymen has really not been completely sketched in without looking closely at the hill that rises behind the Assembly grounds and, stretching one's imagination, noticing, perhaps by the tiny pavilion on the left, about halfway up, the eyes of the Central Government carefully surveying all the activity just described. Raising one's gaze to the top of the hill, one notices a second pair of eyes-- the eyes of the Central Committee of the Nationalist Party--surveying the eyes of the Central Government as well as what the Central Government is surveying. Finally, as the bus pulls out for Taichung City, one can imagine the mysterious cloaked figure from the national security

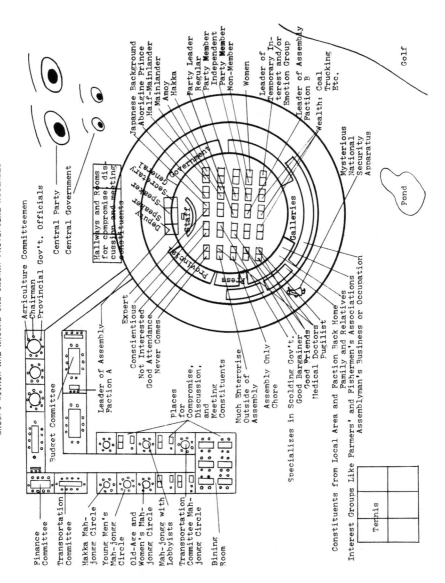

GROUPS WITHIN AND AROUND THE TAIWAN PROVINCIAL ASSEMBLY

5

apparatus disappearing behind a tree, which completes
the picture.

*   *   *

This study will concentrate on the political environment in which the provincial assemblymen carry on their
activities. The conception used here of the political
environment in which any group of assemblymen carry on
their activities has been formed by such legislative
studies as those by Donald R. Matthews, Charles L. Clapp,
and John C. Wahlke,[1] in conjunction with a combination
of the group and systems approaches. The latter two are
organizing devices frequently used by political scientists.

Under these sources of influence, the political environment of Taiwan's provincial assemblymen can be con-
ceived of as a system of groups centered around influenc-
ing--and being influenced by--the individual assemblymen.
The bulk of this study examines each group in the system
as it is related to the individual assemblymen.

For purposes of analysis, the groups that together
form the political environment of the provincial assemblymen have been divided into three categories. The first
category, dealt with in Part I, is composed of groups that
center themselves around support for or opposition to
Taiwan's governing elite. These include the mainlanders,
the minority of Taiwan's population that most enthusiastically supports the governing elite; the elite's Nationalist (Kuomin) Party (tang), as it appears on the central
and the local levels; the government, as it appears on
both levels; the governing elite's supporters within the
Provincial Assembly; and the opposition to the governing
elite, as it appears inside and outside of the Assembly.

The second category, dealt with in Part II, introduces
groups that center themselves around competition for local
political resources. Although there is much overlapping
of membership between these local groups and the elite-
related groups in the first category, the roles actors
play in the local groups are informed by different goals
and techniques than are the roles played by these same
actors in the elite-related groups. These local groups
are the local electoral faction, the lineage, the in-laws,
the surname group and clan, the territorial group, the
ethnolinguistic group, the friendship group, and the cere-

6

monial brotherhood. For convenience, the Assembly faction
is also dealt with in Part II.

The third category of groups, introduced in Part III,
contains those that have been stimulated into existence
by economic development. These groups are the assemblyman's own economic enterprises, economic enterprises that
hire assemblymen to represent them, economic enterprises
that must influence assemblymen indirectly because they
cannot hire their own assemblyman, and Taiwan's govern-
ment-sponsored people's associations.

In analyzing the assemblymen's relationships to these
various groups, four approaches to the study of Taiwan
are used--approaches that analysts have frequently used
individually but that they have rarely used in combination.
Thus, the most popular approach to the study of Taiwan--
the conceptualization of Taiwan's politics as a confrontation between the mainlander-supported governing elite
and the Taiwanese--has been supplemented with the work
of anthropologists, who have shown that the Taiwanese
comprise a complex group of people and are not simply a
homogeneous mass to be conveniently set off against the
governing elite. To these two approaches have been
added insights into the effect of economic development
on Taiwanese political behavior; and finally, most tenta-
tively, psychological theories (really guesses) concerning
Chinese political behavior, which appeared to add depth
to the above approaches, have been introduced.

In Part IV of this study, the three categories of
groups and the four approaches to the study of Taiwan are
brought together in a general model of democratic political
development. This model provides an explanatory description of a large number of historical and contemporary
political systems that share the characteristics of Taiwan's
political system. According to this model, Taiwan's political system is now in a fledgling stage of democratic
development through which many established democratic
systems have passed, through which some democratic systems
are now passing, and during which many fledgling democratic
systems were truncated by power elites that found the
characteristics of the developing democracies intolerable.

*   *   *

Given the focus on groups centered around influencing

7

and being influenced by Taiwan's elected assemblymen and given the placing of Taiwan's assemblymen interest-group system in the context of a general model of Western-style electoral democracy in its fledgling stages, the main comparative referents for this study will be historical and contemporary political systems that share the Taiwan political system's fledgling, Western-style, electoral-democratic characteristics. Therefore, although this study will frequently be dealing with political behavior that is unquestionably Chinese, the reader should be aware that the Western-style electoral-democratic referents of this study will rarely lead to comparisons with politics as it is now carried on in contemporary mainland China.

The reader should also be aware that the great bulk of the research for this study was completed before the 1971-1972 explosion of events, which included "ping-pong" diplomacy, former U.S. President Richard Nixon's visit to mainland China, and the expulsion of Taiwan's government from the United Nations. In general, Taiwan's political system has not changed significantly since the early 1970s, and this study does indicate where it has been changing. Unless specifically stated, however, what is being described is Taiwan's political system as it existed in a period of internal prosperity and stability, and wide-ranging international acceptance, before the events of the early 1970s shocked all of Taiwan's inhabitants--elite and mass, mainlander and Taiwanese--into a greater unity and shocked Taiwan's governing elite into greater (if still hesitant) attempts to open up the political system to more participation by the Taiwanese within a more democratic atmosphere.

In terms of research methods, the evidence for much of what is reported in this study came from interviews. These interviews, taking the form of informal conversations, were guided by a standardized series of questions in combination with a feel for the most productive line of questioning at a given moment. Interviews ranged from single hour-long sessions in the relatively formal atmosphere of an interviewee's office to repeated informal contacts in a variety of surroundings, often including the interviewee's own home. In all, hundreds of hours were spent in Taiwan's various counties and cities conversing with provincial, county, and city assemblymen; provincial, county, and city assembly staff workers; citizens active in local political campaigns; local newspaper reporters;

government and party officials from the central, provincial, and county-city levels; local and foreign social scientists; and foreign officials stationed in Taiwan. Many hours were also spent in talks with members of Taipei's mainlander community.

Because evidence from these interviews stands behind most assertions in this study, because of the need to save space, and because it will often be inappropriate to reveal information concerning the time or place of interviews and the identity of interviewees, footnote citations will usually be limited to those sources that bolster or expand upon interview evidence. The reader may assume that interview evidence stands behind all unfootnoted assertions and quotations.

PART I

GROUPS SUPPORTING OR OPPOSING TAIWAN'S GOVERNING ELITE
AS FACTORS IN THE PROVINCIAL ASSEMBLYMEN'S ENVIRONMENT

Part I presents those groups that are centered around
support for or opposition to Taiwan's governing elite.
In the Provincial Assembly hall, representatives of these
groups are found concentrated at the seats of the assemblymen and facing the assemblymen from the government
benches. One can also imagine them surveying the Assembly
grounds from the hill that rises behind the Assembly hall
and lurking behind the nearby trees and bushes.

Of the four approaches to the study of Taiwan, the
most appropriate in analyzing these groups conceives of
Taiwan's politics as a confrontation between the governing
elite and the Taiwanese. Thus, Part I introduces the
mainlanders, the minority of Taiwan's population that most
enthusiastically supports the governing elite; the elite's
Kuomintang (KMT), as it appears on the central and the
local levels; the KMT-controlled government, as it appears
on both levels; the governing elite's supporters within
the Provincial Assembly; and the opposition to the governing elite, as it appears inside and outside of the Assembly.

Chapter 1

THE GOVERNING ELITE'S SUPPORTERS

The Average Mainlander

In order to control a political system's most powerful offices--through electoral or nonelectoral means--a
governing elite must have enthusiastic support from at
least some part of the governed population. Taiwan's
governing elite, which originally governed on the Chinese
mainland, receives its most enthusiastic support from
individuals now on Taiwan who had lived under its rule on
the mainland. These people, politely known as <u>wai-sheng</u>
<u>jen</u> (outside province people), less politely known as
barbarians or mountain people, were either transferred

11

to Taiwan to take over the government after the Japanese surrendered in 1945 or fled to the island after the 1949 Communist victory. Together with their children there are approximately 2½ million mainlanders on Taiwan today.

Many of Taiwan's mainlanders are not representative of the general Chinese population. Before coming to Taiwan, they had received Western-type educations and were brought close to the ideas of Christianity and modernity. Others are ordinary soldiers. Recruited from and representative of the general population, they had little formal education and less familiarity with such Western ideas as Christianity and modernity.

As a whole, the mainlanders did not become a rich ruling class, repressing and exploiting an improverished Taiwanese population. Many mainlanders insist that the farming people are better off. And if they exaggerate, it is true that business is very much in the hands of commercially oriented Taiwanese. Certainly most big businessmen are Taiwanese.[3]

Most mainlanders, educated and oriented toward government work, are less motivated or trained for commercial ventures. On Taiwan, they constitute a large proportion of the bureaucrats in the provincial and Central Governments and fill many positions as teachers and university professors. In general, they remind one of straight-salaried American families in the late 1940s, struggling to make the payments on the material goods of middle-class life (TV, motorscooters--automobile ownership is rare but growing--kitchen appliances to substitute for the increasingly more expensive maid), perhaps by having both husband and wife work, perhaps by having the husband hold down two jobs.[4]

It has been suggested that the overstaffing of the bureaucracy with mainlanders was necessary as a welfare measure to provide for the livelihood of the vast number of middle-class refugees. Such a measure, of course, could not help but tie the mainlanders even closer to the elite's regime.[5]

Although the salaries for bureaucrats and some teachers are sufficient for the maintenance of a middle-class lifestyle, retirement pay for these groups has been less adequate. Despite progress in this regard, many white-collar mainlanders still hang on to their jobs long after normal retirement age, blocking the advancement of younger people in their institutions.[6]

The soldiers, the other group of mainlanders, made a different type of adjustment to Taiwan. Ordered there by the governing elite, some of these men were drafted in Fukien and shipped across the straits moments before the final retreat.[7] Without formal educations, the soldiers often came to Taiwan as individuals, leaving family and possessions back home.[8]

While they were still in the service, the army was the closest thing most soldiers had to a family. Their loneliness affected their relations with those among whom they worked and lived.[9] As the troops aged, the government confronted the problem of integrating them into Taiwan's civilian society, often finding land for them to farm or economic development projects on which they could work. Many soldiers even found wives among the Taiwanese. The mainlander-Taiwanese families thus begun, plus the resettling of the soldiers in many parts of Taiwan, initiated a slight countertrend to Taiwan's prevalent social segregation between mainlanders and Taiwanese.

Although governmental efforts on behalf of the soldiers were relatively successful, few deactivated soldiers have attained the middle-class lifestyle of civilian mainlanders. There are even deactivated soldiers who have not been touched by these efforts. In general, however, these governmental efforts have provided additional incentive for retired servicemen to become strong supporters of the elite's government and of the government's current (1978) President, Chiang Ching-kuo, who has been especially identified with these efforts.[10]

As for those soldiers still in service, the bulk hold the rank of commissioned or noncommissioned officers. Most privates are young Taiwanese and the young sons of mainlanders. For these officers, poverty is still a threat. The budget of the overly large army provides little for the families of officers, commissioned or noncommissioned. Their plight is reflected in the actions of provincial assemblymen, who frequently call upon the government to improve the lot of these families.

Although the mainlanders--soldiers and white-collar

13

groups alike--are closer to poverty than to riches, they
have benefited greatly from Taiwan's growing economy.
Because the mainlanders lived under the governing elite
when China's economy was collapsing, they tend to attrib-
ute Taiwan's economic success to a marked improvement in
elite performance. Their appreciation for this improvement and their general gratefulness for living in a flour-
ishing economy both reinforce their support for the governing elite.

In a number of other respects, however, the psychological state of the mainlanders is a troubled one.
They have been living on Taiwan for a long period of time,
cut off from home, in a foreign province. Such a situation is much more disturbing to a Chinese, brought up
to identify closely with the traditional home town of his
ancestors (not necessarily the place he or his parents
were born), than it is to a mobile American. When a
Taiwan-born son of a mainlander is called a Taiwanese
by an American, the refusal to be so identified comes
strong and fast. The Taiwan-born mainlander quickly in-
sists that he is of the province of his ancestors.[11]

The above uncomfortableness is normal under any circumstances in China. But the circumstances in Taiwan are
abnormal. Although the passage of time and the drawing
together of Taiwan's population in response to the island's
increasing diplomatic isolation is progressively ameliorating the situation, mainlanders still fear physical harm
from their Taiwanese neighbors. This fear rises out of a
dangerous imbalance of government personnel. All high policy decisions affecting the lives of Taiwan's 13½ million
Taiwanese are made--and usually also carried out--by a
governing elite recruited from the 2½ million mainlanders.
The increasing numbers of Taiwanese in the government has
yet to change this imbalance noticeably.[12] The mainlanders
fear that the Taiwanese may sometime try to correct this
imbalance by force. And even if they physically survive
the correction, they still fear living under subsequent
Taiwanese rule.

These fears are heightened by stories about the 1947
Taiwanese revolt against mainland rule (the Erh Erh-pa,
February Twenty-Eight Incident). According to pro-Taiwanese sources, this was a time when mainland troops went about
the island not only slaughtering the indigenous Taiwanese
leadership but also indiscriminately killing anyone who

happened to be on the streets.[13]   The stories that mainlanders hear, however, are quite different.   The word
"hear" is important, since most mainlanders came to Taiwan
in 1949 or after; they themselves did not witness the
events.   It is said, for example, that all the Taiwanese
barbers plotted together to wait until the exact moment
when the clock struck the hour of revolt and then cut the
throats of the mainlanders they happened to be shaving at
the time.

Such tales serve to frighten the mainland community
into drawing even closer together and into separating itself even further from its Taiwanese neighbors.   And despite the growing tendency of the two groups to draw together in face of the increasingly threatening international
environment and despite the growing numbers of Taiwanese
in what before were exclusively mainlander positions, the
mainlander community is still very close together.   Given
identities of occupations, places of work, and places of
residence, as well as differences in regional dialect and
feelings of exile, the mainland community is ingrown enough
without the added stimulus of fear.   And this ingrownness
makes it even harder for Taiwanese to gain positions within
the group or to feel comfortable dealing with the group's
members.[14]

The differences between the two groups are reinforced
by mainlander opinions about the Taiwanese.   Previously
quite extreme, these opinions are continually moderating
under the influence of time and the heightened unity of
Taiwan's inhabitants.   As originally held, these opinions
posited that fifty years of Japanese rule has spoiled the
Taiwanese, leaving them with a slavelike mentality.   This
was especially thought to be the case for Taiwanese women.
The province itself was alleged to have been outside the
mainstream of current Chinese history and, therefore, to
be culturally and materially backward.[15]   Even now, after
many years of uplifting rule by "we educated experts"
from the mainland, Taiwanese are still considered by some
to be either simple peasants or uncouth businessmen.[16]
The academic background and traditional prejudices of the
mainlanders were clear as it was carefully explained to
this author that Taiwanese businessmen who manage to begin
from nothing and wind up with millions of dollars were not
necessarily capable.

Extreme versions of these opinions carried over to

15

the mainlanders' feelings about the Chinese cultural heritage. Given that the bulk of civilian mainlanders that came to Taiwan were educated and that most Taiwanese were not, the holders of these opinions saw themselves as the protectors of ancient Chinese tradition on an island of nonappreciation.[17] Nor did the mainlanders show much appreciation for Taiwan. Their deep homesickness fostered the belief that nothing Taiwan had to offer compared with what was on the mainland. Neither the scenery, the cities, nor the people of Taiwan could measure up to mainland standards.

One argument the mainlanders make--that given their low level of education, the Taiwanese are not ready for democracy--is worthy of further discussion, although not necessarily along the lines the mainlanders would follow. It is possible that some habits and customs shared by both the mainlanders and the Taiwanese will make the adoption of stable democracy difficult--for example, the Chinese difficulty of separating disagreements over policy issues from the complications of personal conflicts and loyalties. Such habits and customs are exemplified by the vehemence of factional disputes among the Taiwanese. The emotions involved in these disputes may overpower commitment to the behavior necessary for democracy--behavior that most Taiwanese politicians have learned well in over thirty years of practice at the local level.[18] No one can be certain that these habits and customs would destroy democracy if it was actually practiced more freely on Taiwan, but certainly a problem exists. More light will be shed on this problem later on in this analysis.

In addition to the mainlander's role as most enthusiastic supporter of the governing elite, the average mainlander also plays an important role in regard to Taiwan's subsystem of elections and elective offices. The population of civilian mainlanders is large enough and concentrated enough geographically so that a few mainlanders can always be elected to seats in Taiwan's various local assemblies.

For example, Taipei City, as the seat of the Central Government, is the home of many mainlander government workers. Many mainlanders also live in the surrounding Taipei County. They commute from the suburban county to the city, often on busses especially assigned to their respective departments and bureaus. Another example of

16

a concentration of mainland votes is in Tainan City. As a consequence, the Tainan City Council has what has been informally designated as a "mainland seat."[19] Indeed, near most government installations there will be officially provided lodgings housing a block of mainland votes.[20]

The votes of the civilian mainlanders are supplemented by the votes of the soldiers. Some claim that even the votes of Taiwanese soldiers can be counted on. The argument is that if the Taiwanese are in the military, all their actions, including voting, are subject to the orders of the base commander. If this is so, the elite's local KMT candidate would be delighted to have an army base in his district.[21]

Two additional sources of mainland votes are homes for disabled veterans and the very poor families of the mainland soldiers. Many constituencies have concentrations of these families. Often, since they are not a part of the Taiwanese social structure where they live, they become the deciding vote between otherwise equally balanced local factions.[22]

The Central Organization of the Kuomintang

In addition to enthusiastic support from at least some part of the governed population, in order to control a political system's most powerful offices, modern governing elites often depend upon political party organizations. On Taiwan, this organization is the Nationalist Party (KMT). The men and women in the central organs of this party, under the direction of the party's Director-General, Chiang Ching-kuo (Chiang K'ai-shek's son and successor),[23] form the core of Taiwan's governing elite.

One reason these men and women have been able to maintain themselves in power is that the party has armed them with a highly self-legitimizing version of modern Chinese history.[24] According to this version, the party's founder, Sun Yat-sen, conducted a series of legendary struggles to overthrow the "foreign" Manchus; to expel other foreign aggressors from Chinese territory; to establish a unified, democratic, economically sound nation; and to bring China to its rightful place of respect among the nations. Sun died after accomplishing only his first goal, the overthrowing of the Manchus.

17

Chiang K'ai-shek is seen as succeeding him to the leadership of the party and carrying on these struggles. The party's version of modern Chinese history credits Chiang with bringing a semblance of unity to the nation by defeating the warlords and decimating the Communists. Chiang is also credited with driving foreign aggressors from Chinese territory, especially the Japanese, and with laying the foundations for democracy, economic growth, and international respect.

Unfortunately, the party's version of history continues, because of a resurgence of Communist strength--a resurgence aided by the devastation caused by the Japanese, the perfidy of the Russians, and the naiveté of the Americans--Sun Yat-sen's revolution suffered a severe setback. The KMT, along with the Central Government it had created, was driven from all of its mainland provinces and was left with only the island province of Taiwan, plus a few islands off the coast of Fukien. On Taiwan, the central organization of the KMT and the Central Government had to crowd themselves in alongside the already existing provincial party and government.

The party sees these latter events as a tragedy not only for itself but also for all the Chinese people and for the civilized world at large. But, recalling the spirit of an earlier group of Chinese warriors (forced to retreat into the tiny state of Chü and almost annihilated before it counterattacked and completely defeated the enemy), the KMT has created an optimistic ideology out of its severe setback.[25] According to the KMT's optimism, the crowded conditions of both the Central Party and the Central Government existing together on the same island with the provincial party and government are temporary. Soon, with Taiwan supplying the initial striking force, the KMT will return to the mainland. The people there will rally around it, and together they will overthrow the hated Communists and resume building the China Sun Yat-sen dreamed of.[26]

Another reason the elite members in the KMT's central organs have been able to maintain themselves in power has to do with the organizational structure through which the counterattack is supposed to be effected. In 1924, after many setbacks and much disappointment, the present organizational structure of the KMT was adopted, with the aid of Russian advisers. These advisers helped reorganize

18

the floundering party along the lines of a typical Leninist
party, only substituting the ideology of Sun Yat-sen for
that of Karl Marx.

Thus, the party had a hierarchy of legislative con-
gresses and administrative committees beginning at the
district level and rising through county and provincial
levels to a national congress and secretariat, along
with provisions vesting the power of the national congress
in a central committee when the congress is in recess and
the power of the central committee in a standing committee
when the central committee is in recess. It provided
for party cells in all significant nonparty organizations
responsible for guiding these organizations and for reporting on their activities to the party. It also incorpo-
rated democratic centralism and a stated policy of toleration for the expression of individual opinions along with
strictures against organizing intraparty (factional)
support for one's opinions. The KMT retains this organization on Taiwan today.[27]

The Central Government

Basis of Legitimacy

As has been seen, the Central Government's offices
are controlled by Taiwan's governing elite through KMT
members holding office within the Central Government,
reporting back and responsible to the party. And these
officeholders justify their own--nonelectoral--power over
Taiwan through the KMT's self-legitimizing version of
Chinese history.

This justification is based on the claim that in
establishing the Central Government on the mainland, the
KMT followed democratic procedures allowing for the repre-
sentation of all of China's vast population. As the claim
is elaborated, through these procedures a truly representative constitutional assembly was convened in 1946, and
the current constitution of the Republic of China was
adopted.

Soon after, in accordance with the new constitution,
nationwide elections were held. In November, 1947, the
National Assembly, a combination of a constitutional
amendment convention and an electoral college, was elected

19

for a term of six years. In early 1948, a Legislative
Yuan, or Parliament, was elected for a term of three years,
and a Control Yuan, a body established to investigate and
oversee the operations of government, was chosen for a
six-year term. In its turn, the National Assembly followed
these elections by choosing the President and Vice-President
of the Republic. Both officers were chosen for six-year
terms. In this manner, the key elective offices of the
Central Government were filled.

Unfortunately, just as the government was being set
up on this legal and democratic foundation, a tragedy
occurred:

> Even before implementation of constitutional
> government, the Chinese Communists began their
> open rebellion. With the aid of international
> Communism, they succeeded in seizing the main-
> land in 1949. The only legal government of the
> Republic of China, deriving its just power from
> the people through popular election, had to
> move to Taiwan to continue the struggle.[28]

Given the governing elite's professed desire to
adhere to the principles of legality and democratic rep-
resentation for all citizens of China, the resurgence of
the Communists, driving the government from thirty-four
of its thirty-five provinces, left the governing elite
with a great dilemma: Until most of the lost thirty-four
provinces were retaken, how would it be possible to have
another set of elections when the original terms of elected
officials expired? It certainly would not be possible,
according to the elite's reasoning, to allow only those
people in the remaining province to elect the entire
national government. Citizens of Taiwan only have the
right to elect their own province's representatives;
they cannot elect representatives from Hunan or Shantung.

It was finally decided that the only way out of the
dilemma was to suspend general elections for the Central
Government, allowing those elected in 1947 and 1948 to
continue in office until new elections could be held on
the mainland.[29]

This decision, of course, had some problematical
consequences. First, no satisfactory method was provided
for replacing elected officials as the inexorable aging

20

process began to diminish their numbers. As a result, the membership of the Legislative Yuan has declined from 760 legislators to 434; the membership of the National Assembly, from 2,691 to 1,344; and the membership of the Control Yuan from 180 to 72.[30]

Second, this decision provided the governing elite with a legal- and democratic-sounding justification for perpetuating its control over the offices in Taiwan's Central Government. Although this may sound legal and democratic, however, it is electoral only in a historical sense, for it is not based on periodic votes of the Taiwanese. They were outvoted thirty-four provinces to one in 1947 and 1948. The 1947-1948 votes of the thirty-four provinces give the elite's representatives in the Central Government offices the right to rule the thirty-fifth province. And the logic of the argument can never permit the officeholders to stand for reelection before the Taiwanese electorate.

Three points are noteworthy with regard to this justification. The first is that originally the post-1949 arrangement left the Central Government of China with virtually the same territory to govern as the Taiwan provincial government had. Only the tiny island groups of Quemoy and Matsu remained outside Taiwan Province, under the nominal control of the Fukien provincial government. This caused many problems with regard to unclear lines of power and responsibility, as well as too much government and too many governors.

On July 1, 1967, however, Taipei City was administratively removed from Taiwan Province by the Central Government and raised to the status of a province itself, as a special municipality. Many reasons were given for this action. According to the government, the following is the explanation:

> According to Article 4 of the City Organization Law promulgated by the National Government, a city can be elevated to a special city if it meets one of these three tests:
> 1. Seat of the Central Government,
> 2. Population of over 1,000,000,
> 3. Possessing special political, economic and cultural importance.
> Taipei fulfills all three requirements . . .[31]

21

More cynical reasoning has it that the people of Taipei
had too frequently elected the anti-KMT candidate as
mayor; thus, the city's status was changed to prevent
this from recurring.[32] (Mayors of special municipalities,
and governors of provinces, are appointed by the Central
Government.) Cynics further argue that by dividing the
island into two administrative jurisdictions, each forced
to compete with the other for scarce resources parceled
out by the Central Government, the Taiwanese would be
easier to divide and rule.

Another possible reason for the changing of Taipei's
status is that the division of Taiwan into a province and
a municipality in a sense solves the problems created by
having a central government and a provincial government
overlapping on the same small island. With this change,
the Taiwan area becomes more like any normal country, with
a central government as the link and arbiter between the
country's provincial-level units. It can now fulfill the
normal central government functions of enforcer of inter-
province standards and leader in all united efforts.
Administratively the picture looks far more rational if
under a central government there is more than one significant provincial-level unit. It now can be argued that
there are two significant units under the Central Government. The argument can even be stretched to Quemoy and
Matsu and hold that there are three units. Rumor has it
that there may even be a fourth, since there may be plans
to take the city of Kao-hsiung out of Taiwan Province and
raise it to a special municipality also.

The second point with regard to the government's
justification of its rule is that, although the governing elite has remained firm in its decision to hold no
new elections for seats in the National Assembly, Legislative Yuan, and Control Yuan representing areas of China
now under Communist control, it has agreed to periodic
elections for those Taiwan, Quemoy, and Matsu seats that
have been vacated in these organs and for those extra
seats that Taiwan and the offshore islands now deserve
because of their increased population. Thus, although
very little new blood has flowed into the elective organs
of the Central Government since 1947-1948, since 1969
the still proportionately small Taiwan and offshore island
delegations to these organs have been kept at full complement through a series of elections.[33]

The third point relates to the great lengths to which the governing elite goes to legitimize its government on the international scene and to use whatever recognition it can obtain there to justify further to the people living on Taiwan its government's position as the legal, democratically elected government of all of China.

The government-published China Yearbooks give some indication of these efforts, extensively reporting any type of recognition that the Central Government obtains abroad. This reporting includes such major events as the visit of the government's (1967) Vice-President, C. K. Yen, to the United States; the visit of President Banda of Malawi to Taiwan; and the establishment of the World Anti-Communist League. The tone of this reporting is highly flattering and glorifies the Central Government's positions and spokespeople.34 Nor are minor events forgotten. The attendance of Vice-Minister of Foreign Affairs (1966) H. K. Yang at the independence ceremonies of Botswanaland and the visit of Luxembourg's Minister of Economic Affairs to Taiwan are also recorded.35

These reports are vividly presented to the people on Taiwan. On the cover of the January 27, 1968, issue of the weekly magazine Liao-wang Chou-k'an is a picture of Chiang K'ai-shek's son Wei-kuo giving a letter from Chiang to General Franco in Spain. And recent changes in American policy toward Communist China were reported at the bottom of the front page of the Central Daily News (Chung-yang Jih-pao). Most of the page was reserved for reporting the visit to Taiwan of President Mobutu of the Congo.36

Ground Rules for the Provincial Assembly

The KMT's self-legitimizing version of Chinese history, by justifying the control of the elite's party over the offices in the Central Government, has given the governing elite the right to determine the basic ground rules under which the Taiwan Provincial Assembly may exist.

Originally there was an authority higher than Taiwan's central governing elite that was supposed to determine the ground rules. This authority was the constitution. According to Article 112 of the constitution,

> A Province may convoke a Provincial Conven-
> tion to enact, in accordance with the General
> Principles of Provincial and Hsien [County]
> Self-Government, Provincial Self-Government
> Regulations, provided the said Regulations are
> not in conflict with the Constitution.[37]

The language of the constitution with regard to provincial assemblies was, of course, very general. Moreover,
it left much to be defined by ordinary legislation (i.e.,
the General Principles of Provincial and County Self-
Government). But, based on the sections of the constitution concerned with subnational government and glancing
at the actual experience of subnational government on
Taiwan,[38] one can envision the framers' intentions of
establishing a network of legislative assemblies, each
with its corresponding government.

These assemblies would begin with the lowest level of
(a) the neighborhood (lin), rise up step by step through
the increasingly inclusive levels of (b) the urban precinct
(li or ch'ü) or rural village (ts'un), (c) the county-
subordinated city (hsien-hsia shih) or less urbanized
township (chen) or rural district (hsiang), (d) the pro-
vince-subordinated city (sheng-hsia shih) or rural county
(hsien), and end with (e) the Central Government-subor-
dinated city (yüan-hsia shih) or more rural province
(sheng). In general, this network would be characterized
by assembly control over the government at its own level,
though the higher-level assemblies and governments would
retain authority over their lower-level counterparts.[39]

But the system just described, although based on the
generalities of the constitution, with hints gleaned from
the practice on Taiwan, is not the system as it really
exists. The governing elite is not acting according to
the constitution. Its government has never enacted the
General Principles of Provincial and County Self-Government.
Thus, there is nothing that a Provincial or County Convention can enact Provincial Self-Government Regulations
in accordance with.

The reason the General Principles have not been enacted
is expressed by Liu Yen-fu as follows:

> . . . first plan for the existence of the nation,
> and only later put into practice local self-

24

government. The main portion of the territory
of the Republic of China is on the mainland.
Taiwan Province does not come to more than a
group of faraway islands. It has only one-
sixtieth of the nation's population and only
one-one-thousandth of the nation's land area.
Of our more than ten million compatriots on
Taiwan, . . . there is not one who is not a
descendant of the Yellow Emperor. . . . How
is it possible to forget the retaking of the
mainland and the saving of our mainland compatriots?

Just at this time of desperate need to unify
strength to mobilize for counterattack, . . .
to increase democracy and promote self-government means for the local area to splinter its
strength . . . Every time there is a local election,
the conflict of factions, the battle of the
campaigns, the struggle of political parties,
although among brothers, it is as if the opposite
were so . . . Only the office currently being
contested is thought of. The great national
disasters are thrown to the back of the mind.
To expand the application of local self-government is just enough to tear apart the strength
needed to protect Taiwan and to counterattack
the mainland. . . .

. . . Where is the profit that the people have
obtained from the instituting of local self-
government? . . . Only pursuing the aggrandize-
ment of one's own power and endangering the security of the nation, how can this not aid the
bandits or the actions of the bandits? . . .

. . . the General Principles of Provincial and
County Self-Government is the unified standard
law of self-government for the entire country.
Naturally it is not possible to rely only on
Taiwan to enact them . . .

Finally, . . . in order to increase the effectiveness of the emergency mobilization provisions,
power limitations were placed on the Legislative Yuan in the hope that actions taken in
meeting emergency needs would not be obstructed

by the Legislative Yuan. While at the level
of the Central Government the use of the Legislative Yuan's power is still being limited,
how is it possible to broaden the provincial
legislative power at the provincial level?40

Instead of the Legislative Yuan's enacting the General Principles called for in the constitution, the provincial and local governments of Taiwan were established
through orders of the Executive Branch (Yuan) of the Central
Government, with the status of an experimental pilot
project. 41

Despite this shaky foundation, however, the actual
legal powers of the Provincial Assembly do not appear
unreasonably limited. The Assembly's powers, as listed
in the China Yearbook, are as follows:

1. To pass regulations concerning the rights
   and obligations of the people;
2. To approve the provincial administrative
   budget and to screen the provincial accounts;
3. To decide on disposal of provincial property;
4. To review proposals of the provincial government;
5. To hear administrative reports of the government and to make interpellations;
6. To submit proposals for administrative reforms;
7. To consider petitions from the people;
8. To exercise other functions provided by law.42

But this reasonable scope of power shrinks as one
probes further. Two Executive Branch regulations specifically subject the decisions of the Provincial Assembly to
review by the Central Government. And additional regulations limit the Assembly's power to control the provincial
government, giving the Central Government the right to decide
disputes between the two. The effect of these additional
regulations is to make it legally possible for the provincial government to do almost anything it wants to,
despite the opinions provincial assemblymen may have on
the matter, as long as Central Government support is forth-
coming.43

It is noteworthy that in comparison to the lower-
level assemblies of counties, cities, townships, and rural
districts, the Provincial Assembly has less power over

26

and against its corresponding government than they do.
These lower-level assemblies also cannot pass regulations
conflicting with those passed by higher-level bodies,
and there is a heavy presumption of upper-level guidance
for lower-level governments and assemblies written into
the laws and regulations. 44

Still, despite this heavy presumption of guidance,
when one of these lower-level assemblies overrides its
corresponding government, the government cannot appeal
to higher authority. It must accept the decision. For
counties, cities, townships, rural districts, etc., the
phrase "however, if the government [of the level in ques-
tion] still feels there is that which is obstructive and
impossible to put into practice, it may petition [the
government of the next highest level] to investigate and
handle the matter" is not appended to the requirement that
"if upon reconsideration, two-thirds of the present and
voting assemblymen insist on the original decision, the
government [of the level in question] must accept it." 45

A final question is why are there greater limits on
the Provincial Assembly than on assemblies at lower
levels? Interviews indicated that this was felt to be
the safer way. The lower bodies are all Taiwanese--Tai-
wanese-elected assemblies versus Taiwanese-elected mayors.
And the jurisdictions of these bodies are over small,
countywide or townshipwide matters. When it is a matter
of Taiwanese against Taiwanese, over concerns of local
interest only, it is of no consequence if an assembly
prevails.

But to allow the Provincial Assembly to prevail over
the provincial government is an entirely different matter.
The provincial government is (even after Taipei City was
removed from its jurisdiction) the government of almost
all the territory over which the governing elite retained
control. And the provincial government is really a government of mainlanders, ruling on behalf of the governing
elite over the Taiwanese. The elite's self-legitimizing
version of Chinese history could not allow the elite's
provincial government to be overridden by Taiwanese, especially given the elite's expectation that its government
would usually be overridden in favor of nonnational, narrow
Taiwanese interests. Nor would the aura of elite rule by
a minority of mainlanders be able to maintain its psychological impact if the spectacle of Taiwanese votes overriding mainlander decisions became a frequent occurrence.

27

This reasoning should help in finding a different answer to the question of why the General Principles called for in the constitution have not been passed and the pilot-project status of Taiwan's provincial and local governments ended. The answer is based on the constitutional requirement that under the General Principles, the provincial governor is to be elected by universal suffrage.[46] It is hard enough for the mainlander elite to maintain legitimacy under the present arrangements. Imagine maintaining legitimacy against an individual elected by virtually all the citizens in the ruled territory.

Secret Police in Provincial and Local Politics

In addition to the above, Taiwan's governing elite places constraints upon the provincial assemblymen--as well as on their fellow politicians in provincial and local politics--through the activities of a secret police force.

The gathering of information concerning Taiwan's secret police is hampered by a number of difficulties. The secret police, after all, are secret. They do not act publicly nor open their files to public scrutiny. Few writers about Taiwan can even prove the existence of a secret police, much less fill pages with information concerning their activities.

Another difficulty is that the topic of secret police activities is a very sensitive one. It is not proudly listed in the index of the China Yearbook. Although the governing elite's supporters will admit to the existence of an FBI-type of organization and defend the necessity for its existence, the idea that such an organization makes Taiwan a police state is heatedly denied.

The topic is also sensitive in another way. Secret police are frightening. They make citizens fear for their lives. Few people will freely discuss what they know about them. If the topic is discussed, the information given must be disguised so that it cannot be traced back to its source.

A final difficulty, given the nature of the topic, is that what this author has to present concerning it may be no more than the figments of an imagination oversocialized

28

in the ways of idealized democracy. At least one veteran of Taiwan studies has cautioned those socialized in democracies against allowing their imaginations to create a secret police presence behind every tree and doorway they pass by. Not only, therefore, is there the difficulty of finding no concrete evidence of secret police activity on Taiwan, there is also the reverse difficulty of one's imagination finding evidence that does not exist.

Given the difficulties that hamper the collection of information about the secret police, it is with some uncertainty that this author presents the following gleanings concerning secret police activity on Taiwan as it relates to Taiwan's provincial and local politicians. It is necessary to present this information without footnotes, referring to sources as vaguely as possible.[47]

This author's first gleaning concerning secret police activity on Taiwan is that provincial and local politicians--and everyone else on Taiwan--exist in an atmosphere alive with the suspicion that there are secret police, and that these secret police are probably watching and listening. Awareness of this atmosphere began to grow in the author's own mind when, upon hearing that his research had to do with current politics on Taiwan, many joked about how he was probably being followed. The atmosphere of suspicion thickened when acquaintances related a visit by mysterious government men inquiring about what the author was up to. (Why not ask the person directly, the author wondered?)

Similar evidence came from tales by old Taiwan hands about the part-time informer in every corner grocery store. It also came from advice on how to explain this research project so that the interviewee would have something safe and convincing to tell the secret policeman who would follow up the author's visit. Suspicions hardened when an occasional interviewee begged the author to record nothing on paper and to deny that politics was discussed, even though nothing consequential was said, and warned the author against loose talk on the telephone.

Of course, the suspicion that Taiwan has an active secret police force will affect the behavior of local politicians even if that suspicion is not based on hard evidence.[48] But the author's second gleaning concerning this topic is that the evidence is hard. Taiwan does have an active secret police force. The acts of this police force serve not only to sustain the suspicion of its existence but also to place all political activity under surveillance, to report inappropriate activities to the governing elite, and--upon the orders of the elite--to intervene directly in the lives of those judged to be engaged in inappropriate activites.

Two targets or surveillance were specifically mentioned: the individual who actively seeks elected office and the same individual once he has attained elected office. If the person seeking elected office is a member of the KMT, according to informants, some type of police organization must pass on his fitness before the party will consider his nomination. If the person is not a member of the KMT, his fitness is still reviewed by the police. At least enough may be found about the non-KMT candidate to blackmail him into only mild opposition to the elite's rule. Perhaps enough will be found to force him to renounce his independent status and join the elite's party, accepting its discipline. Perhaps enough will be found to eliminate him altogether.

Once he has attained elected office, the individual continues to be a target of surveillance. For the provincial assemblyman, for example, it is said that spies are stationed within the Assembly buildings themselves. (Given that the Assembly buildings are already saturated with government officials, newspaper reporters, KMT members, and sundry occasional observers, one wonders if stationing secret policemen there is not redundant featherbedding.)

The author's final gleaning concerning Taiwan's secret police summarizes the concrete and atmospheric results of secret police activities for provincial and local politicians. For at least some politicians, the result is a constant, nagging fear that at any moment of the day or night a knock on the door will signal arrest and imprisonment. For virtually all politicians, the result is that, in one way or another, everyone limits his actions to accommodate the probability that he is being monitored.

The Kuomintang at the Provincial and Local Levels

The form of the elite's Central KMT and Central Government are duplicated at the provincial and local

30

levels. But the content of these lower-level organizations
differs from their parent organizations. This section
will describe the differing guises that the KMT takes on
at these lower levels.

The Provincial and Local KMT
as Agent of Taiwan's Governing Elite

The most important guise of the KMT at the provincial
and local levels is that of agent for carrying out the
governing elite's policies. The way in which this is done
with regard to controlling elections and other areas of
political activity will be discussed below.

Controlling Elections

The policy of controlling Taiwan's elections has
already been touched upon in the descriptions of the basic
legal and other constraints--including secret police
activities--that the governing elite has placed on Taiwan's
provincial and local politicians. In its capacity of agent
for the governing elite, the provincial and local KMT
imposes additional constraints aimed at furthering this
policy.

One such constraint arises from the KMT's power over
the mass media. Most of Taiwan's magazines and newspapers
sing the praises of KMT-approved candidates and generally
disparage the opposition. In this way, for example, KMT
candidate Hsü Chin-te, as mixed up with factions as any
person running for office, is not pictured as a faction
leader but as "one of the area's leading personages":

> Hsü Chin-te is currently a Provincial Assembly-
> man and President of the Board of the Taiwan
> Mining Company. His education is specialized
> and deep. Both his character, ability, and
> talent are superior. His manner is open and
> friendly. He is one of the area's leading
> personages, with an extremely strong mass base.

Cheng Sung-lui, on the other hand, gets a different press:

> Cheng Sung-lui is currently a Provincial
> Assemblyman. He claims to be of the anti-
> Western Hsü faction. In the past he was very

31

> close to the China Democratic Socialist Party.
> In general it is felt that his education and
> knowledge are ordinary. Moreover, he has no
> mass base. The only thing he can really rely
> on a little is that his relations with the
> lower level of society are rather close. He
> is also skilled in taking advantage of local
> factions. Moreover, he uses violent language
> to stir people up, fetching the sympathy votes
> of the curious masses. But local factions
> and the psychological curiosity of the masses
> are quite fickle. The average citizens have
> no good words for him. If they still want to
> vote for him is certainly questionable. It
> seems that reelection is not in his grasp.[49]

In addition to this propaganda support of KMT-approved
candidates, constraint also comes from KMT-controlled
votes. Orders are sent out to every KMT member, and word
is passed to sympathizers on how they should vote in each
election. As already indicated, among the sympathizers,
mainland-born soldiers, their families, and the civilian
mainlanders count heavily. The KMT may also be able to
deliver the votes of soldiers stationed in a given area,
making the political officers responsible for the soldiers
voting as the KMT desires.[50]

Indeed, the position of the KMT on the island, controlling all significant power and communications, gives
it a pervasive influence over many ordinary Taiwanese
voters as well. And if such constraints as these are not
enough to sway votes, the KMT candidate can always resort
to vote buying or other questionable methods to tip the
balance. Many informants felt that KMT-approved candidates
had less to fear from breaking election laws than did their
non-KMT competition.

An element of the KMT's electoral strength was described as follows by a local reporter:

> In relation to the party nomination, its votes
> are few in comparison to nonparty votes. But
> the Taiwanese are disunited, fielding many
> candidates. Therefore, the party can usually
> outpull the nonparty candidates. They get
> a majority, but they are divided, and the party
> has definite votes it always gets . . . gets

32

> most, not a majority. Who votes? Mainlanders,
> public servants (there are many of these),
> dependents of soldiers . . . like Assemblywoman
> P . . . the government through representatives
> like her gives them enough to get their votes.

An example of the results of this strength was given by an official describing the career of one provincial assemblyman. After running unsuccessfully four times as a nonparty candidate, the assemblyman thought, "Well, if I'm going to make it in politics here, I have to join the party," which he did, and then won election.

Given the constraints placed by the provincial and local KMT on the other parties' or nonparty candidates, the effectiveness of which is proven by the overwhelming majority of KMT-nominated candidates dominating all elected legislative and administrative posts on Taiwan, the KMT nomination becomes a great prize, the awarding of which gives the party great power over the behavior of local politicians.[51] Moreover, as non-KMT politicians are fond of pointing out, it gives the KMT politician an extra hurdle to jump over:

> Not only have to get elected. You have to be
> nominated. And that means a lot of activity
> . . . have all those levels to influence.

> The KMT member has to spend money twice. . . .
> bribe to be nominated and then to be elected.[52]

In its drive to win as many elections as possible, the party adds to this battery of constraints attempts to co-opt all electoral politicians with good prospects of winning and attempts to ensure that these vote-getters remain in politics. These efforts perhaps explain the strange statement by one assemblyman that he "received a government order to be a people's representative." Less strange in this regard are the following statements:

> Now the party does not want me to get out.
> I do not want to register, but they will do it
> for me and then we'll see.

> There is no way. I didn't register, but they
> probably will push me to run again.

33

> Many people rely on a politician's enterprises
> for a livelihood. Therefore it is his economic
> base, and (likewise) his political base. And
> the party wants to take advantage of his power.

Informants suggest that the party strives to balance its policy of co-optation with attempts to convince formidable opponents to step aside so the KMT candidates will not be endangered:

> The party already asked me not to run for mayor.
> They will fix me up with something if I don't.

> The KMT fears someone who is getting many votes
> who is not one of their people. They pressure
> people.

Another constraint employed by the party to control elections is a morally based, emotionally toned demand for party loyalty and discipline. In this respect, the party acts much as did the old-line, regular Democrats in New York City when they were faced with the insurgencies of reformers. Members of both groups expressed a strong feeling that their organization had some kind of emotional right to the loyalty of its members, and that there was a real problem of morality for those who refused to recognize this right. Those who break party discipline, therefore, risk censure as moral lepers.

> "In a year of drought one sees the filial son.
> When power becomes unstable, one sees the loyal
> official." "In the cold of winter it is the
> leaves of the fir and cypress that are the
> last to fall." The good or bad of an indi-
> vidual cannot be seen in ordinary times. He
> must be tested. Only then can the real good
> man be differentiated from the false gentleman . . .

> In the current city-county assemblyman and rural
> district-township mayor elections, of those
> who opposed discipline and competed for elec-
> tion, about half won and half lost. For the
> losers, given that their loyalty and sincerity
> toward their group (party), their comrades,
> and their friends were insufficient, their
> rejection by the voters was a misfortune that
> comes under the heading of censure brought

on by oneself, punishment that is deserved.
For the winners, they indeed had to exhaust
all their strength and make use of every method
and treasure at their command in order to leap
over the mountain and sealike obstacles they
had already placed in their own way. Now one
only hopes that at this point they will stop
practicing their black arts once and for all,
that they will not simply turn to another battle-
field and write a continuation . . . To oppose
discipline and compete for election is incor-
rect and unrighteous behavior. But if one is
able from now on to put down his butcher knife,
what misfortune will be able to prevent him
from becoming a Buddha? It is only to be feared
that the gall to do bad things will ever increase,
gradually causing the eye to see no legal restraints, and the person to have nothing that
he would not do and nothing that he would not
take.[53]

Finally, if all these constraints fail, the party
can always resort to organizational discipline, the worst
being the expelling of the offender from the party.[54]   The
possibility of the party's going beyond organizational
discipline, resorting to more sinister constraints, was
also indicated by informants.[55]

At times the party gets overzealous and goes too
far in its attempts to control elections, bringing a reaction down on itself and causing its own defeat at the hands
of a nonparty candidate or a party member running against
the party-nominated candidate "against discipline." An
official close to the situation gave the following examples:

The government (for example, the last time in
Taipei and this time in Kao-hsiung) goes all
out against the nonparty candidate and gets
an antiparty reaction. So it goes further
into a hole and gets an even bigger reaction.
And therefore it reacts further until the people
are all riled up. Then if they do not let the
nonparty man win, perhaps there will be an
insurrection. Thus they let him win, making
the decision in the middle of the night . . .
like what happened in Taipei City . . . [where
they] gave it to Kao in the middle of the night.

35

Controlling Additional Areas of Activity

The basic legal and other constraints that the governing elite has placed on Taiwan's elections are accompanied
by constraints that extend beyond elections to all areas
of Taiwan's fledgling democratic system. As agent of the
governing elite, the provincial and local KMT has been
instrumental in the imposition of a number of these constraints.

For example, the choice of the speakers and deputy
speakers for Taiwan's rural district-township, county-city,
and provincial assemblies is often dictated from outside
by the party. Concerning one contest for the deputy speakership of the Provincial Assembly, the following comment by
a provincial assemblyman is illustrative:

> If it was a free vote, Li Chien-ho would win
> because he can buy votes in the Assembly.
> But after the party nominated, it was an open
> ballot. You had to carry your open ballot
> past the party men from where you marked it to
> the ballot box.

The reaction to a deputy speakership contest in the T'ao-
yüan County Assembly indicated that the party will view
its efforts as having failed, even if it wins these positions by a close vote--especially when some of the opposition comes from its own members.56

Other activities internal to Taiwan's assemblies are
also controlled. The party caucus in the Provincial Assembly does not vote on decisions. Each member may speak
his piece, but the party organization outside the Assembly
makes the final decision.

> People have different backgrounds in the
> Assembly, but they do not have any influence
> on legislative behavior. It is the orders
> from the party that are all-important. Perhaps
> some complain, but in the end they toe the
> mark . . . except for those who are quitting
> the party, or after the party refuses to nom-
> inate them anyway.

For those occasional instances when a member defies
the party, there is punishment.

36

This year, on June first, when the Provincial
Assembly voted on if it should or should not
stop meeting to protest the Central [Govern-
ment's] taking back the Bureau of Inspection
[from the provincial government's jurisdic-
tion], both of these women voted to stop meeting to protest.

In regard to that vote, Lin Ts'ai Su-nü, after
it was over, told the party that her vote was
an unintentional mistake. Her original idea
was not to oppose the Central [Party's] policy
intentions. Thus, although she was not nominated,
her own request to sign up for the election
was received with understanding. Moreover,
she obtained election as an alternate commit-
teeperson. As for Liang Hsü Ch'un-chü, because
during that incident of opposing the Central
Government's taking back of the inspection
power, she intentionally supported recessing
to protest, she did not get the support of the
delegates for this election of provincial com-
mitteeperson. 57

Perhaps in order not to appear too punitive, the Provincial Assembly's party leader told this author the following:

The party leadership group in the Assembly
discussed the giving of prizes to good party
members as well as punishing them for not
following. The party keeps a careful record
of their behavior.

Informants disagreed on just how much legislative
behavior the party attempts to control with these constraints. Some claimed that the party controls almost
everything. But the majority of informants felt that the
party's control was limited to certain basic policies
crucial to Taiwan's governing elite. Much more is left
free to the forces of the political marketplace.

[There is a] two-level system. On basic national
policy there is no independence. But on things
that are not so important there are all sorts
of divisions in the Assembly . . . often based on
individual interest or the interests of constituents.58

37

Finally, in addition to controlling behavior within Taiwan's assemblies, the party also keeps a firm control over behavior within its controlling agent, the provincial and local KMT itself.

> The KMT higher-ups still control who is named
> to the party committee. Yes they are elected,
> but the nomination is from the top. All is
> arranged beforehand. [It is] still dictatorial.

> Taiwan is not completely democratic. Party mem-
> bers are not so free to always speak their minds.
> In the United States you can vote for any party
> in spite of your party membership.

The Provincial and Local KMT as Mediator between Taiwanese Electoral Factions[59]

Besides the guise of agent for carrying out the governing elite's policies, the party at the provincial and local levels also appears in the guise of mediator between the many Taiwanese local-level electoral factions. Given the apparent fitness of the approach used so far to analyze Taiwan's fledgling Western-style electoral democracy--that of Taiwan's politics as a confrontation between the mainlander-supported governing elite and the Taiwanese--one may find it surprising that the mainlander elite's KMT has come to be a mediator between Taiwanese electoral factions.

In this section, the confrontation approach will be supplemented by two of the three other approaches to the study of Taiwan noted in the introduction--a psychological approach based on certain speculations concerning Chinese political behavior and an anthropological approach based on certain more solidly researched theories--in order to provide one possible explanation of why the KMT has been able to fulfill this mediator role successfully.

In Part II of this analysis, local-level Taiwanese electoral factions will be described in detail. Here it is sufficient to note that many of Taiwan's local areas are divided among Taiwanese electoral factions, competing with each other for control of such elective public offices as mayor, assemblyman, and president of the local Farmers' Association.

38

Related to this is the possibility that this competition, now channeled into electoral campaigns, will get
out of hand and violence will result. Behind this possibility lies a history of violent village-level conflict,
which was especially manifest before firm police control
was established in the countryside and which momentarily
reappeared within the power vacuum created by the transfer
of Taiwan from Japanese to Chinese sovereignty in 1945.

Such a history of violent social disorder is not unique
to those living on Taiwan. All Chinese are aware that their
society has frequently lapsed into violence, both on the
gigantic scale of the overturning of national political
regimes and on the smaller scale of local-level group conflict. Nor is awareness of comparable lapses unknown to
members of most other societies in the world.

Exaggerated Chinese Fear of Disorder and Violence?

According to the speculations of some social scientists,
additional aspects of Chinese psychology lead the Chinese
to be much more fearful of the possibility of outbreaks of
social disorder and violence than individuals of other
societies with violent histories would be. Lucian W. Pye
and Richard H. Solomon, for example, trace this exaggerated
fear of social disorder and violence to the early socialization and later reinforcement of the Chinese personality
as it relates to authority figures and the control of aggressive emotions.

Pye and Solomon argue that the Chinese child grows up
under great social pressure to obey his elders. The slightest show of hostility toward his parents, especially toward
his father, is severely punished. The punishment is that
of shaming--a punishment that implies loss of social position in the group, and loss of social position further
implies loss of the protection that the group extends to its
members. This protection is important, the child is carefully taught, because only protection that comes from personalized family and familylike groups, led by fathers,
elder brothers, or comparable figures, will be reliable in
the dangerous, enemy-filled world in which the child will
spend his grown-up years.

Nor does the importance of the group to the individual
end with these practical considerations of protection.

Apparently, the individual's entire concept of self is heavily dependent on his position within the group and on the group's support for this position. The possibility of loss of position within the group, therefore, threatens the individual at the very basis of his personal identity--a possibility that is likely to cause great emotional stress, if not panic.

But it is inevitable that from time to time the child will feel hostile, especially toward his father's exacting demands and harsh discipline. Later, feelings of hostility toward superiors in the other protective groups in which the individual participates during his lifetime will also be difficult to avoid.

The individual, therefore, must suppress his aggressive emotion or face the threat of losing the most important support of his physical and mental well-being. Indeed, he becomes so convinced that aggressive emotions are bad and so fearful of their existence within himself that he resorts to a variety of psychological defense mechanisms to keep his aggressions within or to deny that they exist within.

But especially the defense mechanisms of projection and displacement only increase the individual's uneasiness, encouraging him to feel that his surrounding environment is filled with ill will and threats. Therefore, the individual's attempts at suppressing his emotions even further increase his need for protection and his fear of rejection by his protecting superiors if his true feelings become known to them.

In order to cope with this situation, the individual develops the exaggerated fear of social disorder and violence noted above. Social disorder and violence are the exact conditions that the individual has learned to avoid, both from the explicit instructions of his mentors and from his use of the psychological defense mechanisms of projection and displacement. It is these conditions that the individual knows he needs the group's protection to guard himself against.

Moreover, social disorder and violence are the conditions most likely to confront the individual with unexpected circumstances, catching his emotions off guard and/or forcing him to improvise his behavioral responses.

40

But being caught off guard or having to improvise one's behavior are just the circumstances that often result in inadvertent responses, revealing the true emotions of the individual. And the price of such revelation--loss of group support--is ultimately what is to be avoided.

As a result, the individual has good reason to avoid social disorder and violence and to strive for group approval. Finally, Pye and Solomon argue, the individual finds that both of these purposes can be served by limiting oneself to a set, stereotyped behavior pattern based on a rigid interpretation of group norms. By so limiting oneself, the individual makes it unlikely that he will meet with anything unexpected, socially disorderly, or violent. And if he does, such behavior will ensure that the group will come to his aid, protecting him from the dangers lurking in others and aiding to keep his own emotions in line. [60]

A similar line of reasoning concerning why the Chinese have an exaggerated fear of social disorder and violence has been suggested by David K. Jordan. Jordan has speculated that the Chinese child, originally coddled and spoiled, suddenly experiences extreme pressure to grow up as fast as possible. A gap thus develops between what the child wants to be (fantasy) and what society demands that he be. Given the great punishment of shame that society threatens, he develops fear that society will find out what he is really like inside. This leads to a personality syndrome involving repression and fear of spontaneity that might inadvertently reveal his true opinions. It also involves resentment at having his true self repressed. On the outside, stereotyped behavior is encouraged, revealing only what one knows will be approved.

A great fear of aggression and violence also develops. The aggression and violence one fears may be that of others, which threatens to cause the release of one's own pent-up aggressions. It may be the pent-up aggressions within oneself, projected onto others. Or it may simply be one's own pent-up aggressions, perhaps merged into one's resentment, which, upon being revealed, will be punished.

This fear and resentment is compounded by growing

41

up in an extended family, where one learns to make fine distinctions of where to behave how and what to say to whom. The child learns to be on guard, and carries this behavior into adulthood.[61]

The speculations of Pye, Solomon, and Jordan concerning why the Chinese have an exaggerated fear of social disorder and violence are among the more extreme and controversial explanations of this phenomenon, based as they are on Freudianlike theories of aggression, relationships with authority figures, the use of psychological defense mechanisms, and the subconscious. Other explanations of this exaggerated fear of social disorder and violence rely on more straightforward concepts. These explanations do not necessarily conflict with the above speculations. Intellectually they often can be combined. More skeptical scholars, however, may prefer to keep them separate.

The explanation suggested by Donald R. DeGlopper, for example, begins by noting simply that social harmony and organic unity are very highly valued in Chinese culture. The problem with this very high valuation of social harmony and organic unity, as DeGlopper sees it, is that it has gone to such an extreme that, when confronted by socially disordered or violent situations-- which inevitably occur despite cultural disapproval-- the Chinese are likely to display more anxiety than the outside observer would normally expect.[62]

For an individual fitting the pattern of DeGlopper's more straightforward explanation or for an individual adhering to such psychologies as those postulated by Pye, Solomon, and Jordan, conflict and competition-- situations often pregnant with the possibility of social disorder and violence--become very distressing. With repression of emotion and avoidance of conflict common, perhaps the number of actual conflicts are relatively few. But given the building pressure when repression and avoidance reach their limits, one would expect a conflict, when it does come, to be heated.

"Potentially Conflictive Peers"
in Chinese Society

Explanations such as these of the Chinese indivi-

42

dual's exaggerated fear of social disorder and violence
lie behind Solomon's conclusions concerning the relationship between "potentially conflictive peers" in Chinese
society. In general, the effects of the psychological
patterns described above cause the individual to live
in fear of conflict breaking out and cause him to feel
unqualified to handle conflict when it occurs. According to Solomon,

> In 79.5 percent of the cases in which our
> respondents describe peer group differences
> of opinion or conflict, the outcome is such
> a "splitting up" or breakdown in cooperative
> relations. There is virtually no expectation
> that peers, among themselves, can bargain and
> compromise their differences and maintain group
> solidarity. And compounding the problems of
> such a breakdown in relations is a residue of
> antagonism . . . [Footnote 49: . . . Chinese
> have a significantly higher expectation of
> conflict in peer relations than Americans . . .
> they do not see cooperation maintained once
> conflict has occurred. Americans are taught
> that limited conflict is a natural aspect of
> ongoing social relations, whereas the Chinese
> tradition has stressed the elimination of con-
> flict as necessary for the maintenance of group
> solidarity . . .]
>
> This concern that aggression is always liable
> to burst forth in interpersonal relations,
> leading to "confusion" (luan), is a constant
> theme in our respondents' interpretations of
> social relations . . .
>
> . . . such an attitude toward interaction with
> one's peers, and the expectation that differ-
> ences of opinion could lead to uncontrolled
> conflict and violence, worked to fragment lat-
> eral social ties and weaken integration of the
> society.[63]

Given the fear of conflict breaking out between
peers and the feeling of incompetence peers have concerning their ability to deal with conflict when it does
occur, the traditional method has been for peers to rely
on "a strong and unitary authority" to maintain harmony

or to restore harmony if conflict breaks out. On this point, Solomon writes concerning

> . . . the expectation that the only way that
> social order and harmony can be maintained
> is through the action of a strong and unitary
> authority who will impose order and unanimity
> upon potentially conflictive peers. A strong
> authority enables the individual to avoid the
> personal responsibility of facing up to points
> of contention, and at the same time ensures
> that "disorders" will be dealt with strictly . . .
>
> Social problems are thus seen as capable of
> being resolved only within the hierarchical
> pattern which we have described as being
> central to Chinese conceptions of social order.
> There is no expectation that peers, among them-
> selves, can bargain and compromise differences
> of social opinion or interest. Interpersonal
> competition is seen as leading to an inevi-
> table conflict to attain a position of domi-
> nance, for not only are security and social
> order conceived of as attainable only within
> the hierarchical pattern, but an individual's
> social identity is also seen as defined in
> terms of who is deferring to (or caring for)
> whom.[64]

Even in normal Chinese society--that is, within hierarchical groups--the fear of social disorder and violence would cause trouble, as Pye and Solomon go on to
point out.[65] But there is even more trouble if there
is no clear hierarchy, forcing the Chinese to deal with
one another as peers.

"Potentially Conflictive Peers"
and Mediators on Taiwan

This problem of peer conflict manifests itself in
the Chinese society on Taiwan. Modernization has brought
the weakening of traditional authority (hierarchical)
relationships, leaving more egalitarian relationships
in its wake. As the number of these egalitarian relationships increase, the problem of settling disputes
between status equals (i.e., peers) increases propor-

tionately.

Thus the normal relationships of brothers or subordinates, in terms of which conflict can be handled,
have been greatly weakened. Instead, unrelated equals
often face one another in dispute. They have to deal
with each other in another way.

One solution, when there is no readily available
authority figure at hand, is simply to press the search,
not stopping until somewhere, some semblance of an authority figure able to encourage agreement is found.
Often, however, when such an authority figure is finally
found, he is not the ideal "strong and unitary authority"
mentioned by Solomon above. Instead, his position is more
tenuous, and his actions make it more appropriate to
label him a mediator.

DeGlopper points out some of the difficulties in
even finding such a mediator in his discussion of a model
dispute and the type of mediator necessary at each level
as the dispute escalates into a major conflict. For a
small incident (a bicycle knocking over a fruit stand,
for example), with both sides afraid and uncertain, unsure
of the power position of the other party, and with un-
conscious fears of violence bringing on shame, both sides
will want to get out of the situation as quickly as possible. In the experience of both parties, once a blow
is struck, all will escalate very quickly (fitting the
theory of the repression of aggression until uncontrol-
lable feelings explode into fury). [66] There are no rules
about hitting others, except that one does not do so.
When it happens, the worst is at hand.

The disputants, therefore, meeting face to face,
are frightened. But they cannot back down. Given their
predicament, any form of mediation, even from a foreigner
passing by with no knowledge of Chinese or the situation,
will be accepted to get the parties out of the immediate
danger with face.

But with the initial incident over, the possibilities of escalation remain strong. Out of danger, each
party thinks over the original settlement. "Could I have
gotten better terms? I am stronger! Have I lost face?"
The answers to these questions are very important.

If the party has publicly lost face because his portion in the settlement was too small, the whole point of avoiding violence is lost. Violent situations are avoided in order to avoid the punishment of shame that comes from revealing one's inner aggressions. But if one is being shamed for not revealing aggression (i.e., avoiding a potentially violent dispute), the original inhibitions cancel out. And one is greatly shamed when he, as the stronger party in a dispute, has received less in compensation than his weaker adversary. Therefore, if one does feel shamed, and is stronger, the dispute must be reopened.[67] The original incident may have been trivial, but the loss of face is not.

Given such reasoning, one or both parties return, often reinforced with relatives and friends, to renew the argument. Each side escalates the dispute, with beatings or stabbings, until force settles the matter or the police step into the issue. (Note that the child has learned that protection comes only from personal relations. Courts and police are far more dangerous allies. Thus, unless the police step in on their own, the dispute will continue until one side proves that its personal relations are more powerful than its adversary's.[68])

DeGlopper, therefore, sees a pattern of encounter, withdrawal, and return with greater force. The initial issue is often trivial, and each settlement of the dispute lasts only until either party becomes dissatisfied and has the means to do something about it. The dissatisfied party will reopen the dispute with greater force, if possible. Thus, if the settlements do not represent the balance of forces, they are likely to be quickly overthrown.

Congruent with the conception of the contest as a matter of power rather than moral or ideological persuasion, DeGlopper notes that the arguments disputing parties often use against each other are not appeals to cultural values or general public opinion. Instead, reasoning appeals to self-interest, stressing the power relations of the parties, not right and wrong: "This affair is too small to get hurt over. And we have more men than you."

For the purpose of this discussion, the most important point is that, as the dispute escalates, the qualifications that the mediator must possess also escalate. For this same reason, as the units involved in the dispute become larger, the difficulty of finding a successful mediator increases.

To fulfill the requirements for a mediator in a dispute that has already escalated to some degree, the individual must be related to both sides, be relatively neutral, and have a social position high enough to command the respect of both sides. His social position should be so high that the participants will feel uneasy about not coming to a settlement, thus insulting the mediator. The mediator himself must be able to make a settlement that never clearly indicates who was wrong or who was right. It must be a compromise within which everyone's face is saved.[69] Finally, the mediator must have some power. Sometimes he is the guarantor of the settlement. His prestige or other power must be adequate for this.[70]

Between many groups on Taiwan, such mediators are easy to find. Between two small families within a larger village, there is no problem finding individuals who meet these requirements. Within villages with more than one surname, which also divide into economic status groups, temple associations, and crop-watching societies, leadership cuts many ways, and there is always someone who fulfills the requirements of a mediator.

If the village has sent out an individual who has become important in supravillage politics, his return visits to the village may be used to arrange who will run for what office and under what conditions who will withdraw. Even in the provincial and county assemblies, there is much overlapping of groups and a number of prestigious individuals to fill roles as mediators.

Within each of Taiwan's many local-level electoral factions, the members are already very embarrassed over their conflicts and are happy to have the faction leader settle the matter. The leader also wants unity and is happy to act to obtain it. Indeed, the maintenance of harmony through authority is one of the main functions of prestigious individuals in general within Taiwan's many organizations and communities.

47

It is only when an area is split between two hostile factions that there is likely to be no one who is impartial and yet not too distant from the disputants. It is between such groups, therefore, that Taiwan's major local-level conflict resolution problem lies.

Competition for elected office between political factions is the most salient example of local-level conflict on Taiwan. This continuing conflict is the situation most likely to result in the social disorder and violence so feared by the Chinese. And this fear is all the more credible, given that it is these disputes between factions for which qualified mediators are so difficult to find.

The basic problem is that there are no mutually recognized authorities between factions. They are conflicting peers. As such, the factional leaders themselves do not know how to deal with each other in any satisfactory bilateral way.[71]

KMT Mainlanders as Mediators between Taiwan's Factions

All of these speculations and theories regarding the Chinese in conflict and their need for mediators have been introduced as a prelude to demonstrating why the mainlander KMT officials assigned to the provincial and local levels are very fit for the role of mediators between Taiwan's local-level electoral factions. In view of the hostility that grew up between many Taiwanese and mainlanders, one may be surprised to find mainlander KMT officials as successful mediators between Taiwanese electoral factions. Certainly mutual hostility exists. But, as will be discussed more thoroughly in subsequent chapters, such hostility is to be found to a greater degree where the two populations are in frequent contact.

In the countryside, where there are few mainlanders, this hostility is much less of a factor. The politically significant populations in the countryside are all Taiwanese, and the important political issues have little to do with who controls Central Government decision-making in Taipei. In the countryside, who controls the mayor's office and Farmers' Association is what is important, and the only competitors for these positions

are factions of Taiwanese. The heatedness of such competition and the history of violence associated with it
often overshadow any mainlander-Taiwanese hostility.

This situation is encouraged by the governing elite
and its KMT, which distribute patronage and use other
means at their command to keep the Taiwanese factions
alive and competing with each other. In this way, Taiwanese attention is concentrated on competition with
other Taiwanese and not on competition with the elite's
KMT. Moreover, post-1945 economic progress, often attributed in the countryside to the elite's KMT and government, combined with the threat of coercion, also serve
to orient Taiwanese toward local politics and away from
anti-KMT activities.

Given these conditions, the KMT mainlanders appear
in an unexpectedly advantageous position with regard to
filling the role of mediators between local Taiwanese
electoral factions. After many years of representing the
KMT in the countryside, these mainlanders have become
closely related to the members of all local factions.
They are also seen as neutral, since, unlike most politically involved Taiwanese, they are not identified with
one faction more than with another. Finally, the great
power of the KMT has earned them prestigious status and
the acknowledgment by members of the various factions
that they are capable of guaranteeing the dispute settlements that they sponsor.

Therefore, although Taiwanese factions compete for
membership on the party committees at the local levels,
it is only the mainlanders who can claim to be neutral
and fulfill the felt need among the factions for a mediator. In this way, the existence of the local KMT
becomes very important to the agreements and thus to the
interests of the local Taiwanese factions. The KMT
takes root in the understandings and give-and-take of the
local society. This is especially so since, through its
nominating power, it controls the door to most political
success. Most ambitious politicians thus join the party,
and most factions are largely Taiwanese factions within
the KMT.

Among the KMT factions, it is therefore not the
Taiwanese-faction delegates on the local party committees
but the mainlander party workers at each level who do

their best to mediate and balance the interests of the factions with regard to membership on the party committee and nominations for office, trying to maintain a balance of power.

> The party usually sits in with the two factions and gets agreement on who gets the Farmers' Association and who gets the town hall, etc. . . . worked out and not necessarily a real election. It is not that they fought for control and one won the Farmers' Association and one won the Town Hall.

Consequences of Mainlander Mediation

This mainlander ability to fulfill the role of mediator has certain consequences for the local political situation. With their qualifications for mediating, the KMT mainlanders can make sure that disputes between factions do not get out of hand. Indeed, it has been suggested that the leading responsibility of mainland officials at the local level is often to keep factional disputes from blowing up. The officials are constantly settling disputes, as any traditional mediator or authority figure would do in any Chinese community. Some observers go so far as to claim that the mainland officials "are constantly trying to keep the factions from breaking out into bloody war." Thus, the KMT's local mainlander officials may be an important force for social peace on Taiwan, fulfilling a role of neutrality and power that, if they were not there, the Taiwanese left to themselves might be unable to fill.

A second effect of the KMT position may be less altruistic. Their mediation efforts provide the KMT's mainlander officials with an additional means by which to keep factions alive and constantly competing with one another. This too can be a force for social peace, since no faction is ever allowed to lose so badly that its members may be driven to desperation and violence against the members of the winning faction or even against the mainlanders. Instead, the mainlanders seem to try to co-opt all factions, giving each enough to satisfy it.

But in keeping each faction alive, the KMT keeps the Taiwanese divided against each other, instead of united in the one faction that might result if competition was unrestrained--a faction of all Taiwanese against the KMT mainlanders. Thus one is left with the impression that everyone in Taiwan who displays the ability to lead a faction is co-opted and bought off.

> . . . if one [faction] is too weak, they would
> shift it so that it may be given patronage.
> Or they would try to put another one together
> . . . [to] make sure that they both keep existing.

Failures of Mediation Efforts

The party is not invariably successful in its mediating role, however. From time to time the KMT-arranged candidates fail to win elections. An official close to such situations notes that when this happens, it is usually because the party failed to handle the factions correctly.

Each faction is composed not only of party members but also of nonparty individuals that it can send out in the regular election if the faction does not receive the party nomination. If necessary, a faction can even send out a party member to compete for election "against discipline" and fight the party's nominee. Thus, in electoral terms, the party does not have to satisfy every faction, but it must satisfy all those that have many votes. The KMT-controlled votes plus the votes controlled by the faction of its nominee must be enough to override the aggrieved faction. Alternatively, the losing faction must be given a substitute prize so that it will not seriously challenge the party's nominee. Otherwise the party may find itself in a severe contest in the election itself. An example of KMT failure to arrange elections successfully follows:

> In relation to Chu Yü-ying, the KMT nominee,
> according to the predictions of all circles,
> he would easily win the county mayor's precious
> seat. But the results of the voting were exactly
> the opposite. Very many could not avoid feeling
> ten thousand parts amazed. But analyzing at
> a deeper level, the loss of Chu Yü-ying is shown
> to be because of the carelessness over one matter
> . . .

51

The first move in Chu Yü-ying's defeat was the
inability to pull tight the support of the
Ch'en Hsing-sheng faction. Chu Yü-ying's
father, Chu Sheng-ch'i, was one of the important generals of the eastern camp. During
his term as Hsin-chu's first- and second-term
people-elected county mayor, he made many
political enemies with the western faction's
Ch'en Hsing-sheng and other personages.

When the KMT held registration for competition
for the party nomination for county mayor, the
western faction supported Ch'en Hsing-sheng's
registration. Moreover, on the list of the
Provincial Central Committee, according to what
is said, his name was listed as first choice.
Who would have thought that, in passing through
the Central Party approval gates, all of a sudden, his battle was lost . . .

Eight o'clock at dawn of the fifth, Ch'en
Hsing-sheng hurriedly returned to Hsin-chu,
alone went to the Election Office . . . and,
with a hand as swift as the clap of thunder
that gives no time to cover the ears, took
an already filled out Election Candidate
Registration Cancellation Application, signed
it, and applied his fingerprint . . . After
his old mother heard the news, she was angered
to the point of fainting to the floor. The
collective feelings of the Ch'en lineage of
Kuan-hsi Township were also stimulated to anger
. . .

After Chu Yü-ying obtained the party nomination to participate in the election, his father,
Chu Sheng-ch'i, came out as a campaign worker.
Moreover, he recruited a group of his old,
deeply faction-tainted lieutenants, arousing
the alarm of the western faction's Ch'en Hsing-
sheng, among others . . . Even if the votes of
Ch'en Hsing-sheng's faction were not cast for
Liu Hsieh-hsün, all they had to do was not
cast them for Chu Yü-ying, and his total would
be lessened. This is the first reason for
Chu Yü-ying's defeat.[72]

52

As a means of avoiding entanglement in too many such factional disputes, as well as to protect itself from overly strong antiparty candidates, the party has devised three alternative nomination procedures. The party generally follows the procedure of nominating a candidate for every office in contention in an election district. The party may, however, nominate fewer candidates than the number of offices being contested, or it may nominate no candidates, allowing any number of party members to compete against each other and against nonparty candidates for the available offices.

KMT spokespersons claim that the choice of which procedure to use is unrelated to factionalism. They argue that "partial nomination" is used when "nonparty circles indeed have just, worthy, and able candidates," who should be allowed to win. The procedure of not nominating any candidates is used "if in an area there are no nonparty personages running, or although there are nonparty personages running, the KMT feels their organizational foundation and social relations are good."[73] More cynical reasoning, however, describes the motivations for the choice of nominating procedures as follows:

> Full nomination: nominate whole slate . . .
> means they were able to get all the factions
> together. Partial nomination: they nominate
> some of the slate but leave other positions
> open to give some outside man who is very
> worthy an opportunity to win and serve . . .
> means that this man is too strong and they
> do not want to suffer the embarrassment of being
> defeated by him in the election. Free election:
> they can't get factions together on candidates
> and the only recourse is to let them fight it
> out in the election.[74]

The Provincial Government

The Provincial Government as Agent for the Governing Elite

At the provincial and local levels, the provincial government, like the KMT, appears in a number of different roles. And, again like the KMT, one of its most important roles is that of agent for carrying out the governing elite's policies. Below, this role will be exemplified in terms of how the provincial government reenforces the basic legal and ideological constraints, the secret police constraints, and the constraints imposed by the provincial and local KMT in carrying out the governing elite's policy of controlling the activities of Taiwan's nonelite politicians.

According to one interviewee, the government and party combined efforts to control his electoral activities in the following manner: "[I] won for town mayor the first time, and they brought the case to court and the party took it away from me. The second time I won they drafted me and sent me to Quemoy."

The government's right to disallow portions of candidates' formal political platform statements gave rise to the following example: "Wu I-wei has his clever methods though. This time his political platform was full of rejections. But all of them were quotes from the constitution."

In an interview, an assemblyman showed this author one of his campaign leaflets that had two sentences marked in red. The government had ordered these deleted. The two sentences translate into English as follows:

> [under experience]: Elected as a provincial
> assemblyman for the Taiwan Provincial Assembly's
> second term. Election was declared null and void.

> [under "Each of you please listen to how little
> brother was wronged"]: In the 52nd year [of
> the Republic], just before elections were to
> be held, thorough planners obtained for him
> a jail sentence of four months. The times did
> not permit [name of assemblyman] to be an official.

In reference to this assemblyman, it was noted, "These things come up into court always just around election time for X . . . last one was a five-year-old case that came up around election time."75

As the point is made in the following cartoon, the government enforces the laws that make it illegal to attack the government or criticize other candidates during an election.

This propensity of the government to use the election law to hamper disapproved candidates was summed up by a number of informants--for example, "A nonparty candidate breaks the election law and they will really get him . . . not a party man."[76]

Finally, the propensity of the governing elite to use such agents as the provincial government to control both electoral and other activities within Taiwan's fledgling democratic system is illustrated by the following statement concerning government control over non-elite politicians who are also big businessmen:

CARTOON OF ELECTION LAWS

Translation: The provincial assemblymen's election war has already entered into high tide. There are some candidates who purposely upbraid and scold the government and criticize the pros and cons of their opponents in order to wrest forth ballots. This is an illegal way to campaign. Mr. Candidates, please be careful.[77]

55

Big businessmen have to deal with government
regulations and need their benevolent inter-
pretation--for example, Assemblyman Y and the
insurance business . . . And government regulations can mess them up if they do not go
along. [They] have things on them.

As with the KMT, the government's actions can also
go too far, bringing a reaction that causes the loss of
an election. The following example describes the consequences of the enforcement of a government regulation
stipulating that unless two-thirds of all candidates for
a given office in a given election district agree, candidates may only make public speeches in meetings arranged
and chaired by government officials.

Within the subtle shifts of this county's mayor
election situation, the element that created
the most profit for Liu Hsieh-hsün came on the
18th, when Liu was preparing to begin activities with his campaign truck. In the square
in front of the Kuo-min Theater he was restrained
from setting up his sign and his loudspeakers.
Many city dwellers and simple folk who had come
in from the countryside, who did not understand
the election laws, upon seeing that Liu Hsieh-
hsün was unable to use an election truck to
campaign, developed resentment. As a result,
each one became a voluntary campaign worker
for Liu Hsieh-hsün.

The local personages who supported Liu Hsieh-
hsün, upon discovering that the more the authorities restrained them, the easier it was
to pull out votes, then regardless of being
restrained, sent out the campaign truck . . .

. . . Liu Hsieh-hsün, in Chu-pei Village,
prepared to give a speech on the street, opening up his political displays. But before
he was able to begin speaking, he was stopped
by the police. Although the soapbox speech
was not successfully begun, still many votes
were successfully obtained--originally they
were prepared to lose Chu-pei Village by 5,000
votes. On the contrary, they won it by over
3,000 votes. This time's loss of a soapbox

56

speech, how much help did it give to Liu
Hsieh-hsün? Everyone can see for himself.[78]

Between the Husband's Sister and Mother,
It Is Hard to Be a Wife [79]

In addition to appearing as an agent of the governing
elite, the provincial government often plays the role of a
middleman. Much like the county magistrate in traditional
China, the position of the provincial government is under a
governing elite that most of all wants stability from its
provinces. It expects the provincial government to keep
peace and order. If there is any disturbance within the
provincial government's jurisdiction, the governing elite
will blame the provincial government for not doing its job.

Thus the provincial government cannot just assume that
in disputes with the various groups over which it has jurisdiction the elite's Central Government will automatically
support it. Instead, if the provincial government finds
itself turning to the center for aid too often, the center
will want to know why the provincial officials cannot handle
things alone. It will want to know why there is so much
dissension within the provincial government's jurisdiction.

In this way the provincial government is encouraged
to come to agreements and satisfy all parties that have
the ability to create dissension before grumbling gets
out of hand and the Central Government begins to ask
questions. Moreover, because of this situation, local
groups, including those the Provincial Assembly repre-
sents and the Assembly itself as a group, find themselves
with a certain amount of power to extort. If the provincial government does not give them what they want, they
can blow up the situation and bring wrath down, perhaps
on themselves, but also on the stubborn provincial government.

The Provincial Government as Lobbyist
before the Provincial Assembly

Another role that the provincial government assumes
is duplicated in all political systems in which an administration must deal with a legislature of some power.
This is the role of a petitioner. In such political

systems, the administration often must seek cooperation from the legislature. In the specific case of Taiwan's political system, this need for cooperation raises special problems for Taiwan's provincial government. These problems arise because the governing elite and its KMT only take a stand on those policies that they consider to be of premier importance. The many other policies that the provincial government is trying to get through the Assembly are left to fend for themselves.

Occasionally, this leads the government to seek special help from the party in order to induce Assembly cooperation on matters considered of lesser importance by the party. More generally, the government goes directly to the Provincial Assembly to obtain its cooperation.

> Pressure groups [are] not well developed.
> This kind of influence on Taiwan is small.
> Most important is administrative lobbying.
> Government officials come in droves . . .
> very pervasive.

> The nine-year compulsory education bill passed
> and officials had to entertain. It is bad
> that officials are entertaining the assembly-
> men all the time.

Things do not always go smoothly when the government goes directly to the Provincial Assembly to obtain its cooperation. The provincial government is made up of a large number of small offices, many headed by obscure, nonprestigious bureaucrats. It is terrifying for these individuals to be called before the Provincial Assembly and be subjected to the public scolding and budget-cutting power of the assemblymen. Nor is it only the wrath of the assemblymen they fear. According to the principle that higher-ups expect their subordinates to head off trouble in their area of responsibility before it becomes public and gets out of hand, the higher provincial officials will also become angry with the object of the assemblymen's displeasure.

> Why power over budget? Certainly the governor
> is not worried that the budget will not pass.
> Of course it will. But if a department has one
> hundred units under it, it is the little fellow
> who heads the unit who is scared that the assem-

blymen will destroy his unit or his projects.
If assemblymen object, the department head is
likely to become angry and ask why he did not
prepare his answers better . . . or clear things
first with the assemblymen . . . or why he wants
the money anyway. In other words, the idea is
to go smoothly. And your responsibility is not
to let trouble happen . . . And simply, without
a fuss he may have his salary or project cut
out from under him. Or with a fuss he may be
fired.

Therefore the government is not solidly united.
And it is not assemblymen against the government, but an assemblyman against individual
government officials . . . or the entire Assembly
against one. And this changes the balance of power.

. . . coupled with fear of face and publicity
. . . an assemblyman's biggest power . . .
[is an official's] fear of attack during the interpellation period . . . fear of attack and
damaging of self-respect is the motivating factor
. . . an official being attacked in front of
his underlings makes a mess of his authority.[80]

Moreover, given a government composed of a large
number of small offices together with scarce resources,
one can expect that, from time to time, the unity of the
government will be disrupted as the units fall into
quarrels over who gets how much from the Assembly. Such
quarrels are common to all large administrations that are
beholden to a legislature.

An extreme example of such a quarrel took place between Taiwan's provincially owned banks and the Provincial Railroad Bureau. This quarrel was rumored to involve
"all kinds of rescue activities, either in the light or
in the darkness," including a large feast with "good
food and Western liquor making assemblymen clouded and
confused in mind" and "bills habitually incurred in dance
halls" being paid by "third parties." These efforts of
the provincial banks apparently caused "very many assemblymen to change their original intentions." Even the
Railroad Bureau's most consistent supporter in the Assembly "was like a wooden buddha, with no expression on his
face and no words leaving his mouth" during the Assembly's

debate. In the end, the Assembly's deputy chairman, with "a manner and attitude . . . of the representative of the related banks, . . . used strong-arm and powder-puff tactics to push unyieldingly for . . . capitulation."[81]

The Provincial Government as Representative of Governing Elite Attitudes

The final role in which the provincial government appears is as a representative of governing elite attitudes about government, democracy, and the Assembly. Officials of the provincial government seemed to have a sincere desire to do a good job for the government and for the public. But exactly what doing a good job means is influenced by the socialization these officials experienced as their traditional civilization was confronted by the invasions of Western imperialism.

The shock that governing elites throughout the non-Western world received when their civilizations and pride crumbled before the invading West had a profound effect on their thinking. In their search for a method to restore "wealth and power" to their nations, many members of these elites sought to discover the secrets of the West and to emulate them. One school of thought came to believe that the wealth and power of the West came from a combination of science and democracy. Thus the secrets of science plus the energy liberated by democracy, combined, would bring wealth and power back to their nations. The many tragedies that occurred following the invasion of the West led many elite members to abandon at least the democratic portion of this school of thought. The disappointed often turned to authoritarian ideologies, such as Communism, as new saviors. But among those elite members who fled Chinese Communism and came to Taiwan, most still held to both the scientific and the democratic portions of this school, in thought if not in action.

Given this background, it is not surprising that in talks with Taiwan's government officials, democracy was still understood to be basically a means to the end of wealth and power, not an end in itself.[82]

As reinforcement to this conception of democracy, the view of democracy learned by non-Western elites was one of harmonious and rational discussion leading to

60

mutual agreement.[83]   This was the direct antithesis of
what seemed to be a major factor in their civilizations'
decline--intranational competition and conflict.   For
those holding this view, it is very difficult to conceive of democracy as involving often bitter competition
between interest groups, with partial and tenuous com-
promises leaving basic disagreements unreconciled, hope-
fully taking place within a broader consensus.   Indeed,
as will be seen in Part III of this study, Taiwan's governing elite takes an extremely hostile view toward the existence of interest groups.

A final factor in this insistence on a view of democracy as a nonconflictive, rational process may be the
fear of conflict and irrationality hypothesized above as
being associated with Chinese political psychology.   This
factor, of course, would only be relevant to those non-
Western elites such as Taiwan's that adhere to the above-
described syndrome of Chinese political psychology.

Combined with this view of the efficacy of a nonconflictive, rational democratic morality for restoring
wealth and power to their nations is the non-Western
elites' conception of themselves as being especially
successful in living up to this morality.   Of course,
many outside observers do not agree with the elites'
self-conception.   The reason for this blind spot in the
elites' measurement of their own behavior may be found
in the elites' assumption that their experience and education are so superior to those of the ordinary people
of their countries that they must be behaving better as
a matter of course.

For these elites, this experience and education
included the participation in political movements aimed
at the restoration of wealth and power to their nations.
Within these movements, the elites underwent emotional
experiences that dramatized noncompetitive and rational
moral values.   Through these dramatic movement experiences,
the elite members apparently came to believe that the movement's cadres (i.e., the elite members), who struggled
for so long, must have already been tested and proven to
be especially qualified to be exemplars of these values.
This conception of elite members as exemplars of moral
values is illustrated in the following description of the
justice and fairness of Taiwan's administrative personnel:

61

> Administrative personnel are national public
> affairs personnel. Certainly they do not rep-
> resent any party, faction, group, or area
> interest. They completely base themselves
> on the standpoint of serving the entire body
> of the people.84

In addition to confidence in the ability of its own members to be exemplars of its conception of democratic morality, non-Western elites also have confidence in their members' ability to apply the method that was to complement democracy in restoring wealth and power to their nations--science. Government officials on Taiwan, for example, considered themselves technical experts in the Western scientific tradition. They had college-level educations and had spent many years in their work. Per- haps they reflect a general attitude of administrative officials in all governments--Western and non-Western-- who spend their time developing broad plans for dealing with society's many problems.

According to such officials, these plans are "cor- rect," since they are made by "neutral experts" who apply "scientific-technical principles" to social problems, producing "apolitical doctors' prescriptions." The fol- lowing quotation mirrors the attitude of the elite's mainlander government officials in this regard: "These people wouldn't know what to do without the large number of mainlander experts in the government . . . The main- lander experts are really responsible for this island's remarkable progress."85

Thus, the provincial government representatives of Taiwan's governing elite, through learning that democ- racy is a nonconflictive, rational process that can aid in restoring the wealth and power they so deeply desire for their nation, through faith in science as a companion method for restoring wealth and power to their nation, and perhaps through traumatic fears of conflictive po- litical processes causing social disorder, in similarity to other non-Western governing elites, became socialized to measure political behavior against the extremely high standards of a nonconflictive, rational conception of de- mocratic morality and a technical-scientific conception of policy-making competence.

Unfortunately, in the face of these deeply felt needs

62

and high standards, nonelite electoral politicians are perceived by non-Western governing elites as displaying conflictive, irrational, immoral, and incompetent behavior. In terms of competent policy making, for example, elites see assemblymen as encouraged by ill-informed constituents to use their untrained and emotional (democratic) laypeople's hands to throw the experts' (scientific) work into disarray. The anguish of Taiwan's elite in this regard is illustrated by the following quotations:

> . . . the decisions of the Provincial Assembly are not "completely good and completely beautiful." This is because the people who make up the Provincial Assembly, provincial assemblymen, are produced from the citizens of the counties and cities. Their election is because of either individual prestige or the support of political parties. Thus it is very possible that the winner understands absolutely nothing about administrative affairs. After taking office, although from the report of the provincial governor and from interpellation he may obtain knowledge of the provincial governing situation, still, in relation to actual conditions, there is likely to be that which is not clearly seen. Therefore, that which it decides is not necessarily practicable. Or although practicable, it misses the big picture, leaving one with a "perceive tree, miss forest" feeling.

> Assemblymen represent the interests of their local areas, occupational groups, parties, and factions. For them it is difficult to avoid "selfishness higher than public interest."

> Originally, the yearly budget prepared by the provincial government aims to attain various kinds of political goals. Because, when it undergoes the review of assemblymen, the amount of each allocation is disrupted by increases and decreases, the original goals for the year definitely become hard to obtain. They must await supplementary budgets passed later in the year or will have to be supplemented in the next year's budget, thus being delayed. Is this not clearly increasing the burdens of the people?[86]

Assemblymen always support the people against
the government.

In regard to the assemblymen's conflictive and immoral behavior, the anguish of Taiwan's elite is illustrated by the following:

The progress of the local area and the quest
for the greatest happiness of the people re-
quire a stable political and economic situation for attainment. But if, because of
the problem of interests arising from the
Assembly's determination of the allocation
of the budget's various items, the representatives of the various parties, factions, local
areas, and groups, in hopes for private profit, increase the depth of the hatred between
them, increasing the antagonisms of politics,
the greatness and deepness of the influence
on the future of the local area will be hard
to estimate.[87]

Non-Western elites find themselves in a dilemma.
They have been socialized to believe that democratic
and scientific behavior that adheres to given standards
will restore the wealth and power they deeply desire
for their nations. Yet the behavior of democratically
elected politicians is perceived by the elites to
threaten these standards, and the restoration of wealth
and power along with them. Given their socialization,
it is understandable that the elites easily lose patience, concluding that the voters and those elected
by them are not yet mature enough to adhere to the necessary standards. Therefore, until the voters and politicians learn to adhere to elite standards, they must
be constrained, both for their own good and for the good
of the nation.[88]

On Taiwan, for example, constraint is accomplished
by a deus ex machina--the government. Staffed by what
the elite perceives to be its own moral and competent
members, the government is seen as standing outside and
above the fallible human element.[89] In the following
illustration, it is implied that in the face of the
assemblymen's immoral and incompetent threat to throw
the government's expertly prepared budget into disarray,
current constraints are insufficient, and additional

64

constraints will be needed.

> The goal of preventing the Assembly from pro-
> posing increases in allocations of the govern-
> ment's budget is to stop assemblymen from
> greatly inflating the budgetary statistics in
> order to ingratiate themselves with their
> various voters or in order to represent the
> interests of their various professions, groups,
> parties, or factions, thus increasing the
> burdens of the people. If within the overall
> amount of the budget prepared by the provin-
> cial government, the Assembly has the power to
> readjust the amounts of the various allocations,
> increasing some and decreasing others, this
> will of necessity cause a "you wrangle, I grasp"
> situation between the assemblymen when the
> budget is being worked on. In the end, the
> dividing up of the public treasury as if it
> was booty would result. Moreover, because the
> use the Assembly makes of this adjustment
> power to cut or reduce budgetary items is
> equivalent to decreasing the budget, there
> is no doubt that reduction and cutting increases
> the burdens of the people.[90]

Further, freedom must be constrained even if no
problem has yet arisen. Thus, the voters and their electoral politicians may have done a very good job, so far.
But given their nature, they are not likely to continue.
Therefore, to "prevent the calamity that has not yet happened" (fang huan wei jan), measures to limit their activity had better be taken before they act again.

> It is fortunate that the Taiwan Provincial
> Assembly has until now been rather careful
> and reasonable in regard to the disposition
> of the budget. The problems resulting from
> the adjustment of the budget referred to
> above have not yet been serious. But to pre-
> vent the calamity that has not yet happened,
> it seems that an effective preventative reg-
> ulation must be instituted.[91]

What is most disturbing is that although some argue
the need for constraint in terms of the immaturity of
the electorate, many argue for constraint against the

65

nature of democracy itself, as shown in previous quotations:

> . . . the decisions of the Provincial Assembly
> are not "completely good and completely beautiful," . . . because . . . provincial assemblymen are produced from the citizens of the
> counties and cities.

> Assemblymen represent . . . interests . . .
> For them it is difficult to avoid "selfishness
> higher than public interest."

Such circumstances, however, are inseparable from the
nature of electoral democracy. Instead of accepting this
as a fact of human nature and trying to develop a concept
of competitive group politics to accommodate human nature
within a framework of consensus, Taiwan's elite, as an
example of non-Western elites in general, is encouraged
by its socialization to insist on a Rousseauian general
will-type of democracy in which the general will, magically comprehended by government experts, is used to
force the selfish group representatives into a freedom
of unity.

Given attempts to go beyond the control of assemblies to control of the types of individuals elected to
them (through the establishment of quotas and minimum
qualifications, for example), one sees another misconception of the nature of democracy. Democracy is a system in which the voters select leaders through free,
competitive marketplace politics. No amount of preselection by some deus ex machina can make a political
system a better democracy. Nonpopular preselection is
by nature authoritarian. The more authoritarian a
political system becomes, the less democratic it remains.

Governing Elite Supporters
within the Provincial Assembly

Institutionalized Form

In addition to its agents within the secret police,
the provincial and local KMT, and the provincial government, Taiwan's governing elite has relied on a group of
agents within the Provincial Assembly itself in its

endeavors to control and limit Taiwan's nonelite politicians. In its institutionalized form, this group displays a convergence of democratic and dictatorial party methods. The purpose of the democratic method is to ensure that within legislative assemblies each political party has its organization of leaders to lead the rank-and-file members in the assembly. The purpose of the dictatorial method is to ensure that every significant organization in the society has a party cell within it to oversee and guide the actions of the entire organization.

In terms of both methods, therefore, the elite's KMT is supposed to have its leaders organized within the Provincial Assembly; and since the overwhelming majority of assemblymen are party members (about 85 percent), the KMT leaders are supposed to oversee and guide the actions of the entire Provincial Assembly.

The assemblymen in formal leadership positions within the Assembly are organized into a Party Group Executive Committee, which consists of the speaker, the deputy speaker, the chairman (chao-chi-jen) of each of the Assembly's six standing committees,92 the party secretary (shu-chi), and his two assistants (fu shu-chi). The latter three are party, not Assembly, officers.

With the power of the governing elite and its agents standing behind it, this group is dominant in the Assembly any time the governing elite chooses to turn on the power. At such times its dominance is the dominance of a transmission belt, transmitting overwhelming power from an outside source.

It is not that the assemblymen in formal leadership positions have no power of their own, however. They are important allies, whose power, if withheld from the battle or turned against the governing elite and its agents, can make things very uncomfortable for the mainlander rulers. This is what happened when the Central Government reasserted its jurisdiction over the inspection of manufactures and farm produce, taking this jurisdiction back from the provincial government. It also happened when the government administratively removed Taipei City from Taiwan Province, making it a special municipality.93

67

The power of the assemblymen in formal leadership positions does not come only from their status as trusted agents of the elite. They are also Taiwanese, tied into their society through networks of personal relationships that they have transformed into political support. This is especially true for the speaker, who not only usually obtains more votes than any other assemblyman in the general elections but also is chosen by the elected representatives for his position of leadership.

Although everyone knows that the governing elite stands behind the scenes pulling most of the strings, the speaker is still recognized as one of the highest elected officials in the province, the closest anyone comes to the position of an elected governor--a position that the mainlander rulers allegedly fear so much. Perhaps he does not have the kind of power that the mainlanders hold, but his elected position does not render him insignificant.

This same point is true on a lesser scale for the Assembly's other formal leaders. The deputy speaker and the committee chairmen are all chosen by their Assembly colleagues, and each one has solid voting support in his local area. Moreover, some of the Assembly's formal leaders have vast personal fortunes. This gives them some obvious additional advantages.

Given their position of support from both above and below, these leaders find themselves performing a middle-man's role. For the speaker this is manifested in the same types of hopes held by other middlemen discussed above. Basically he wants no trouble. "I hope everyone will take large problems and turn them into small problems, take small problems and turn them into nothing."[94]

That many of the speaker's large problems will not turn into small problems, however, is noted by a number of informants. They all referred to the dislike that speakers usually have for their middleman's position and their frequent desire to retire from it. "Speaker is the hardest job . . . in between all assemblymen and the government. [It brings] pressure and no one likes the job. Huang Ch'ao-ch'in got out and Hsieh would like to get out, but they won't let him."[95]

Mainlander Assemblymen

Behind the assemblymen in formal leadership positions stand four sets of individuals in the Assembly
that more or less support Taiwan's governing elite. One
of these sets, the mainlanders, are the strongest allies
of the elite in the Assembly: "Mainlanders support government policy down the line, and that is all there is
to it!" [96]

The background of the mainlanders is indicative of
the type of votes they attract and the type of policies
they support when elected.

> Li Hsien: . . . member of the first graduat-
> ing class of the Whampoa Military Academy.
> Within the army he previously served with a
> rank of lieutenant-general as an assistant
> army commander, an educational commandant,
> a chief secretary, an assistant commander-
> in-chief, as a high-level lieutenant-general
> adviser to the Ministry of Defense, and in
> other important positions . . . This time,
> in obtaining the nomination of the KMT and
> entering the campaign, he will receive the
> voting support of military, governmental,
> and educational personnel, as well as the
> support of military dependents. [97]

Interviews with mainlander assemblymen and discussions with others familiar with them revealed that in
general they held to the views of the ordinary mainlanders
and the mainlanders' governing elite. For example, faith
in the government's reasonableness was balanced by lack
of faith in the ordinary Taiwanese voter:

> On Taiwan it is too fast . . . have to go
> through a training period for democracy
> before you can put it into practice. And
> on Taiwan the training was not enough to
> begin what was already begun. It has to do
> with the standards in education of the voters.
> Taiwan is too low . . . have to guide the
> people until they choose better.

The mainlanders also held reservations about the assem-

69

blymen themselves.

> Especially in county assemblies, often have
> laughable situations because of these low-
> level people. The Provincial Assembly also
> has them.

> Difference of mainland experience and others.
> Local orientation . . . Taiwanese assemblymen
> are more [inclined to] aid small places than
> mainlanders who see the bigger picture . . .
> "The frog who only stays in one well sees
> the sky as a very small thing."

> In the Assembly the Taiwanese do not know this
> [the greatness of the mainland] . . . do not
> feel this . . . do not care at all.

> They lack manners and I try to teach them.

> The quality of most assemblymen is pretty low.
> The Mandarin of many of the assemblymen is
> terrible and they are at home only in Japanese.

In relation to the mainlanders in the Assembly
there are two final points of interest. First, there
is enough social distance between them and their Taiwanese colleagues to cause them to act with care within the
Assembly.

> Mainlanders have to be careful. Do not put
> up a front and irritate other assemblymen and
> make them angry. Have to have a decent atti-
> tude.

> For example, on the age limit from sixteen to
> eighteen for bar girls, etc. He supported
> raising it to eighteen, but spoke so bitingly
> and impolitely--"would you send your daughter?,
> etc., etc."--that everyone became angry and it
> ended in a fight. Actually, without such
> irritation it would have been passed without a
> formal vote.

Second, the experience of the mainlanders before they
arrived on Taiwan is likely to cause them to see a great
improvement in the ability of the elite to govern well.

70

Thus they are likely to look on Taiwan's current political and administrative situation with general approval. This attitude of approval will not necessarily be shared by colleagues who have lived under more efficient administrative systems before 1949.

Half-Mountain KMT Assemblymen

For those who do not like them, the mainlanders are known in the Taiwanese dialect as a-sua, translatable into something like "mountain barbarians." To these same people, the Taiwanese who lived much of their lives on the mainland are called bua-sua, "half-mountain barbarians."

> Bua-sua . . . is a curse word. When the Japanese came, [they] called them hsi-ga (four feet) in Taiwanese. And it means the same thing that they called mainlander-Taiwanese when they came back. The worse name went to the mainlanders.

Within the Assembly are a small number of these Taiwanese with mainland backgrounds. They form a second set of strong supporters for the governing elite. They left Taiwan to avoid Japanese rule: "not wanting to live an unfree life on a Taiwan seized and ruled by Japanese devils, she secretly went to Peiping."98

While on the mainland these Taiwanese became closely identified with the governing elite and its policies, carrying this identification with them back to Taiwan.

> There she met [her husband]. Together they participated in the movement to recover Taiwan, devoting themselves to "resist Japan, save country" work . . . Eight years of the war of resistance defeated the aggressor Japanese, and hand in hand the couple returned to liberated Taiwan, devoting themselves to the work of reconstruction.99

That they are still closely identified with the elite is demonstrated by the sources of their votes.

> Huang Kuang-p'ing grew up on the mainland and came into politics through the army. His votes

71

are military men. No problem . . . Wherever
he goes, he has those votes. Look at his
background--half-mountain!

Still, despite their close identification with Taiwan's elite, some of these assemblymen have worked hard
to build up nonelite bases of support. They began with
their preexisting networks of families and relatives.
On top of these they built businesses, establishing
economic roots and a following of employees.100

The building of a political base among Taiwanese
constituents, in conjunction with the continuance of an
originally close relationship with the governing elite,
has placed the returned Taiwanese in a cross-pressured
position similar to the one in which the formal legislative leaders find themselves.101 Indeed, one would
expect that, given their close identification with the
elite and their ability to win elections, these returned
Taiwanese would frequently be chosen as formal leaders
by the elite's KMT. For the Assembly's third term (1963-
1968), this was the case for four out of the Provincial
Assembly's eight returned Taiwanese.

The ambiguity of the position of the returned Taiwanese, and even the ambiguity of the mainlander assemblymen's position, will be further discussed in the following Chapter's description of Assembly opposition to
the governing elite. The other side of the ambiguity,
however, the tendency to have faith in and look well on
the current political and administrative situation, is
illustrated as follows:

>If the request is reasonable, the government
>officials will help the assemblyman help his
>constituents. If not . . . no.

>They [the returned Taiwanese] are used to the
>Chinese way of government. And their stan-
>dards are what they knew on the mainland (not
>as good as here). And in comparing, they are
>still nor satisfied, but not so dissatisfied.

Ordinary Taiwanese KMT Assemblymen

Another set of individuals within the Assembly that

serve as general supporters of the governing elite is composed of the ordinary Taiwanese KMT assemblymen. Subtracting mainlanders (six), returned Taiwanese (eight), and non-KMT members (nine), the ordinary KMT Taiwanese make up the Assembly's remaining membership (forty-seven out of seventy in 1966-1968). Whether from fear of the power of the elite's KMT, especially in terms of their renomination, or out of actual conviction, the ordinary Taiwanese KMT assemblymen generally support their party. Below, two such assemblymen enthusiastically express their feelings on the matter:

> The KMT means well . . . no bad intentions.
> They want to find the best in society for lead-
> ership . . . someone who people will support.

> If you just criticize the officials, putting
> on a "I am a fantastic people's representative"
> front, they will be very nice to you on the floor,
> but will not follow it up. They will follow it
> up if you have your good reasons and do not
> speak ridiculously.

Supportive Non-KMT Assemblymen

A final set of supporting individuals is said to consist of those non-KMT assemblymen who, because of financial pressures, are from time to time persuaded to vote with the party. Informants were only able to identify convincingly one assemblyman as falling into this category: "Z is a 'good' nonparty man, and he can get what he wants from them. And because of his big business, he is under their thumb and they can control him." Even in his own words this assemblyman appears cooperative:

> I do not make a differentiation . . . Taiwan
> . . . mainland . . . it is all the same in my
> behavior toward them. Also the same with non-
> party and party . . .

> After all, people living in Taiwan are not
> bad off . . . enough to eat . . . and some
> comfort . . . and you can live . . . And the
> standard of living is better here than in many
> other areas of the world.

> . . . get things done and not only talk big
> like Assemblyman X [another nonparty member].
> In the Assembly they request my support for
> something and naturally I can expect a return
> opportunity.   Only in this way can I be an
> effective assemblyman and take care of my
> locality.
>
> I do not just attack and attack . . . really
> speak little . . . and will admit the party is
> correct when it is, but will bring out where
> it is wrong.
>
> The KMT has bad points, but also has good points
> . . . would never get the chance I now have
> under the Communists to run.   And you can speak
> your piece here.

Still, even in Assemblyman Z's case these cooperative
words were balanced by other statements, as will be noted
in Chapter 2.[102]

Chapter 2

THE GOVERNING ELITE'S OPPOSITION

Taiwan's governing elite, the elite's KMT, and the elite's other agents, as powerful as they are, do not have the field of provincial and local politics completely to themselves. There is a weak but persistent opposition.

Opposition Politicians and Their Constituencies

Taiwan's opposition politicians and the constituencies that support them are of a diverse nature. In some cases an opposition politician may receive support from his voters for reasons unrelated to his opposition to Taiwan's governing elite--his opposition being a personal choice that does not reflect the desires of his constituency. Such a personal choice may even be a matter of refusing to support the elite in an isolated case because one or another of its policies directly threatens the politician's private interests. Even if the politician's opposition does reflect the desires of his constituency, these desires too may be only to protect threatened interests in isolated cases.

In other cases the motivation for opposition may be related to the KMT's problems of nominating candidates when two powerful local Taiwanese factions demand the same office. The choice of the candidate of one faction, without mollifying the other faction, may cause the other faction to send out a candidate from its own ranks to compete with the party in the election.

But in written material about local elections in Taiwan reference is often made to an antiparty source of votes independent of factional conflicts or isolated situations of particularistic interests. It is these votes that are the core of antielite opposition, with factional conflicts and particularistic interests adding or subtracting votes depending on local circumstances.

According to knowledgeable informants, this core of antielite opposition is small and localized, being centered in the cities, where public awareness and contact with mainlanders are high.

75

> Cities have (not countryside) an antiparty
> vote of 15% or 10%, which you can depend on.
> [This is] ideological. [It is] different
> in the countryside.
>
> Taiwanese kids [from the countryside] . . .
> go to Taiwan University [in Taipei City]
> feeling they are Chinese, but everyone treats
> them like Taiwanese . . . In the countryside
> they think they are Chinese.[103]

Moreover, according to informants, this core of antielite opposition is not only limited but also often split. One anti-KMT candidate's comments on this problem follow:

> Hsin-tien was my vote source, but Cheng Chen-
> te took it away. Only Cheng Chen-te, the
> woman perhaps, and Hsieh A-shu should have
> run. But there is no way to get the nonparty
> people together in Taipei County. [They are]
> all too independent.
>
> [It is] hard for nonparty people to get together
> because everyone is a prima donna.
>
> [There were] so many nonparty candidates that
> they took votes that were originally mine.

Part of the explanation for the small size and the disunity of this core of antielite opposition is that some nonparty politicians are not core members--they do not share an ideology based on opposition to Taiwan's governing elite. Therefore, they are not interested in uniting for the furthering of antielite goals or for increasing the size of the antielite coalition.

Most nonparty politicians, however, do share an antielite ideology. But this ideology is often overridden by ambitions to attain the many nonideological rewards offered by successful players of the local politics game.[104] This overriding of ideology by nonideological ambition is facilitated by the strength of the status quo (as it appeared to electoral politicians and to the general voter in the 1966-1968 period that this study was researched).

Such factors as the governing elite's ability to play local factions off against each other, to satisfy electoral politicians and their followings through the wide distribution of local political patronage, to keep the economy producing comparative well-being for the general population, as well as to frighten through the threat of coercion, had convinced many antielite politicians and potential voters to concentrate on more private goals instead of futilely butting their heads against the elite's great stone wall.[105]

In the following quotation, an informant further details the strength of the local political status quo, noting that only extraordinary circumstances would translate verbal approval of radical rhetoric into voting or other concrete political behavior.

> [The] typical Taiwanese revolutionary is a
> Taiwan University graduate in political science
> whose parents were landlords who received
> degrees in Japanese schools. [He is] out of
> touch with society.
>
> The politicians in the factions [who are non-
> revolutionary], through systems of relation-
> ships, votes, etc., are knit into the society
> and because of this, only they count.
>
> If the situation were different, Taiwan perhaps
> would be very unstable. Like if the old man
> died and no one knew what was happening, or
> if the Communists take the offshore islands.
>
> But otherwise incendiary elements get applause
> and shouting affirmation from giant crowds
> . . . and no votes, and [with] incendiary state-
> ments that you would expect to set off a riot,
> things do not go anywhere.[106]

The Opposition's Ideology

The content of antielite ideology is difficult to determine. Information given by informants is influenced by the possibility of severe punishment for too much opposition.[107] Moreover, informants are but a small group. Given this situation, it was physically and politically

impossible to obtain a reasonable sample of opinion.
The only people from Taiwan free from fear are the large
numbers of students and former students now living in the
United States and other foreign countries. But they are
divorced from the local situation geographically and
intellectually. Thus, the following description of Taiwan's antielite ideology cannot be taken as definitive.
Indeed, given the constraints on research prevailing on
Taiwan, no description of Taiwan's antielite ideology
can be taken as definitive.[108]

Normal Desire for Best Deal Possible

Part of Taiwan's antielite ideology expresses the
normal interests of any ruled group for the best deal
possible from its rulers. Reporters and KMT assemblymen
agreed that many of the demands made by non-KMT assemblymen are motivated by this concern. This motivation appears
to be latent in the rest of the electorate and its representatives, for KMT members within the Assembly express
the same type of demands (though less frequently and less
dramatically).[109] Indeed, most of the efforts of most
assemblymen show that, in general, a better deal for the
governed is their main expressed concern.[110]

Effect of Government by Outsiders

Added to the basic relationship of ruler and ruled
in Taiwan is the problem that the rulers are outsiders.
Such a difference between ruler and ruled can result in
a spectrum of feelings among the ruled. At one extreme
is an acceptance of the superiority of the outsiders.
At the opposite extreme are demands for replacing all
ruling outsiders with native rulers.

Certainly Taiwan has those who have been indoctrinated
well enough to accept the KMT's ideology, and thus the
right of the mainlander elite to rule. There are also
those who accept the KMT's ideology but, basing themselves
on that ideology, see room for much more democracy (Taiwanese Power) within its framework. More extreme are
those who see the mainlanders as alien rulers, an obstacle
to the political independence of Taiwan from mainland
rule--KMT or Communist.[111]

78

Some of those on the independence side of the spectrum have even gone to the point of declaring the need for the cultural as well as the political independence of Taiwan from the Chinese world. Such demands open up the problem of cultural identity for Taiwan's inhabitants, a problem that reaches to the emotional roots of each inhabitant's psychology.[112]

Given the lack of encouragement of free thought (some would say any thought) on Taiwan, it is even conceivable that some Taiwanese have formed no opinion regarding rule by outsiders.[113] More disturbing, whatever the state of opinions, is the possibility that no mainland or Taiwanese politician will ever permit the development and testing of these opinions through free discussion. Either the elite will continue to enforce obedience through the techniques described above or a violent opposition will frighten everyone into a new line. Unfortunately, it is even possible that, given freedom of choice, the lack of democratic training and the factionalized state of political behavior on Taiwan will make it impossible for the Taiwanese to resolve the question peacefully among themselves.[114]

Expressed Opinions of Assemblymen concerning the Elite's Rule

Given the constraints on research prevailing on Taiwan, it is impossible to state what proportion of Taiwanese fall into each part of the opinion spectrum concerning acceptance or rejection of Taiwan's outsider ruling elite. What can be stated--and exemplified--is where the expressed opinions of Taiwan's provincial assemblymen fall on this spectrum.

In general, these opinions fall in the portion of the spectrum that accepts the KMT ideology but sees the possibility of much more democracy within its framework.[115] The presentation of these opinions that follows contains quotes from assemblymen in all categories: nonparty members, party members who tend to be independent in their actions, nonindependent party members, and even mainlanders.

Although nonparty members lead in the opposition, the fact that other assemblymen also join in suggests that the 10-15 percent opposition vote may only be the small

manifestation of a much larger, latent Taiwanese opposition; that, in general, there is a socializing experience
that orients all assemblymen to argue for the legitimacy
of their role and for the general powers of their body;
and that, among mainlanders, there is not simply a proelite
reflex but also a liberal strain of thought that has led
them both to flee the Communists and to criticize the
Nationalists.

General Support for
Basic Elite Policies

General support by all assemblymen for basic elite
policies can even be found on the censured antiparty
campaign leaflet noted above (page 54). But this support
is often stated along with the implication that the governing elite's image of itself as omniscient guide for Taiwan's democratic development is not congruent with the
actual effectiveness of the elite's democratic developmental policies.

> [We need to develop the] ideal of two parties
> in Taiwan and a democratic China. Then we can
> really go back to the mainland and have a repu-
> tation to gain support.

> The basic national policy . . . returning to the
> mainland . . . I support it. If you are to
> get back to the mainland, you have to correct
> all the deficiencies and firm up your base.

Denial of Governing Elite's
Morality and Competence

Other statements, which directly contradict key
attitudes held by Taiwan's governing elite, dispute the
morality and competence of the elite's government officials.

> In the past the government had many experts.
> But these are all phoney experts. For example,
> population recording had population recording
> experts, and on the mainland there was not one
> province that had population records. They
> came to Taiwan and then became population experts.

80

Local administration had local administration
experts. But there was not one province in
which local administration was up to par.
But they came to Taiwan and also became experts
. . . These kind of experts we have plenty of.[116]

Government officials do not understand (although
there has been much improvement in their attitudes from the past). Still they feel they are
the experts. They do not understand the Assembly
system, in which every level and circle in society
must be represented, no matter what.

If the several Central Government officials
are so great, how were they able to lose a
population of four hundred million, leaving
over only twelve million . . . The greatness
of the President is recognized all over the
world. But there are some officials who, if
given power, then only think of themselves.
If they earn some money, they would rather
save it in foreign banks. I do not believe
these officials are capable of doing a good job
of governing. Otherwise, why are the national-
owned enterprises so far behind provincial-
owned enterprises?[117]

Similarly, the idea that assemblymen are less competent than the elite's officials is disputed by the
assemblymen.

People's representatives are close to the
people and see things clearly. Members of the
Legislative Yuan up in Taipei see nothing.

When I myself was an administrator, I welcomed
the criticisms of each assemblyman, since
they were closer to their individual districts
than I could ever possibly be . . . and they
knew what was going on better.[118]

Denial That Increased
Democracy Is Harmful

The assemblymen also dispute the elite's contention
that the scope of elections and elective offices cannot

be broadened on Taiwan because it will detract from
Taiwan's ability to counterattack against the mainland.

> . . . According to Article 108 of the con-
> stitution, "The General Principles of Provin-
> cial and County Self-Government should be es-
> tablished . . ." This basic bill for the es-
> tablishment of the local self-government system
> until today is still being held up in the organ
> responsible for Central Government legislation,
> the Legislative Yuan. It is in cold storage.
> I do not know for what reason. This representa-
> tive feels that although the only area that is
> now carrying on self-government is Taiwan Prov-
> ince, still the success or failure of Taiwan's
> putting into practice local self-government is
> not solely related to the interest of the people
> of Taiwan. It also is related to the attraction
> or repulsion of the hearts of the people living
> on the mainland and the wresting forth of inter-
> national aid and support.[119]

Demands for Legitimacy

These statements of opposition to elite ideology
lead to a demand for the recognition of the elected
Assembly's legitimacy to decide matters that now are
decided by the nonelected elite.

> Because the colleagues of this Assembly are
> elected according to law, of course it is the
> only organ of the will of the people representing
> the Province of Taiwan. Besides this, is there
> any other organ that represents the will of the
> people of Taiwan Province? If there is not,
> then the opinion of our Taiwan Provincial Assem-
> bly should receive respect first and foremost.
> Our government takes the will of the people as
> its guide . . . If it does not take the will
> of the people as its opinion, is not everything
> finished? That would be equivalent to the
> manner of a Hitler . . . Thus, the Taiwan
> Provincial Assembly is now the institution for
> the expression of the opinion of the people of
> Free China. This cannot be denied. As far
> as the national assemblymen and the members of the

Legislative Yuan and the Control Yuan elected
in the past, they also are people's representatives elected by the voters of the entire
country. But in what place are their current
voters? Who do they represent?[120]

Assembly as Party out of Power

Behind this demand for the recognition of the assemblymen's legitimacy may be not only the logic of democratic political philosophy but also the assemblymen's
very human feeling that they are being shunted aside--
that the Assembly itself is the party out of power.

> The government does not take the Assembly
> seriously. Sometimes it privately tells the
> Assembly and proclaims the law without seek-
> ing Assembly approval. Sometimes it asks the
> Central Government to put it into effect over
> the head of the Assembly. And it does not put
> into effect the bills of the Assembly, or only
> partially puts them into effect.
>
> In most county assemblies there are two factions,
> the government-supporting faction--the faction
> that won the county mayor elections--and the
> government-opposing faction. But in the Provin-
> cial Assembly there is only an out-of-power
> faction, and all the assemblymen are part of it.

Welfare of Taiwanese

In a broader context, the assemblymen do not argue
only for the legitimacy of their own organ. They extend
their arguments to the welfare of the Taiwanese they
represent.

> I stand on the ground of the people of Taiwan
> Province . . . Taiwan Province is a small island.
> Now it is as if it is being divided into two
> provinces. Taipei City is the richest financial
> city of the entire province. If severed from
> us . . . [how] will Taiwan build itself in the
> future? What will happen to education? Especial-
> ly after the counterattack to the mainland is

83

successful, originally rich Taiwan Province will
become a poverty-striken province. For everything we will have to beg the Central Government for aid.[121]

This province has been liberated for over
twenty years now. Higher and technical education are now extremely common. Thus, although
the number of this province's citizens in the
various [governmental] organs are few, those
with talent and ability are many . . . although
it is said that examinations are objective,
still very few [Taiwanese] receive their benefit.
There should be no quotas in government personnel
practices. "Only talent as the criterion" is
the great principle for personnel policy.[122]

Radicalization since 1968?

The above are just some of the statements and categories of Assembly opposition to the governing elite's
1966-1968 status quo. These moderate statements were
generally made for public consumption, however, and it
is conceivable that private feelings were much more
radical.[123] Moreover, since the author's 1966-1968 research, given "ping-pong" diplomacy, the governing elite's
defeat in the United Nations, and former President Nixon's
trip to Peking, the situation is different. Thus, either
because radical feelings were kept private in 1966-1968 or
because the situation was different and opinions had
changed, reports from Taiwan soon after the shocks of the
early 1970s indicated a radicalizing of opinions and actions.

"You Americans . . . dropped two atom bombs
on Japan, But you did a far worse thing
against Taiwan . . . What did you drop on us
when the war was over? Chiang K'ai-shek."

". . . the feeling of Taiwanese resentment
against mainlander rule--this sense that if the
world were just, we would be the rulers and
not the mainlanders--exists in every Taiwanese
heart . . . all of a sudden you may find this
whole seemingly impressive structure of police
and agent and informer crumbling away."[124]

84

Reformers would like to abolish the whole
present national government structure here
and have a new single government for Taiwan
. . .

. . . heads of student unions at Taiwan National
University issued a manifesto that contained
the implied threat that if reforms were not made
. . . the young people of the island would turn
against the Government.

And at a meeting of Taiwanese with [1971]
Premier and Vice-President C. K. Yen recently,
Kang Lin-hsing, a 32-year-old member of the
popularly elected Taipei City Council, made
a bold speech in which he stressed the Government's lack of support among the Taiwanese and
demanded reforms.[125]

Whether these statements represented a general trend
toward radicalism on Taiwan or were merely representative
of the feelings of small, isolated groups is difficult
to say. In any case, similarly tentative evidence indicates that after the first shock waves of the early
1970s wore off, there was a strong countertendency to
accept the leadership of the Chiang Ching-kuo government as long as it strove to keep Taiwan factually (if
not ideologically) independent of the Chinese mainland
and slowly moving toward a greater political role for
the Taiwanese.[126]

Characteristics of Opposition Politicians

The rather tame opposition that the author found
on Taiwan, expressed mainly by the nonparty members of
the Provincial Assembly but on occasion by their colleagues also, obtains much of its character from six
personal characteristics of the opposing individuals.

The first characteristic derives from the pre-1945
experiences of most Taiwanese. These experiences were
very different from those of the mainlanders and the
returned Taiwanese. The mainlanders and returned Taiwanese had become used to the elite's way of government.
Their standards are what they knew on the mainland.
The post-1945 situation on Taiwan was a great improve-

85

ment to them. But for the Taiwanese who spent the pre-
1945 period on Taiwan or in Japan, the perspective is
very different. "Their basic attitude is to contrast
the administrative disorder (luan) of Taiwan today with
the efficiency of Japan and come out criticizing the
present government on those terms."

The second characteristic shared by many opposing
individuals is that many politicians with pre-1945
Japanese backgrounds were trained in Japan or on Taiwan
as medical doctors. This training has resulted in giving
them a special place among their fellow Taiwanese. Under
Japan, the policy was to allow only a small number of
Taiwanese to continue on to higher education, and those
only in the more technical disciplines. Thus, until
recently, there were few among the Taiwanese who had
gained the respect of their fellows by satisfying the
cultural requirement of superior learning. Among the
few, medical doctors had the highest respect. This and
other points about the medical doctors' special position
on Taiwan were made by many informants:

> Power of a doctor . . . people hold a doctor
> in high respect. They see that he has passed
> that academic hurdle. He must have brains
> . . . has money. And many people come to see
> him.

> My independence from being a doctor.

> The KMT . . . fears doctors and independent
> people more than anyone else . . . they cannot
> control them.

> The government can really put pressure finan-
> cially on anyone but doctors. Therefore it
> fears them.

The third characteristic shared by some of the
opposing individuals concerns their claim to be associated with no parties and no factions (wu-tang wu-p'ai).
Actually, many self-labeled nonparty nonfaction politicians are in factions. The problem is that no matter
what one's ideology, few politicians in Taiwan--KMT
or non-KMT--can get elected without the support of a
local-level Taiwanese electoral faction. It is likely
that the nonparty nonfaction label is used because it

sounds good in Chinese and because both elite and public opinion look upon factions as illegitimate--no matter how necessary. Almost all faction members deny their membership in factions as a matter of course.

But for some of these nonparty nonfaction politicians, even the claim of being nonparty is erroneous. They are nonparty, if party is spelled with a capital letter, since they are not in the KMT. But they often belong to one of the two tiny political parties existing alongside the giant KMT--the Young China Party (Ch'ing Nien Tang) or the China Democratic Socialist Party (Min She Tang). Since these parties have little organization and less prestige, however, the non-KMT politicians and others prefer to view all non-KMT politicians, whether in one of the small parties or not, under the clearly independent "nonparty" label.

Fourthly, for some of those who are not medical doctors, other sources of wealth may permit a certain amount of independence. Although wealth may tie the wealthy to the fortunes of a politically vulnerable business, this is not inevitably the case; and if it is the case, the vulnerable but wealthy politician is not without weapons of his own.

A fifth characteristic that may permit a certain amount of independence is a supportive source of votes. In this regard, informants make the following observations:

> [They] dare to speak because a fight between them and the government gets them votes.

> Assemblyman Y dares to speak and oppose the party. He is more interested in the reaction of his powerful vote source than in party support.

> Nonparty men purposely oppose. It is their source of votes and raison d'être.

The final characteristic shared by at least some opposing individuals is the loss of land they sustained as a result of the governing elite's land reform programs (thus, the revolutionary offspring of former landlords referred to on page 77 above). Below, Martin Yang describes two political paths taken by landlords who lost their land during the reform. The second path led to active political opposition.

> At one extreme stood all those who tried to keep and multiply their former power and positions by identifying themselves with, or submitting themselves to, the current political authorities or the ruling party. These people had wholeheartedly supported the present Government and its party by offering their loyalty and means, and by complying with all legislation and all programs instituted by the Government. As their reward many gained political favor and appointive positions at all levels.

> At the opposite extreme were those who did not want to support the Government and the ruling party. But neither did they want to give up power and position. These people also resorted to political means to get what they wanted, but instead of going over to the Government and its party, they turned in an opposite direction. They worked hard to create something like an opposition party. They identified themselves as champions of the political feelings and interests of those groups which had a grudge or a complaint against the authorities. When they felt more or less assured of the needed support, they stood for election to all kinds of public offices. Many of them succeeded.[127]

Power of Opposition within Assembly

What factors operate to translate the above statements of opposition and conditions of personal political independence shared by a minority of assemblymen into power within the Provincial Assembly?

One factor is the ability of nonparty politicians to speak more freely than those subject to party discipline. This gives the nonparty politician not only more potential to threaten the face of officials during the interpellation period but also the opportunity to express the opinions of the KMT politicians who have been ordered not to speak. Quotations involving restraints on party members and the corresponding freedom of non-party politicians follow:

> The loss of Ch'en Wu-chang was contributed
> to because, as the KMT-nominated candidate,
> his behavior and speech could not but respect
> certain limitations.[128]

> I am not in the party and thus can say things
> the party members cannot. Sometimes they ask
> me to speak for them. They all give me their
> time periods and I speak three or four times
> a day.

> Hsieh A-shu is a young nonparty nonfaction person.
> In speaking, he can express what his heart
> desires. In action, he has no restraining
> fears.[129]

A second factor contributing to the power of the opposition is its ability to use the rules of the Assembly, especially the rules for a quorum, to force the acceptance of their ideas.

> Voting is also very troublesome. Very rarely
> are there enough members to vote on the matter.
> A call for a [role call] vote can really set
> things back.

> Also power when the government needs something
> fast.

Third, on occasion the nonparty assemblymen are able to expand their numerical strength by convincing colleagues (and government officials) of the justice of their arguments: "Kuo Yü-hsin was correct on the equalization of land rights bill. Therefore we amended it."

If the opposition should expand to a majority of the assemblymen, it can then avail itself of the general power of the Assembly already described. Such powers as the right to approve the provincial government's budget, the power of interpellation, the power of rich assemblymen against poorer civil servants, and the power to bring disputes into the open in the press come into play or are strengthened. These powers are not great, but they can be troublesome to the governing elite and its agents.

Weakness of Opposition within Assembly

Still, despite the opposition's ability to be troublesome, either on its own or in its expanded version, in general its impact is quite limited. The causes of this limited impact are to be found in the weaknesses of the opposition as well as in the strengths of the governing elite and its agents. Evidence suggests that nonparty assemblymen frequently cooperate with one another to form a core around which a larger opposition can expand, but this cooperation is not complete.

> In the Assembly, the Young China Party members
> . . . used to get together, but no longer . . .
> Now three don't meet with them . . . Four do
> . . . get together frequently. Eat together
> and plan.

> Nonparty nonfaction . . . all independent . . .
> isn't any organization. In the Assembly every-
> one is his own faction.

> Nonparty nonfaction members are not united
> . . . too busy fighting among themselves.

An attempt to explain this lack of cooperation between nonparty politicians has already been offered on pages 76-77 above.

Even if there is success in expanding the opposition to a majority of the assemblymen, the constraints imposed upon the power of the Assembly, dealt with previously, must also be contended with. Some representative reactions of assemblymen to them follow:

> Not much power . . . cannot propose any real
> legislation . . . therefore very limited . . .
> and government can ask reconsideration . . .
> and as a last resort it can run to the Central
> Government. Even things that are within its
> jurisdiction, the government does not do them
> all. Therefore the real great power is the
> interpellation. One reason for the general
> interpellation is to get everyone to pay attention.

It was not clear in the language of the laws
and so I asked, and they said that you cannot
pass bills with regard to laws. Most resolutions proposed are suggestions or requests for
action in one place or another. They do not
write laws; the government does that.

Not satisfied . . . after questioning on a
matter, one must keep asking to see if it is
done. Influence small . . . budget threat
small . . .

Two weapons . . . propose resolutions . . .
interpellation. Proposed many times . . .
for ten years sometimes before it goes through.

An additional aspect of the weakness of the entire
Assembly, noted by the assemblymen themselves, was the
lack of technical resources (time, staff, office space)
available to the members.

. . . the Committee's time is insufficient.
And especially small matters are cursorily
reviewed and approved.

Even the budget . . . no time for a penetrating
analysis. They always have to have the budget
passed very quickly. Naturally they try to
give most attention to the more important items.

More important than the lack of technical resources,
however, a major criticism of the Assembly voiced by the
assemblymen is that there is indeed much truth to the
governing elite's perception of their colleagues as incompetent, an incompetence that makes it difficult for
the Assembly to be taken seriously by the elite and by
the voters.

We propose too many resolutions. Therefore
the government does not look upon them as important . . . our own fault. Even though we
do not have a great deal of power, if we concentrated on a few important resolutions, and
know what we are doing with them, the government would be hard pressed not to accept them.
But last time we proposed around a thousand
resolutions. And half came back as not in the

jurisdiction of the government . . . hurts the
prestige of the Assembly.

Assemblymen throw away their power . . . They
speak foolishly, destroying their interpellation power.

Cannot just propose resolutions pushing the
government to do ten things for every district
. . . must also think of the problems of the
amount of money the government has and its
general plans for the whole province.

Too many assemblymen are country bumpkins . . .
do not understand finance, etc. . . . not understand importance of the budget, and do not
understand it or see it only piece by piece.

An assemblyman should see the broad picture,
not like Assemblyman X who just wants you to
repair road A and road B . . . tiny ones somewhere in his county.

Despite their self-criticism, however, assemblymen
and other observers do find reasons for why they display
this incompetent behavior.

And you sort of have to [propose many reso-
lutions], because, if the other assemblyman proposes and is successful for his constituents and you have not proposed anything,
they all point to you and say, "what's the
matter?" Therefore you have to propose also,
and in the end no one gets anything.

The behavior in regard to proposing resolutions and the ability to influence fellow
members on a vote would be very different if
the Assembly actually had power to make its
decisions stick. All the resolutions and the
ease of influencing colleagues stems from
the limited powers.

An additional reason for this dysfunctional behavior
is that the elite's KMT displays little interest in enforcing discipline upon its members within the Provincial
Assembly regarding such matters as the number of resolu-

92

tions proposed or the narrowness of interpellation questions asked. As indicated above, the KMT only concerns itself with those matters that the elite considers to be of premier importance. Other matters are left to a freer play of provincial and local political forces.

Given that the governing elite professes to consider Taiwan's democratic development to be a matter of premier importance, however, this lack of concern for enforcing the kind of discipline that would increase the assemblymen's democratic competence calls for explanation. One possible explanation is that the KMT's lack of concern for enforcing discipline is an example of the laxity many political parties have displayed after long periods as the ruling party of a country.

A second possible explanation is that, on one or another level of consciousness, the governing elite is insincere. Deep down it knows that real democracy means that it must release its hold over the government. And either because it fears that no other politicians will be willing or able to pursue its cherished goals of national wealth and power and/or because it wants to preserve its rule for reasons unrelated to the pursuit of national wealth and power, it does not want to release its hold. If this is the case, the elite may well prefer to have the assemblymen behaving incompetently. Such behavior makes it easier for the elite to continue constraining democracy on the grounds of the immaturity of the electorate and the elected.

Finally, a third possible explanation for not enforcing discipline on assemblymen may be that the local-level particularistic pressures (to be described in Parts II and III of this study) under which Taiwan's electoral politicians must operate are so great that if the governing elite wants to allow even the minimal amount of democracy to which it has so far committed itself, the elite will have to permit the politicians to express these pressures through such devices as particularistic resolutions and interpellations.

The opposition to the governing elite, taken as a small group of nonparty assemblymen or taken as an expanded opposition representing a consensus of Assembly members, as weak as it is on its own terms, must also contend with the tactics the elite uses to defeat it. These tactics are commented upon in terms of elections, control of newspapers, ability of the elite to get support from unprincipled opportunists (an admittedly prejudiced category), power of the party to marshal votes in the Assembly, and threat of arrest and imprisonment, as follows.

With regard to elections,

> Two days ago we had the candidates' meeting and eight nonparty candidates wanted freedom to make campaign speeches at any time, anywhere. But five [party candidates] did not. And because of the two-thirds rule, the eight could not get it.

> The five do not want it because they have party votes and do not need it, while if outsiders do not have it, they have no way to get themselves before the public.

> . . . have my own source of votes . . . X City . . . could also get outside of the city, but it is easy for the party to fix elections out there . . . showing you how to vote, etc.

With regard to control of newspapers,

> . . . the two newspapers owned by the provincial government, the New Life and the News, did not print one word concerning the important bill that the Assembly heatedly discussed yesterday. I request the speaker to ask the head of the Department of Information to come before the Assembly to explain the reason. If the newspaper that we own will not print it, what newspaper will?[130]

> The newspapers have reported that we, the Assembly, support the changing of Taipei City's status. What evidence do they have for this? I do not know. In the past it has often been like this. They say that the will of the majority supports something. I do not know whose public opinions they polled. Today the newspapers frequently sing a tune opposite from that of our organs of the will of the people. We are the will-of-the-people organ, representing the entire province's 12 million people . . . If it is

94

made known to the various democratic nations of
the world that our Taiwan has this kind of free
speech, has this kind of organs for the will
of the people, truly it will be a thing of great
shame.[131]

With regard to support from unprincipled opportunists,

President Chiang has called upon us to take
Taiwan as the base for counterattack, to use
the youth of Taiwan as the backbone of the
counterattack, to act forcefully on the policy
of employing Taiwanese talent. None of the
people of the province do not feel thankfulness
from the heart. But in relation to the carrying out of this policy, there seems to be some
problems. Those who are being employed, if they
were not loyal subjects of the Japanese Emperor
during the period of Japanese rule . . . then
they were traitorous running dogs who formerly
served the counterfeit Manchukuo or phoney
Wang Ching-wei regimes. Otherwise they were
local rascals and oppressive gentry. As for
those determined revolutionary souls who did
not hesitate to sacrifice family or life to
serve loyally their ancestors' country in anti-
Japanese activities, one on the contrary does
not see them in important positions.[132]

With regard to power of the party to marshal votes in the
Assembly,

People fear most being scolded and therefore
you can use that as a threat. Also sometimes
they would rather compromise than be stubborn.
But in the end they can get the votes.

The final tactic used by the governing elite to hold
down the opposition is the ever-present threat of arrest
and imprisonment. Despite this threat, there is a certain amount of organization among the nonparty politicians, as indicated by the following statements:

Taipei area [nonparty] people all meet together
once a month. Everyone takes a turn. When
I have them over, it is at the M Restaurant
or a place like that. [We] drink and have fun

95

and the like.

> For this election the organization of Yang
> Chin-hu's campaign headquarters was truly
> quite thorough. It brought together over
> one thousand cadres. At each polling station
> they prepared a team of four men: one man
> took responsibility for checking to see if
> each voter matched the registration book, thus
> preparing evidence for later court action; one
> man carried a lighting apparatus, just in
> case the source of electricity is cut off;
> one man took responsibility for communications
> with superiors and the asking for aid; and one
> man was the head of the team. In addition,
> there was a two-hundred-man emergency aid team.
> A young, twenty-seven-year-old, Chuang Wen-hua,
> who previously, during the elections for third-
> term mayor of Taipei City, aided in Kao Yü-shu's
> [anti-KMT] campaign, took responsibility for
> leading the entire operation. Taking elections
> and treating them as war was previously only
> a slogan. This time in Kao-hsiung City it has
> actually become a reality.[133]

But this amount of organization is severely limited
by previous experience in which the governing elite
cracked down when an attempt to organize an opposition
party formally threatened not only to be very successful
among Taiwanese but also to bring liberal mainlanders
and Taiwanese together in one formidable coalition.
The memory of this and similar crackdowns tends to make
current independent politicians cautious.

> Phone is tapped . . . do not discuss things
> on it . . . Was anyone following you about Taiwan?
>
> I am followed . . .
>
> We only discussed language, and no politics . . .
>
> In the Assembly not only the assemblymen but
> also the staff members have among them KMT
> men who are watching.[134]

PART II

FACTIONS AND FACTION-RELATED GROUPS
AS FACTORS IN THE PROVINCIAL ASSEMBLYMEN'S ENVIRONMENT

Part I of this study introduced one sector of significance in the environment of Taiwan's provincial assem-
blymen--the complex of groups centered around support
for or opposition to Taiwan's governing elite. Part II
introduces a second sector of significance in that en-
vironment--the complex of groups centered around competition for local political resources. Given the power
of Taiwan's governing elite to dispense most of the political resources available, these two complexes are
closely related. Indeed, many nonelite political actors
play roles in both complexes. But the concerns of the
actors when they play roles in one complex stem from
different circumstances than the concerns of the same
actors when they play roles in the second complex.

The analysis of this second complex of groups uti-
lizes those approaches grounded in anthropology, psychology, and theories of economic development that are
mentioned in the Introduction. Part II consists of
four chapters. Chapter 3 introduces local-level electoral factions--the groups that provide the major organizational context within which Taiwan's nonelite politicians and their rank-and-file citizen supporters act.
Chapter 4 provides examples of the kinds of resources
these politicians and their supporters compete for and
the kinds of techniques used in this competition. Chapter 5 analyzes additional groups involved in this competition, with special attention to the ways in which the
citizens within these groups are associated with the
various factions and their politicians. Chapter 6 deals
with the behavior of Taiwan's nonelite politicians in
the two factions that operate within the Provincial
Assembly itself--two nonlocal groups that share many
similarities with the local groups analyzed in Chapters
3-5.

Chapter 3

LOCAL-LEVEL ELECTORAL FACTIONS

The Nonexistence of Factions?

There is, on the surface, a certain amount of evidence suggesting that local-level electoral factions do not exist on Taiwan. For example, in attempting to learn more about Taiwan's factions, the author interviewed many politicians alleged to be heavily involved in them. Yet interviewees responded with little more than denials. The common response, repeated almost word for word, was Wo pu ts'an-chia p'ai-hsi ("I don't participate in factions").

One typical interview took place during lunch in the Provincial Assembly's dining room. Present were an assemblywoman, together with an assemblyman known in gossip and in the press for his relationship to the Lin faction of Taichung County.[135] The assemblywoman was taking delight in pointing to her colleague and praising him for being a "real VIP in his county . . . a real faction leader." The colleague simply shook his head, saying "Wo pu ts'an-chia p'ai-hsi." When asked if she participated, the response came: "Our county is very good. We don't really have factions. We're not like his county!"

Nor is it only the noted politician who will deny participation in a faction. Even rank-and-file members deny participation.[136] Perhaps the most extreme example of denial is a comment by one of Taiwan's political scientists: "The Central Government is strongly opposed to the existence of such factions. This is the main reason for their almost nonexistence."

Thus, there is evidence that local-level electoral factions are the figment of some overzealous imaginations and that no one in Taiwan participates in them. Still, tantalizing gossip from foreign anthropologists in the field plus tantalizing stories in Taiwan's press suggest that local-level electoral factions do, in fact, exist. For example,

Of the local factions of Changhua County, in

99

the city of Changhua itself there is the division between the Red and the Black. In each
rural district and township, all is held within
the Ch'en-versus-Lin system. In each election,
the forts are clearly divided. For example,
in the region covered by Erh-lin, Fang-yüan,
and Ta-ch'eng, there is love of bravery and
fierce struggle. Often there is even the
outbreaking of blood-flowing incidents.[137]

Moreover, evidence presented later in this chapter
and in Chapter 5, below, demonstrates that in some areas of
Taiwan almost everyone participates in local-level electoral factions. Indeed, this evidence demonstrates that,
in a description of the politics of Taiwan's rank-and-
file citizens, it is most useful to equate rank-and-file
citizens with rank-and-file faction members--or, at least,
with voters who are the main supporters of each faction's
nonelite electoral politicians.[138]

This contradictory evidence can best be explained
as a conflict between ideals and actuality. In terms of
ideals, factions are condemned on Taiwan by both the
governing elite and the rank-and-file citizen. For example, note the following comment taken from a magazine
reflecting the attitudes of Taiwan's governing elite:

In the year thirty-nine, the government
held all sorts of elections for public officials
as a part of its program of putting into practice local self-government. And ever since,
from the divisions of elections, local factions
appeared. These alone truly are the divisions
that harm the construction of the national
people. This is because the elements from
which the factions are made have no political
platform. Nor do they have the goal of developing the spirit of freedom and democracy. Their
constituent elements are no more than the
accusations and curses used for the wresting
forth of election ballots.[139]

Explanations of why Taiwan's governing elite con-
demns factions have already been presented. The reason
that Taiwan's rank-and-file citizens join with their
governing elite (and with most other Chinese) in con-
demning factions is their veneration of social harmony

100

and organic unity. This concern for social harmony
and organic unity is experienced through a tradition
of consensus politics. Bernard Gallin describes the
manifestation of this tradition in the village he studied
as follows:

> Traditionally, most decisions in the village
> were made on the basis of consensus . . .
> Given the traditional Chinese desire to main-
> tain peace and harmony, there generally appears
> to have been a desire to eliminate any open
> competition or open antagonism between people
> over such things as decision-making, conflict,
> and the election of leaders.[140]

As Ralph W. Nicholas points out, however, factions are
"conflict" groups.[141] Thus, the conflict of factions
mars the ideal of harmonious village life.

But if factions are ideally condemned by Taiwan's
rank-and-file citizens and if, therefore, no one wants
to admit participation in them, why do so many citizens
actually participate in them? Discussions in the rest
of Part II dealing with the relationship of nonelite
politicians within local-level electoral factions to
Taiwan's rank-and-file citizens will provide an answer.

The Nature of Factions

Social scientists have summed up much of the diver-
sity in political systems by conceptualizing two ideal
group types. These ideal group types are designed to
help in understanding a reality in which many groups
contain elements definitive of both types but in which
some groups contain most of the elements definitive of
only one type while different groups contain most of the
elements definitive of only the other type.

When thinking about politics, most people on Taiwan
label as local-level electoral factions (ti-fang p'ai-
hsi) groups that contain elements definitive of both or
either ideal group type, without distinguishing between
them. According to social scientists, however, the faction label should be reserved for those groups that
contain most of the elements definitive of only one
of these ideal types.

The ideal group type that social scientists think should not be used as a reference for labeling groups as factions is a politically active group bound together by such traits as family ties, in-law ties, residence in the same area, a shared surname, and/or a shared language. Using such terms as primordial, corporate, ascriptive, collective, categorical, or trait group and using such definitions as shared membership in a bounded community, or groups united by the sharing of a distinguishing trait, social scientists differentiate this "trait" group from the second ideal group type, which the people of Taiwan also use as a reference for labeling groups as local-level electoral factions.[142] It is this second ideal-group type that social scientists think should be used as the exclusive reference for defining factions.

The blocks out of which this second ideal group type is built are supportive-exchange dyads.[143] These are two-person relationships founded on the exchange of aid. This aid is based on arrangements calculated by each person to be favorable to his particular individual interests, without necessarily making reference to the interests of others with whom he shares distinguishing traits.

This stress on exchange on behalf of calculated particularistic interests, however, does not mean that the dyads are cold contractual relationships. The parties to a dyad inevitably attempt to add warmth to their relationship, attaching to it labels and feelings associated with intimate family ties (i.e., turning their dyad into a fictive family trait group or stressing whatever traits the two parties actually share).[144]

According to social scientists, a faction is composed of a number of supportive-exchange dyads. Factions of more than two individuals are possible because one person can be a party to more than one dyad. Some dyads that a person is a party to may be with individuals of a socioeconomic status equal to his own. More likely, however, the person will be a party to one dyadic tie to a superior (i.e., a patron) and to one or more dyadic ties to individuals of lower status (clients).

The faction usually takes the form of a pyramid, with one high-status individual or clique at the top

and with voters and/or other supporters at the bottom.
For some social scientists, a faction includes everyone
from the humblest supporter to the highest leader.
Others prefer to limit the definition to the individuals
at the higher levels of the pyramid.[145]

From the humblest supporter to the highest leader,
the glue that holds the faction together is the exchange
of communication and particularistic aid within each
dyad (i.e., between each individual and his immediate
superior and between each individual and each of his
immediate subordinates). Communication and aid are not
channeled around any of these specific links.

The differences between dyadic factions and politically active trait groups, both taken as ideal types,
are marked. One is often born into a trait group, or
becomes a member almost by necessity, because the traits
he shares with others make it advisable to combine for
the protection of interests arising from the shared
traits. A member enters and leaves dyadic factions,
however, solely on the basis of what another specific
faction member can do to advance his own particular
interests, without necessarily making reference to the
interests of others with whom he shares distinguishing
traits.

In pursuing his interests, an individual looks only
to combine with those with whom a favorable exchange of
resources can be made. Although the other party to the
exchange may share specific traits with the individual,
this is not necessarily relevant to the relationship.
Indeed, the parties to the exchange may share nothing
but the possibility of a mutually advantageous exchange
of resources. It is because the particularistic-exchange
relationship basic to the dyadic faction is not necessarily relevant to groups based on shared traits, and
may even be potentially hostile to their existence, that
social scientists see it as important to differentiate
dyadic factions from politically active groups based
on shared traits.

Although the differences between dyadic factions and
politically active trait groups, both taken as ideal
types, are marked, in reality many groups contain elements definitive of both types, as has already been
noted. This is possible because dyadic-faction relation-

ships are established without necessarily making reference to the sharing of distinguishing traits, a qualification that does not rule out the possibility that shared traits will be used as a reference in many cases.

Factions, Jen-Ch'ing, and the Need for a Security System

The description just presented was a general one, applicable to factions as they exist in all types of political systems. The remainder of Part II will be devoted to Taiwan's local-level electoral factions as they are manifested in the specific context of that island's Chinese society.

This discussion of factions on Taiwan will deal with groups that contain elements definitive of one or both ideal group types just introduced: trait factions, defined as politically active groups based on shared traits, and dyadic factions, defined as a number of politically active individuals linked together by distinct two-person relationships, each relationship based on the exchange of politically relevant particularistic benefits and established without necessarily making reference to the sharing of distinguishing traits. For convenience, unless otherwise indicated, groups on Taiwan that adhere closely to the definition of a trait faction or a dyadic faction will be labeled as such, although in reality no group will exactly replicate the ideal type.

The Need for a Security System

Richard H. Solomon hypothesizes that within the complex of attitudes that make up the Chinese orientation to politics is the belief that the goals of security and order are best attained by establishing a personal "dependency" relationship with powerful individuals. According to Solomon, this method of attaining security and order contrasts sharply with the alternative method of reliance upon contractual arrangements built around impersonal institutions. Ideally, in return for personal loyalty to a chosen authority figure, the average Chinese obtains full satisfaction "in a condition of being cared for by others."[146] This observation is associated with a second observation that reliance on "others" who are related to the individual guarantees the best conditions of care possible. Depending on the situation, sometimes the individual feels he can only rely on his closest siblings. Other times, if necessary, any excuse will be found to establish a relationship between total strangers.[147]

To integrate Solomon's discussion with the general description of factions presented above, the specific Chinese strategy of attaining security through reliance on others who are related to the individual combines advantages found in trait factions with those of the dyadic factions' patron-client relationships. This is a case of a patron-client relationship being established "with" reference to the sharing of distinguishing traits (e.g., the family trait shared by siblings). If the individual seeks security by using any excuse to establish a patron-client relationship with a stranger, however, the existence of shared traits becomes questionable. In this latter case, the shared trait may well be pure fiction, invented to add intimacy and warmth to a supportive-exchange dyad that would otherwise be felt as a crassly impersonal series of materialistic exchanges.

That the average Chinese should be concerned about his security is certainly no great revelation. Most political analyses assume that security is one of the most important goals of the vast majority of people. In the Chinese case, Solomon's article, along with the type of conclusions reached by such researchers as Donald R. DeGlopper, support this author's own observations that the Chinese child is consciously socialized into a milieu that especially stresses the insecurity and dangers of human relations, and the need for protection against these dangers. Moreover, this conscious socialization is in addition to the subconscious socialization (in relation to authority figures) already discussed above, in Part I. Under the influence of both types of socialization, one would expect the Chinese individual's felt needs for security to be very great indeed.

The effect of prior socialization on subjective definition of environment is, of course, key in the determining of political behavior. Just as important

105

in this regard are the stimuli that penetrate the individual's consciousness during his actual participation
in the political process. According to admittedly frag-
mentary evidence, the type of stimuli met by many Chinese
in Taiwan's countryside is the reality of factional conflict.

Lawrence W. Crissman, who carried on extensive
research in and around the township of Erh-lin in southeast Changhua County, finds that in many areas of Changhua County, the division of towns into local-level
electoral factions is a given. In some towns, factions
do not limit themselves only to the formal political system but permeate all walks of life, down to where one
buys his medicine and groceries.

> Even though the factions proper are composed
> of wealthy and influential men, the lives of
> ordinary people are sometimes heavily affected
> by factional differences. A large number of
> permanent positions are given in return for
> political support, and who wins an election
> is crucially important to many people. Day
> labor on roads and canals or for the Farmers'
> Associations is also often assigned on the
> basis of factional support. The Farmers'
> Associations are particularly blatant in
> factional discrimination, specially in regard
> to the percentage of moisture acceptable in
> rice turned over for taxes and land payments
> and in allocating quotas for advantageous pro-
> duce contracts.

> In those cases where a village is divided
> along factional lines, the social effects
> can be considerable. People won't speak to
> one another, women won't wash clothes in the
> same place at the same time, and children
> won't play together. Fights between village
> youths are common and each of the factions
> patronizes different village stores.

> Factional allegiance is also a prime deter-
> minant of which shops and businesses are
> patronized in the towns. Most businessmen
> attempt to avoid factional considerations,
> but none are completely successful. The

106

businesses most susceptible to factional division are hospitals and drug stores, wine
houses, taxi companies, rice mills, and butchers.
The earning power of most doctors ensures that
they will engage in politics, and they are
in a perfect position to do favors for people
by reducing fees or even providing free care.
The same applies to druggists, who practice
medicine illegally. Restaurants and wine houses
are patronized mainly by the rich, and are
therefore almost automatically involved in
factional activities, especially since outsiders
who visit the Farmers' Association or the
Local Government must be entertained somewhere.
Entertainment in general is usually involved,
and for a period Erhlin Town had two roller
skating rinks to serve the two factional alliances.
Rice mills, because of their close relationship with the Farmers' Associations and government control of rice, cannot avoid factional
involvement. At one time, when factional
feeling was running high, some people in
Fang-yuan Hsiang would not eat pork bought
locally because all the butchers belonged to
the opposite faction. Purchases of most large
items are also influenced. Ordinary people
buy from shops aligned with their factions
because of a feeling that they will be given
a better price or because they can expect more
credit.

Marriages and friendships are also channeled
by factional membership, and attendance at
funerals and weddings is often determined
likewise. Important temples are heavily involved,
especially the committees which run them.
Some religious celebrations have two separate
operas or puppet shows, one supported by each
faction.[148]

No doubt the above passage contains many extreme
examples. But even on a more moderate level, with or
without the conscious and subconscious childhood socialization hypothesized above, such conflict would cause
the rank-and-file villager to be concerned about his
security. It is this concern with "building a security
system, even for the peasant," that brings him to the

political process and to the factions.149   As Crissman
has put it, the faction is used to control events. The
participants join in order to gain better control over
a potentially hostile environment.150

Jen-ch'ing and the Needed Security System

As noted previously, when people in Taiwan were
questioned about factions, few would admit to their
involvement, much less be willing to discuss their involvement at length. Even when persons willing to discuss the subject were found, few would go beyond the
simple observation that factions are "all a matter of
human emotion" (wan-ch'üan shih jen-ch'ing). The
author was extremely disappointed with these results
until he realized that jen-ch'ing, in addition to meaning
human emotion, also has the connotation of obligation.
Putting these two connotations together, one is led back
to Richard Solomon's hypotheses and to further insight
into how the general description of factions presented
above is manifested in the specific context of Taiwan's
Chinese society.

Jen-ch'ing (obligation to give aid in the future)
and/or aid immediately given are what is exchanged between the powerful authority figure (high-status patron)
and his weaker dependents (clients). The authority figure
"cares for" the dependent, and the dependent in return
gives his support to the authority figure. But this is
no cold contractual relationship. As in the general
description of factions, in the specific case of Taiwan,
the Chinese also shun dependence on impersonal institu-
tional arrangements--it must be a warm, intimate "personal" relationship. Some of the flavor of this "personalization" (roughly the counterpart of "legitimization"
in more legalistic societies) is brought in through the
jen-ch'ing label. It is obligation, but it is human
obligation, a matter of human feelings. Thus, Gallin
finds at the basis of his factions the exchange of jen-
ch'ing. For example,

> . . . by the time of the village mayoralty
> election of 1963 and hsiang chang [rural
> district mayor] election of 1964, the FA
> faction was able to recruit the support and
> actual membership of almost every single family

108

which had benefited from Mr. Shih's assistance.
Not only did the villagers appreciate what
he had done for them, but they also owed him
jen-ch'ing, an obligation to reciprocate for
his former help. Their political help was
the way in which they could now repay this
jen-ch'ing.[151]

In the author's interviews and in the research of
others, the term kan-ch'ing (feeling, sentiment) was often
used in conjunction with jen-ch'ing to express related
ideas. Gallin describes kan-ch'ing as the basis of legitimized (personalized) obligation in traditional Chinese
communities:

In effect, then, it is basically a matter of
structured obligation. The feeling or sentiment results from satisfied or disappointed
expectations of appropriate behavior, and the
expected behavior is behavior appropriate
to the formal relationship of the two individuals within the social structure. The social
order was thus stabilized by a structure of
mutual obligations that paralleled the established hierarchal system.[152]

More support for the contention that jen-ch'ing
and kan-ch'ing connote obligation comes from Yang's
description of the deterioration of kan-ch'ing relationships between landlords and tenants when the landlord-
tenant relationship on Taiwan ceased to be dominated by
insecurities and mutual obligations began to be enforced
by outside parties. Security and impersonal enforcement
made the need for mutual respect of obligation, legitimized through kan-ch'ing terminology, superfluous. The
kan-ch'ing relationship thus atrophied.[153]

Although the landlord-tenant relationship no longer
needed the blessing of jen-ch'ing, other insecurities
grew up in the countryside, however, and these called
into being the authority figure-dependent relationship
of local-level electoral factions based on supportive-
exchange dyads. Again jen-ch'ing was needed to aid in
legitimizing a security-guaranteeing relationship.

Chapter 4

LOCAL POLITICAL RESOURCES AND THE
COMPETITION TO OBTAIN THEM

In order that there be something to exchange within
its dyads, a faction must compete for resources. This
chapter will present an impressionistic survey of local-
level political resources on Taiwan and the competition
to obtain them.

The People Recognize Money, Not Candidates
(Jen-min Jen Ch'ien, Pu Jen Jen)

The smallest resource that rank-and-file citizens
in Taiwan may compete for is the relatively modest sum
many politicians are willing to give in exchange for a
vote.

> From each bank in Tainan County's Hsin-ying
> Township, within the past three days, the total
> of ten-dollar bills that have been taken out
> in exchange for other denominations or that
> have been withdrawn from savings accounts has
> reached over five-million dollars [$125,000 US].
> By yesterday (20th) afternoon, the ten-dollar
> notes of several banks were equally exhausted.
> In Tainan County's county assemblymen and
> rural district-township mayoralty elections,
> there are election districts in which there is
> the secret employing of a "silver bullet offen-
> sive" . . . Sensitive personages feel the mass
> withdrawals of ten-dollar bills from the banks
> within the past several days has a relationship
> with the moves of buying votes and bribing
> elections.[154]

Three months after the county assemblymen and rural
district-township mayoralty elections, this author arrived
in Tainan City (a separate administrative and electoral
unit from the county) to observe the elections for provincial assemblymen and county and city mayors. Almost
before setting foot in the house of his host, a city coun-
cilman, this author received a scolding for coming a day
too late. The day before, he could have seen the

111

stacks and stacks of $10 NT bills (New Taiwan dollars, worth $.25 US at that time) in the headquarters of the various candidates. It was now too late to see the money being given out.

To the inquiry why only $10 bills, the explanation was given that each voter was offered only $40 for his vote. Since the closest denomination was a $50 note, the use of the $50 note would have caused the politician to ask for change. It is very embarrassing to ask for change when giving a bribe.

On vote buying, Crissman (with some exaggeration) writes the following:

> A fundamental feature of Taiwanese elec-
> tions is the fact that all votes are pur-
> chased in one manner or another. The vast
> majority are paid for in cash, the price vary-
> ing from $.25 US to over $2.50 US depending
> on the importance of the office and how hotly
> it is contested. Prices have risen steadily
> for the past ten years at least. Close friends
> and relatives of candidates and primary clients
> of course refuse payment, and they are pressed
> into service buying votes from others. The
> employees of the Farmers' Associations are all
> involved with vote buying for the faction that
> controls their branch, but bureaucrats in the
> Public Offices must be more circumspect lest
> they lose their positions. The votes are mainly
> paid for by the candidates and their primary
> supporters, with some aid from faction leaders
> in the form of loans, but zealous vote buying
> agents will pay for a few on their own. If
> the first price offered is not immediately
> accepted, the buyers will not bargain for fear
> that the seller is not sincere.
>
> Each agent purchases only 25 to 30 votes, and
> instructs the people he buys from to mark their
> ballots in a distinctive fashion so that when
> the ballots are publicly counted he can deter-
> mine who failed to honor their agreement. The
> agents are also present at the polling places
> throughout the period when voting is going on,
> and they pay close attention to who shows up

and who does not. This helps to curtail the
opposition tactic of paying a fair sum to
obtain identification cards (without which it
is impossible to vote) from people known to have
sold their votes to certain candidates they
are trying to keep from getting elected. As
the Taiwanese explain, everybody has two votes,
one for and one against, and if you can't buy
the positive one, you may still be able to get
the negative. Careful records are kept within
each faction of whose votes were bought and
how much was paid for them.[155]

Given the nature of the jen-ch'ing relationship described in Chapter 3 above, it is doubtful that vote
buying is usually a simple cash deal. In many cases,
the exchange between rank-and-file citizen and dyadic-
faction politician is one of a series of resource exchanges
taking place within an ongoing supportive-exchange dyad.
In view of the small sum involved, moreover, the money
paid for a vote is frequently only a token symbol of the
ongoing dyad. The obligation implicit in the ongoing dyad
is to give aid when called for. This is the real significant resource involved, not the small sum of money
exchanged at the time of elections.

Resources from the Private
Assets of Politicians

Duane Lockard, in his book The Politics of State
and Local Government, notes that

The essence of bossism was service for a price
and political spoils were the means by which
the system was kept operating . . . the standard
operating procedure of the old-style boss
was to make himself available to those in
need--whatever the need. Some needed work;
some, a basket of food; some, rent money;
some, advice and intercession when the police
arrested a wayward son. As a social service
agency, the boss was humane and indispensable
to his people.[156]

Although the money nonelite electoral politicians
give when buying votes may be only a token symbol of

ongoing supportive-exchange dyads, the sum total of aid
they give in their contemporary rendition of Lockard's
old-style political bosses does translate into materially
significant resources. It is such materially significant
resources that held together the supportive-exchange dyads
basic to the machines of the old-style bosses and that now
hold together the dyads basic to the factions of Taiwan's
nonelite politicians and rank-and-file supporters.

In order to expend the materially significant resources necessary to hold their factions together, Taiwan's nonelite politicians must often rely on great
amounts of their own money.[157] Vast sums are contributed to such community projects as the building of
schools and the paving of highways.[158] More relevant
to the traditional boss model, large sums are given
directly to individuals in trouble. For example, despite accusations that former Provincial Assemblyman Li
Chien-ho concentrated most of his energy on protecting
his vast coal interests in Taipei County, interviewees
always admitted that he never forgot the voters that
were the mainstay of his power: "Li spends much money.
He helps many farmers in trouble . . . That is his best
source of votes."

Conversely, Assemblyman Wu I-wei's failure to be
reelected was explained by his lack of financial ability
to distribute such materially significant resources.

> You need money to send people gifts when
> there is a funeral, and that sort of thing,
> to keep up proper relations and propriety
> with your constituents. [This is] very hard
> without money. You spend less on yourself and
> give more away. . . . Therefore it is impor-
> tant to have an economic base.
>
> The . . . Wu I-wei type, although competent,
> loses out because they cannot afford the funeral
> type of gift required by propriety all the
> time.

The expense of funerals is often assuaged by local
politicians. Stephen Feuchtwang noted that during an
election campaign, Candidate N visited the village of
Mountain Street only four times--each time to attend and
contribute money for a funeral.[159]

Circumstantial evidence for the importance of funerals to local politicians comes from this author's visit with candidate Ch'en Hsin-fa. Candidate Ch'en was late for the interview; he had been held up because of a funeral he had to attend for a former employee. After the interview, he offered to drop the author off at the bus station, which he said was no inconvenience since he had to go in that direction anyway; that was the way to the funeral of his friend's sister. Even casual observation of a funeral service taking place near the front gate of Taiwan University turned up a wreath from Ch'en T'ien-yu, a provincial assemblyman based nearby.

Health is also an important area of resource distribution. In Erh-lin Township, there is the town hall where the local officials go through their bureaucratic motions, and there is the "real" town hall--a local hospital. The head doctor in this hospital, partly through the resources he dispenses to his many patients, has amassed enough votes to determine who will sit at the desks in the "apparent" town hall.

Crissman contends that this situation holds in many rural districts and townships throughout Taiwan. The real power does not reside in the local Farmers' Association or the town hall. To find the real power, one is pointed down the street to the local doctor's office or hospital. Not surprisingly, in Erh-lin as in other rural districts and townships, there is another doctor's office with another head doctor striving to amass more votes than his more fortunate opponent in the hope that soon he will be able to decide who occupies the desks in the "apparent" town hall.[160]

More indications of the relationship between health service and local politics comes from the author's own travels about Taiwan in search of interviews. In Nant'ou County's Ts'ao-t'un Township, the author confused the building that housed Provincial Assemblyman Li Wutsung's home and hospital with the town hall and other public buildings that were standing alongside it in the center of town. Given the similarity of their facades, the uninitiated might indeed assume that Assemblyman Li's hospital was an official part of the governmental complex.

In Taipei County's rural district of Lu-chou, the author sat with Provincial Assemblyman Li Ch'iu-yüan in his four-story hospital and spent much of the evening talking of Li's ambitions to make his hospital an even greater service center for the community than it already was. Similarly, the headquarters for Assemblywoman Liang Hsü Ch'un-chü's reelection campaign were located in her husband's hospital. Finally, to be introduced to a major supporter of Assemblyman Kuo Yü-hsin of I-lan County, Assemblyman Kuo led the author through the supporter's waiting room to find the doctor upstairs.

Resources from Politicians in Control of Elected Administrative Posts

Two strategic suppliers of resources at the local level are the town or rural district Farmers' Association and the town or rural district government hall (i.e., public office).[161] As Crissman describes it, the rice mill in Erh-lin refuses to sell its rice to the Farmers' Association because the owners of the rice mill are in a different faction from the individuals elected as officers of the Association. The result is that the Farmers' Association is not terribly diligent in enforcing high standards on the rice sold to it by people from its own faction but will only accept letter-perfect rice from the rice mill. At one point, it sent the same shipment of rice back to the mill five times, insisting that the rice was not dry enough to meet specifications.[162]

The politicians in control of the Farmers' Association also have the power to assign crop quotas. This amounts to deciding who sells his asparagus and whose asparagus rots in the field,[163] or at least who sells his crops directly to the Farmers' Association at the regulation price and whose crops are declared unacceptable by the Association, forcing the rejectee to sell cheaply on the open market. The crops sold in this manner end up being bought by the Association anyway, but at a lower price.[164]

As for control of the town or rural district hall, Gallin describes the situation within the village he studied as follows:

> It is clear to all villagers, whether they are members of a large tsu [lineage] or a non-related family, that their security could

116

easily depend upon the willingness of a village
mayor or hsiang chang [rural district mayor]
to support them in time of need. They realize
that an official is no longer selected or elected
by consensus. Therefore, "the mayor," for
example, "is no longer mayor of all the people."
He holds his position primarily to work for members of his own faction or at least for his
personal supporters including those village
families which are neutral of any alignment.
As the middleman between the villagers and the
government agencies, a mayor can arbitrarily
refuse or offer to help a villager who needs
his support to get a loan from the Farmers'
Association or to receive some kind of assistance from the Public Office.[165]

Given the extensive relations the rank-and-file
citizen in Taiwan has with both the local Farmers' Association and the local town or rural district hall, the
control of these two strategic points becomes one of his
central concerns.[166] With these strategic points under
the sway of his faction, not only can the rank-and-file
citizen hope to share in some of the money allocated for
the building of local roads and bridges, but also when
he finds it necessary to deal directly with officials,
they will not make a point of handling his affairs especially slowly or, worse, refuse to handle them at all.[167]

Finally, at a level higher than the rural district
or township, the control of the county or city government,
through the election of the county or city mayor, provides
further opportunities to obtain resources similar to those
handed out through the town or rural district hall.
Unlike the provincial governor (really chairman), who
is an appointed official, the mayors are elected.[168]
Thus, the financial and other powers of the county and
city governments, as with township and rural district
governments, remain in the hands of officials elected
from the local level, not appointed from above.

Resources from Politicians in Control of
Elected Legislative Posts

The legal authority that assemblymen have over their
respective governments is often exercised in terms of

117

passing resolutions, raising problems during interpellation sessions, and personally visiting officials in
attempts to influence governmental outcomes on behalf
of their constituents.

Resolutions

The passing of resolutions in the Provincial Assembly has already been referred to as a relatively ineffective method for dispensing resources to constituents.
Unlike the governments at lower levels, the provincial
government can refuse to implement resolutions, explaining that the offending resolution is really a county,
not a provincial, matter, that funds are insufficient,
etc. Still, such resolutions are continually passed by
the Assembly, and about one-fourth of them are honored
by the provincial government. Two resolutions typical
of those passed by the Assembly follow:

> Resolution to request that the provincial
> government appropriate funds to sink one
> middle-size well in T'ung-le Village, Yüan-
> shan Rural District, I-lan County, in order
> to improve the drinking facilities of the
> residents and benefit sanitation.

> Resolution to request that the provincial
> government instruct the Port of Chi-lung and
> the city government of Chi-lung to construct
> the Mu-shan Bay Fishing Boat Wave Protec-
> tion Dike speedily for the benefit of fish-
> ing boats to stop by and for the benefit
> of the fishing people in general.[169]

In order to give the reader an idea of the kinds
of people provincial assemblymen attempt to aid through
the passing of resolutions, a list follows that summarizes the resolutions introduced in the third-term
Assembly's eighth session (November 14, 1966-March 3,
1967). This list presents all the groups that would
appear to benefit from the various resolutions, together
with the frequency of resolutions urging benefits for
each group. The list is notable in that it indicates
that assemblymen attempt to aid all categories of voters
within their districts.

THIRD-TERM ASSEMBLY, EIGHTH SESSION (November 14, 1966-March 3, 1967)
RESOLUTIONS analyzed in terms of
1. groups resolutions appear to benefit
2. frequency benefits urged for each group

Group	Frequency
SPECIFIC GROUPS	1,220
specific teachers	37
e.g. in rural or aborigine areas	7
teachers in general	19
specific government employees	61
e.g. aborigine area employees	6
public hospital nurses	2
quality employees	7
retiring officials	3
janitors	5
school administrators in general	10
principals in general	6
government employees in general	12
specific people's assoc employees	13
specific govt business employees	10
specific businessmen	298
e.g. truckers	14
one specific airline	28
bus companies	14
drug industry	2
coal mine owners	6
potential auto companies	2
agriculture processing	10
lumber industry	34
paper industry	13
nonfood agriculture	6
taxi companies	6
shipping companies	22
business in general	12
specific farmers	152

Group	Frequency
e.g. sugar	3
banana	2
tobacco	37
pineapple	2
red bean	1
asparagus	2
farmers in general	26
specific fishermen	37
fishermen in general	3
specific laborers	7
laborers in general	3
specific unemployed	27
unemployed in general	2
specific students	99
students in general	7
one specific school	49
specific schools	23
specific local govt or bureau	50
e.g. sanitation office	2
assemblyman's home local govt	14
local govt or bureau in general	15
public-owned business	16
people's associations	17
e.g. Farmers' Assoc	6
Fishermen's Assoc	4
Women's Assoc	2
labor unions	1
specific politicians	25
e.g. national assemblymen, etc.	9
township-rural district mayors	3

Group	Frequency
military families	25
medical doctors	1
unlicensed MDs	1
athletes	5
musicians-artists	3
deaf-blind-crippled	8
frequent travelers between two	
specific points	32
residents disturbed by a local	
business's operations	12
landlords	6
senior citizens	1
motorcycle-car owners	6
typhoon victims	5
women in general	9
low-income people	4
poor areas in general	8
rural areas in general	6
urban areas in general	4
aborigines in general	26
Taiwanese in general	10
SPECIFIC LARGE REGIONS	136
SPECIFIC SMALL REGIONS	136
GENERAL POPULATION	314
INJURY TO SPECIFIC GROUPS	356
EXPAND ASSEMBLY'S POWER	77
CIVIL RIGHTS: expand	65
contract	3
AID BASIC KMT POLICY	71
TOTAL	2,366

Source: Chuan-chi, Volume I, pp. 17-602

Despite these indications, however, informants insist that the theme of factionalism must not be forgotten in interpreting the list. Echoing Bernard Gallin's statement that "the mayor is no longer mayor of all the people" but "holds his position primarily to work for members of his own faction," informants note (probably with some exaggeration) that even resolutions apparently intended to benefit all the people of a given locality or interest group are frequently only intended to benefit the assemblyman's specific supporters.170

Willingness to Speak
(Interpellation)

On Taiwan it is often said that a good assemblyman must have a willingness to speak and a willingness to run about on behalf of his constituents. He does his most important speaking when relevant government officials attend Assembly sessions to answer questions raised by the assemblymen. As with resolutions, these interpellations are used by individual assemblymen to demand action on behalf of their constituents and supporters.

Lists of groups that appear to benefit from these interpellations, together with the frequency of interpellations urging benefits for each group, look much like the list compiled above (page 119) for groups benefiting from resolutions.171

Willingness to Run About

As for the willingness to run about on behalf of one's constituents, Provincial Assemblywoman Wang Kuohsiu proudly showed this author a letter from a crippled child who could not get accepted by a given school. Although he had all the qualifications, he was refused because of his disability. The letter was one of thanks. After Assemblywoman Wang called the situation to the attention of the provincial government's Department of Education, the school reversed its decision.

The Chiang-tzu-ts'ui controversy provided another provincial assemblywoman, Wang Sung Ch'iung-ying, with an opportunity to serve her constituents through her willingness to run about. In conjunction with two of her

120

colleagues, she managed to win relief for a number of
contractors and their clients whose projects and homes
were being threatened by a new regional zoning law for
the Chiang-tzu-ts'ui area of Taipei County.[172]

Finally, the following piece of political propaganda
describes Provincial Assemblyman Kuo Yü-hsin as an
exemplor of the "willingness to speak, willingness to run
about" ideal:

> At the end of last month, when Typhoon
> Chieh-la plundered this province's north-
> eastern region, for I-lan County it brought
> a violent rain, the likes of which have not
> been seen in eighty years. A serious dis-
> aster was thus created: dykes were broken,
> houses crashed to the ground, farms were
> inundated, roads were washed away. A griev-
> ous tragedy of 38 deaths, 29 missing, 10
> serious injuries, and 7 minor injuries was
> created. Over 40,000 people had no homes to
> return to or were completely isolated by the
> waters. The loss was extremely grave . . .

> While the wind was still blowing, Assembly-
> man Kuo Yü-hsin immediately rushed to the
> Provincial Assembly in Taichung. To the
> Interim Committee he presented an emergency
> report, requesting the government to begin
> immediately the work of saving the disaster-
> striken and relieving those in urgent need.
> At the same time, even more a matter of not
> being willing to sit long enough to warm
> the mat, he rushed east and ran west; from
> each and every related organization and depart-
> ment, he wrested forth disaster relief . . .

> Assemblyman Kuo Yü-hsin, because he endured
> to go everywhere, moreover because his heart
> was anxious about soothing the distresses
> of the elders and brothers of his native
> place, came to a point where his eating and
> sleeping became unsettled and his heart anxious
> as a flame. Finally, after continuous exertions,
> because of this he became sick and had to lie
> down. But because "rescuing from a disaster
> is like fighting a fire," he was unwilling

to lie down and rest. Instead he fortified
his spirit and continued to rush about, not
stopping at the sacrifice of his own personal
health, exchanging it for the safety of his
several ten thousands of I-lan brothers.
This "if the people are drowning I am drowning, if the people are starving I am starving," "taking the distresses of the people
as his own" heart of Assemblyman Kuo Yü-hsin
truly moved the citizens of I-lan County.[173]

Success?

In giving examples of the kind of resources an assemblyman brings back to his constituents, the author has
cited a number of written resolutions and verbal requests
of assemblymen. But verbal requests in all of Taiwan's
representative assemblies and resolutions passed by the
Provincial Assembly do not have the force of law. Thus,
it is prudent for an assemblyman to provide some evidence
that the resources he has promised have actually been
given out. The following propaganda, written on behalf
of Candidate Li Chien-ho, provides such evidence:

A tremendous amount of public works has
been wrested forth and constructed through
the efforts of Mr. Li Chien-ho. Figuring
from this term of office of the provincial
assemblymen, there is: the Hua-chiang
Ta Bridge, the underground walkway in the
Pan-ch'iao Railroad Station, the Kung-liao
Ta Bridge, the Jui-fang Chieh-shou Bridge,
the paving with asphalt of the Kung-Ao
Highway, the paving with asphalt of Wu-ku's
Min-i Ta Bridge, the Chui-fen running water
project, the underground walkway at Shuang-
hsi Station, the Hsi-chih to Wan-li Highway,
the Wan-li to K'an-chiao Highway, the opening up of railroad service from Jui-fang to
Shui-nan-tung, the opening of the Chin-Shui
Highway, the walkway on the Keng Tzu Liao
Bridge, the Jui-fang Railroad Station, the
protective bank along the Chi-lung River,
the walkway over the railroad tracks in
front of the Shu-lin High School, etc.,
etc.[174]

122

In view of the overwhelming stress on transportation facilities among the resources Li has obtained for his constituents, it is interesting to note that Li was the chairman of the Provincial Assembly's Transportation Committee. It is also interesting to compare Li's list with a list of resources obtained for his constituents by L. Mendel Rivers, former chairman of the U.S. House of Representatives' Armed Services Committee:

> River's South Carolina district has an Air Force base, an Army depot, a Naval shipyard, a Marine air station, the Parris Island boot camp, two Naval hospitals, a Naval station, a Naval supply center, a Naval weapons station, a fleet ballistic-missile-submarine training center, a Polaris missile facility, an Avco Corp. plant, a Lockheed plant, a General Electric plant under construction and an 800-acre plot of ground that has just been purchased by the Sikorsky Aircraft Division of United Aircraft. The military payroll alone is $2 billion a year. The main gate at the Air Force base is "Rivers Gate," Route 52 through Charleston is "Rivers Avenue," a housing project on the Navy base is "Men-Riv Park."[175]

Resources from Identification with Winning Individual or Group

Individuals in all sorts of cultures tend to identify their own lives with the lives of other individuals and/or with the existence of various groups. Such individuals obtain an emotionally satisfying feeling of pride if the object of their identification meets with some success.

Besides material resources, therefore, a vicarious prestige accrues to those who have a relationship with individuals who win in Taiwan's electoral contests. Relationships to such winners may be of all sorts. It may be the relationship of a rank-and-file citizen to his faction's candidates. The citizen may additionally identify with his faction's candidates because the faction includes or is coextensive with other groups that he otherwise identifies with. The citizen's membership

123

in his family or his relationship to his wife's relatives, to his friends, to his local area, and/or to a given ethnolinguistic Chinese subgroup may each aid in binding him to a faction (i.e., a trait faction, or a faction composed of overlapping trait groups, or a dyadic faction overlapping with one or more trait groups). Finally, apart from the existence of factions, identification with families, relatives, friends, etc., by themselves may cause the rank-and-file citizen to feel pride when a fellow member of one of these groups is successful in the electoral battle.

An example of this kind of identification is found in the Ch'en lineage of Kuan-hsi Township, Hsin-chu County. If you are born into this lineage, you are, almost by definition, in the faction that takes the lineage as its core. The angry reaction of this lineage to the news that one of its members could not be a candidate for mayor of Hsin-chu County was related on page 52 above.

Another example of this type of identification is reported by Arthur P. Wolf. Researching in a small town outside of Shu-lin in Taipei County, Wolf took note that mock elections were to be held in the local primary school to give the children a practical lesson in civics. The teachers nominated one candidate and the students the other (unintentionally mimicking the real nomination process, in which the authorities--the governing elite and the KMT--nominate a candidate to compete against the "people's" non-KMT candidate).

As it happened, the families of the nominees were two very important families in the community. When the campaign got under way, the families began supplying funds to the candidates, who used them to buy ice cream and other gifts to pass out to the young voters. Seeing that the lesson in civics was fast becoming a lesson in the evils of vote buying, the school authorities decided to call the experiment off. But this angered the nominees' parents, bringing them into conflict with the principal. Soon everyone was quite embarrassed, all searching for ways to cover over the incident and soothe ruffled feelings.

In this example, no power or material resource was being contested. It was simply a competition between

124

two important families, neither of which was about to
let a representative of the opposition obtain the prestige of defeating it in an election--even in a primary
school election.[176]

The Superior Man Hates the Idea of Leaving the World with His Name Unmentioned There[177]

On January 24, 1968, an editorial in the Min-sheng
Jih-pao complained about politicians: "If it is not for
name, then it is for profit. If it is not to struggle
for prestige, then it is to wrest forth material gain.
Those for right and justice are fewer than few." So
far, the resources the rank-and-file citizen may compete
for in Taiwan's local politics have been described.
The remainder of this chapter will deal with the resources
that accrue to the active politicians, those who do more
than simply cast their individual vote on election day.
It is the resources coveted by these individuals, the
active politicians, that the Min-sheng Jih-pao editorial
deplores. This section will deal with the first of these
resources, a name.

Besides pride obtained through identification with
the successes of a group or one of that group's representatives, pride in and respect of self is also an
important motive for political behavior. Even at the
most local level, such a feeling of pride can be found.
Arthur P. Wolf tells the story of a man who was really
only a front for a powerful family in the village that
Wolf was researching. When drunk, this man had only one
message: "I'm the precinct headman!" he would repeat
again and again. Wolf sees in this behavior indications
of a basic drive for the prestige of position, even if
the position is quite humble.[178] For many politicians,
if they can ultimately attain the position of rural district or township mayor, they will have had a fulfilling
political life.[179]

The importance of prestige on Taiwan is indicated
by how much local political activity costs the active
politician. Although some politicians do make back their
investment, many seem to be spending money without
prospects of a financial return. Indeed, they seem to be
willing to accept great losses. Money is necessary for
everything from buying votes to buying nominations.

Through money, enemies are convinced not to be so threatening, and friends are convinced to remain friendly. Leaders contribute to community projects and help individuals in need, all with money. The hypothesis is that although it costs a fortune to be a successful politician in Taiwan, many of those willing to spend that money are not doing it for financial return but for prestige.180

In line with this hypothesis, according to Professor Pao Ch'ing-chiu, many Chinese feel that an individual should not be satisfied with his life's achievements simply because he has become financially prosperous. If he has become prosperous, he should go on to attain a good name. This feeling implies an obligation of the rich individual to be of service to other individuals and to the community at large. It is through this service that he will obtain the sought-after good name. This feeling even hints at the necessity of selfless service as a balance against a life of selfish accumulation-- an atonement for guilt and a proof to others that the wealthy person is not simply a greedy miser.181

The quest for prestige is certainly not new to Chinese society. But there is an additional inducement that has come to Taiwan along with economic development, land reform, and political change. Traditional status arrangements, buffeted by economic development and land reform, have been receiving their coup de grace from politicians basing themselves on nontraditional forms of political behavior. These politicians, many from humble origins, have been using these nontraditional forms to nudge aside those traditional leaders who are not adapting their behavior to the new political system.

With other arrangements in decline, elections, with their clear proof of popular esteem, have become one of the few methods available with which to affirm, or reaffirm, one's prestige. As has happened in many other developing countries, with the rupture of old status arrangements, it has become difficult to discern clearly who the status elites really are. Since status remains highly valued, both to previous and potential power holders alike, elections have been seized upon as the new proof that one is indeed of high status.182

Jobs for Supporters

This province's county-city assembly and
rural district-township mayor election campaigns have just begun. Within each office
of each department of the Tainan County
government, for the past several days there
has regularly been the singing of "the empty
city song." Many department heads have gone
out to campaign for others and pull for votes,
leaving no time for concern about their own
responsibilities. The remaining minority
of officials, happy in their leisure, sit
within the office reading the paper and chatting
with one another, or drift outside to sun
themselves. We feel this kind of phenomenon
of elections influencing public matters
must immediately and severely be corrected
. . .

. . . The reason many officials and department
heads of the county government do not stop
at the consequences of breaking the law and
helping others to campaign is because their
present job, for the most part, rests on the
recommendation or introduction of several
"influentiallpersonages." Comes the period
of the campaigns for the various levels of
people's representatives and there is an
urgent need for help. How can related county
government personnel put their hands in their
sleeves and watch from the sidelines?[183]

The above complaint supports the conclusion that
faction leaders use those jobs the faction obtains power
over as resources to be parceled out among their active
supporters. Crissman's research adds further evidence
to this. His informants in Erh-lin were vote buyers who
had to buy votes because they worked in the town Farmers'
Association. Like the county government workers described
above, refusal to work in elections would have cost them
their jobs.[184] Such a situation even affected the educational system. In 1965, the provincial government promulgated a law designed to prevent county and city mayors
from continuing to use their power of appointment to
turn the office of public school principal into a patronage position.[185]

Withdrawing before Superiors
(Jang Hsien)

Although Ch'en Chou Lai-fu, running for the assembly in Kao-hsiung City, bragged about her ability to make dumplings, inviting voters to call on her if they become hungry, the making of dumpling soup is quite another matter.[186]

> Lin Ting-shun also said: during the campaign, everywhere abundantly was the making of dumpling soup, but his own withdrawal from the election definitely has no element of soup making in it. He beseeched those in society not to believe lightly any evil words that cause wounds, words that would cause his reputation to be questioned.[187]

The making of dumpling soup is considered so serious that in one county the following headlines were the result:

> CHIA-I ASSEMBLY ELECTIONS
> FIRST ELECTION DISTRICT RUMORS:
> PEOPLE ARE MAKING DUMPLING SOUP
> OVERSEEING COMMITTEE INVESTIGATING[188]

This is considered serious because the phrase "to make dumpling soup" is defined as "to cause another candidate to withdraw from an election by use of the profit derived from money, things, or other property, [thus] to come to an agreement with him."[189]

If candidates oppose each other in an election, each will have to spend a great deal of money, with no guarantee of winning the election in the end. The loser forfeits not only money but also prestige and control over jobs. Therefore, if candidates present a serious threat to one another, both can win if one allows the other to bribe him into withdrawing from the campaign. The candidate who bribes spends less money for election than if he outbids his opponent in buying votes. He also obtains prestige and the financial and patronage power of office.

The candidate who withdraws obtains both a substantial part of the money his opponent would have used to buy

128

votes and the prestige coming to an individual who others
fear so much that they would rather buy him off than
fight him. He is thus a proven power in the community.
Furthermore, the candidate who withdraws is often offered
additional resources. DeGlopper lists the following
resources commonly offered in Lu-kang Township:

1. A voice in how public funds are spent
2. Money contributed to a given charity
3. A government scholarship to study in the
    United States
4. A guaranteed price for mushrooms
5. Guarantees on a number of jobs for one's
    supporters 190

Resources for the Winners

To discuss the resources obtained by the winners is
to discuss the resources generally available to all citizens who are more or less active in the local political
process. What is different about the winners is that
because they hold elective office, they are closer to
all the above-listed possibilities of resource attainment.
Provincial Assemblyman Li Chien-ho's ability to introduce
resolutions, Provincial Assemblywoman Wang Kuo-hsiu's
influence on an unfeeling bureaucracy, and the power of
mayors and Farmers' Association presidents in the towns
studied by Gallin, Crissman, and DeGlopper make available
to these winners opportunities to recoup the money spent
on making dumpling soup and coaxing votes out of constituents, leave them with possibilities for realizing a
handsome profit on their original investment, and provide
them with the nonfinancial rewards of power and prestige.

Two examples of the type of resources the winners
of Taiwan's elections have obtained for themselves follow:

[Concerning the T'ao-yüan County Assembly]
. . . at the time of review of the 1965 general
county budget, the county entered into it
a $630,000 NT [$15,750 US] subsidy, dividing
the subsidy between each rural district and
township according to the number of representatives each elects to the Assembly,
subsidizing the rural districts and townships
in buying motorcycles . . . These motorcycles

129

were listed as the property of the rural districts and townships. Further, upon the giving
of a receipt, each assemblyman borrowed one
from the rural district or town hall.191

. . . The Taipei County Assembly . . . ignor-
ing the wants of the county residents and the
hopes of the city residents, tabled [Taipei
County's] bill for the prohibition of the
burning of soft coal. According to the fifth's
National Evening Press, of the twenty-six
assemblymen who advocated tabling, the majority
carry on coal-mining operations or are related
to the coal-mining industry, if not the owners
of factories that use soft coal. In order to
sell soft coal, and fearing the raising of
costs in their factories, they fearlessly
turned down a matter that was for the benefit
of all the masses. This "there is I and no
one else" kind of selfish attitude truly
bears alarm and lament.192

The Biggest Winners

As has been seen above, the resources sought by most
of those participating in Taiwan's local politics are
relatively modest. For the least active rank-and-file
citizen, the resource was a certain amount of security
provided through a relationship to powerful individuals
and groups, perhaps mixed with a little pride through
identification and some positive help attainable from
time to time. For one active politician, attaining the
position of precinct headman, with the tiny amount of
prestige it brought, was a heady feat to contemplate.
For most practical individuals, election to the position
of town or rural district mayor was about as high as
their hopes would go. Only a few lucky souls actually
climbed to the heights of a county-city mayor or a provincial assemblyman.

Yet on leafing through the Business Directory of
Taiwan, one finds that at least a few politicians have
set their goals even higher. They have kept climbing,
past the elected posts of mayor and assemblyman, into
the directorships of the provincial government's large
financial institutions.193 Also, since 1969, in accor-

130

dance with the attempts of the governing elite to seek accommodation with the Taiwanese, higher administrative and legislative positions, especially in the Central Government, have become realistic targets for these biggest winners in Taiwan's local political games.[194]

Therefore, for those who have the means and are willing to act according to the governing elite's rules, electoral politics may eventually lead to favorable connections with powerful persons in the party and the government.[195] And favorable connections may lead, in turn, to more prestigious and lucrative positions.

The existence of such career plans in the minds of politicians in Taiwan is evidenced by interviews with young politicians themselves, politicians who appear to have the brightest futures in Taiwan's local politics.[196] It is also evidenced by the following cartoon:

Translation (Title): Step by Step Rising High.
(Figures from right to left): ordinary citizen,
county assemblyman, provincial assemblyman,
high official and illustrious nobleman.[197]

131

Chapter 5

FACTIONS AND FACTION-RELATED GROUPS

This chapter will analyze the relationship of fac-
tions--dyadic and trait--to the many other kinds of
groups important in Taiwan's local political system.

Family and Faction

Most of the local political resources discussed in
Chapter 4 in relation to the rank-and-file citizen in
Taiwan were a matter of the positive rewards and protective measures that combine to form a "security system"
within which the citizen can maintain his livelihood without undue threat. The main method of attaining these
resources, as was noted, is to establish a personal
relationship with a powerful person or group of persons
who would ensure security in return for the various types
of support that the powerful feel necessary to maintain
their own positions.

A question arises in terms of factions, however.
The traditional reliance by the Chinese on his family
is well documented, as is the family as the main social
and political unit of traditional Chinese society. Why
then should the problem of establishing personal relations
for protection ever appear? After all, the Chinese is
born into a family. The relationship could not be more
personal. And is not the family the unit that ensures
the individual's security system?

This perplexity increases when one realizes that
the concept of family in China means more than the immediate family of father, mother, and children. Nor is
it necessarily limited to the extended family of great-
grandparents through great-grandchildren. In China,
family often means a large number of people, perhaps but
not necessarily well organized, who trace their origins
back to the same ancestor. On Taiwan, such lineages,
or tsus, have been known to number as many as 2,000 members. Is this not enough to ensure one's security?198

Families Are Factions?

Although situations in which the citizen obtained adequate security from his family or lineage were previously important aspects of the political system in many communities in Taiwan, it is doubtful that there are many communities in which such a situation persists today.[199]

Of course, there probably still are a handful of communities in which large lineages have remained united. Such united lineages, given the votes they control, will certainly be powerful in any local election district. This power will readily translate into protection for individual lineage members and permit the lineage to operate as an independent trait faction in local political affairs.[200]

Families Join Factions

But although a handful of lineages may be behaving as local political trait factions, most local political factions are dyadic, bearing little resemblance to lineages. It is these dyadic factions that Gallin is writing about when he describes the tendency of the political functions of the lineage to be taken over by the faction. Gallin's main point is that lineages have been losing their ability to ensure the security that their members demand.

Gallin attributes this weakening of lineage power to Japanese success at stifling much of the lineages' operations and substituting their own authority during their 1895-1945 rule in Taiwan, the confiscation of most of the land held by large lineage organizations and by wealthy lineage members during the 1949-1953 land reform program enforced by the returning Chinese government, recent changing economic conditions in the village, and changes in the formal political system.

The most important changes in economic conditions have been rapid population growth, an accompanying scarcity of land, and a drive stimulated by the Central Government toward greater farm output through modernization of agriculture. These economic changes have brought the villagers into a world much larger than their

134

village. They now have to deal with such outside organizations as the Farmers' Association, the Joint Commission on Rural Reconstruction, and the Water Irrigation Association. They must also deal in markets extending beyond nearby market towns.201

As for changes in the formal political system,

> The first change, in [1950], directed that the hsiang chang [rural district mayor] be elected by popular vote of the villagers instead of by the hsiang [rural district] council. The second change followed in 1961 and directed that each hsiang be divided into subdistricts, and each subdistrict elect representatives to the council on the basis of population, rather than each village individually electing its own representative to the council.202

The effect of these changes was that

> Candidates for the office of hsiang chang had to compete for the votes of the greater population rather than for those of the twenty or so hsiang council members. Similarly, an individual candidate running for election to the hsiang council had to face a much larger electorate; the competition was with people from other villages rather than with fellow villagers. This meant that a candidate could no longer rely solely on the support of his own kinship groups or even of a coalition of several powerful tsu groups in his village to be elected. Many of the personal relationships upon which both the hsiang chang and the hsiang council candidates had previously depended could no longer be as effective in the election. The individual candidates for hsiang chang could not possibly have personal relationships with the general electorate of the hsiang as they previously had had with the 22 hsiang council electors, just as a candidate for the hsiang council could not possibly have personal relations with the voters of a whole sub-[rural]district which included from four to seven villages.203

135

As with the new economic situation, this new political situation, by enlarging the world on which each
citizen is dependent, similarly weakened the ability of
the relatively small lineage group to continue to ensure
his security system. Although the rank-and-file citizen
did not lightly reject what continued security his
lineage could offer him, he still felt a need for a more
powerful or larger protector.

Here the governing elite's complaints concerning
the rise of factional politics and immoral political
behavior have relevance. The institution of "open elections made participation by almost anyone possible,"
and success in these elections promised real rewards
to the winners. Thus, "a new kind of people" began to
compete for office. Unlike the traditional "gentry-type
leaders," who based their political behavior "on traditional moral and normative rules," these people "rendered
the older moral rules of political behavior impractical
for the effective achievement of success" by using any
means of bribery and election fraud possible to gain their
ends. 204

This new situation, in combination with the financial
pressures and opportunities created by the land reform
program, caused many traditional gentry-type, respected
leaders to withdraw from local politics, giving way to
these "new kind of people." Decisions to withdraw were
based on one or more of the following reasons: (a)
diminished or complete lack of financial ability to compete in elections, (b) unwillingness to take the financial risks necessary for campaigning, (c) rejection of
the extremely opportunistic behavior increasingly necessary for electoral success, (d) diversion of interests
into farming or nonfarm business, and (e) diversion of
interests away from the local community.205

Other traditional leaders, however, refused to step
aside. Just as, or more, motivated than anyone else to
obtain the rewards offered by the electoral system, they
continued to compete for local leadership positions. 206
But the price of success was the readjustment of behavior,
causing the traditional leaders to become "a new kind of
people" themselves.

These new people, in their search for votes, working
from power bases that transcended the small lineage and

village and that connected widely from town-rural district government and Farmers' Association through the county government to the Provincial Assembly itself, offered themselves to security-minded citizens in terms of supportive-exchange dyads legitimized through jen-ch'ing terminology and sentiment. Through these jen-ch'ing dyads, the new institutions of dyadic factions were built.207

But the above changes--taking place in many developing political systems throughout the world--did not make families and lineages politically irrelevant. Loyalty to lineage, Gallin finds, is still an important factor in his village, especially among the older villagers. Villagers estimate that probably 80 percent of those living in the village still feel it is important to give unequivocal support to their own lineage members in elections. The village mayor felt that a dyadic-faction leader must be very careful not to take lineage loyalty too lightly and make unreasonable and unnecessary demands on faction members. It is still considered unreasonable to urge a villager to vote against a member of his own lineage.208

What has happened in many developing political systems is that an enlarged and more complex political world has brought with it problems of complexity and conflict in loyalties and interests. The result is that, for the individual citizen or nuclear family, security is no longer a matter of simple relation to lineage. But neither is it simply a matter of relinquishing lineage ties for the more secure ties of a dyadic faction. Instead, intralineage relations remain a strong factor in indicating to which dyadic faction a lineage member will adhere.

In Gallin's Taiwan area, for example, "major portions of whole [lineage] groups are recruited into a single faction." Although "factions in the area always cross kinship lines, and even split [lineage] groups," these splits are often based on intralineage rivalries, with lineage leaders bringing their lineage supporters, which may indeed be sublineages of the main lineage, with them into the rival factions intact.209

This analysis of the continued importance of loyalty to family and lineage is also supported by findings more specific to Taiwan's Chinese society and less relevant to the world's developing systems generally. Although ideal-type supportive-exchange dyads are established without necessarily making reference to the sharing of distinguishing traits, the Chinese necessarily make reference to the sharing of distinguishing traits when they establish "actual" supportive-exchange dyads.

The calculations upon which the Chinese base their decisions concerning the establishment of supportive-exchange dyads necessarily make reference to the sharing (or nonsharing) of distinguishing traits because the Chinese have learned that such distinguishing traits as family and lineage relationships, when shared by the parties to a potential dyad, will be one factor vouching for that dyad's chances for successfully serving the interests of its parties.

Of course, two Chinese may still find it in their interest to establish a dyad in which no trait of any sort is shared or in which the shared traits are not at all distinguishing. This is especially the case now that an enlarged and more complex world is involving the individual's interests with greater numbers and kinds of other individuals. If this is the case, both partners will strive to invent fictive shared traits or put an exaggerated emphasis on the less distinguishing traits they do share.

Previously it was noted that in all societies in which dyadic supportive-exchange relationships are important, the invention of fictive shared traits or the overemphasizing of less distinguishing shared traits was motivated by the need to add intimacy to (i.e., to legitimize) a relationship that would otherwise be felt as a crassly impersonal series of materialistic exchanges. According to this analysis, a second motivation more specific to Chinese society also exists--a motivation to create the distinguishing shared traits that both parties have learned will vouch for the likelihood that their dyad will successfully serve their respective interests.210

Additional evidence for the continuing importance of family and lineage in Taiwan's local politics and for the necessity of inventing or overemphasizing shared traits when clearly distinguishing shared traits do not already exist comes from the author's own field

138

research. Informants frequently mentioned the importance
of having many family members if one is to be successful
in Taiwan's elections. This observation, moreover, was
bolstered by the enormous number of family members--
some of quite distant (i.e., less distinguishing) and
perhaps theoretical (i.e., fictive) relationship--sur-
rounding almost every politician the author interviewed
in Taiwan.[211]

Family as Leader and Core of Factions

Besides the two relationships of small families and
larger lineages to factions discussed above--the family
as a trait faction and the family (split or, perhaps on
occasion, whole) joining a dyadic faction for protection
in a new world that it, by itself, is not powerful enough
to control--there is one more type of relationship of
family to faction on Taiwan.

In his article on factions, Ralph W. Nicholas notes
that "Leadership may be provided not only by a politically
powerful individual, but also . . . by a 'clique' based
in an influential family."[212] Thus, in all societies
in which factions exist, the family may be related to a
faction because it provides leadership to the faction.
Such a faction may be a "one-trait" family-lineage faction, a multitrait faction, or a combination trait and
dyadic faction.

If a small leading family is part of a very large
and still united lineage, this lineage is likely to form
the core of the faction's support. Such a large lineage,
unlike the small lineages that Gallin found in the village
he studied in Changhua County, may well be large enough
(2,000?) to have a still strong political potential.

A "leader-core" lineage with which the author is
familiar is the Ch'en lineage in Hsin-chu County's Kuan-
hsi Township. Here, according to one lineage member,
approximately 2,000 people identifying with the same
ancestor form the basis of the faction's votes. The
leadership, members of the lineage who received medical
degrees in Japan, remain in the background, providing
funds and designating other members of the lineage to
compete in elections for the votes of the general population against candidates from rival lineages led by

other sets of Japanese-trained doctors.

Although the lineage vote in itself is not overly large when it comes to competition in larger election districts, the lineage is large if thought of in terms of a campaign organization. Such a lineage, if it is still substantially united and if there are those within it ambitious enough and with access to enough funds, can become the center of a team that competes against similar teams for local political resources.

What makes the team broader than the lineage is that, as Nicholas notes, "a [dyadic] faction leader . . . makes use of all possible ties to draw supporters into his faction."[213] Thus, the lineage base of 2,000 is called upon to make use of all the various personal relations at its disposal outside of the lineage to en-large its base of support. According to the above-men-tioned Ch'en lineage member, the lineage's base had been so broadened in the late 1960s that its main competitor in Kuan-hsi Township, a Liu lineage, withdrew from active competition. As seen above (pages 52, 124), the atten-tion of the lineage had expanded beyond Kuan-hsi Township in an attempt to capture the position of mayor of all of Hsin-chu County.

Besides the Ch'en lineage, newspaper reports and interviews indicate that the Yü family of Kao-hsiung County, the Hu family, leader of the river-north faction in Tainan County, and perhaps Li Chien-ho's family in Taipei County are also providers of faction leadership. (In these latter cases, however, the author does not know whether an intermediate large-lineage core exists between the small leadership family and the rank-and-file faction supporters.) A staff member of the Provincial Assembly mentioned seven assemblymen who he felt were in the third-term Assembly thanks to the support of such leader-ship families.

Relatives

The beginning student of the Chinese language learns that the word ch'in-ch'i means relatives. Relatives, he may assume, include anyone related to him: cousins, uncles, grandparents. But, he also learns, Chinese do not simply have cousins, uncles, and grandparents. They have paternal and maternal cousins, paternal and maternal uncles, and paternal and maternal grandparents. Moreover, if he ever spends time in Chinese society, he will discover that paternal cousins, paternal uncles, and paternal grandparents are often not considered relatives (ch'in-ch'i). They are family. A significant distinction is made between family and maternal cousins, maternal uncles, and maternal grandparents. These latter are relatives.

The discussion above dealt almost exclusively with the family, even if this was a family so large that it included over 2,000 people, all clearly descended from the same ancestor. These families constituted the factions in themselves, joined larger factions as a unit or in segments, or became the nucleus of factions. This section will be concerned with maternal relatives and their relationships to factions.

In all societies, maternal relatives have traditionally been looked upon as an important asset for the building of the personalized security system that the citizen feels necessary to surround himself with.[214] Given changing economic and political conditions, the consequent broadening of each citizen's political world, and the citizen's resulting need for a broader security system, the importance of extrafamilial maternal relatives has grown alongside the growth in the importance of extrafamilial faction relationships.[215]

The result of this growing importance of maternal relatives, besides bringing with it a problem of dual loyalty between the demands of family and relatives, has been to make available another personal link that the dyadic-faction leader, be he a lone individual or a representative of a family, can use in recruiting supporters. On Taiwan, for example, the frequent mentioning of the need for many family members to be successful in politics and the constant meeting of enormous numbers of family members around politicians being interviewed were paralleled by the mentioning and meeting of large numbers of ch'in-ch'i. Therefore, when such families as the Ch'en clan of Kuan-hsi Township try to gather support for their candidates, many in-laws are called upon for aid.[216]

Such ch'in-ch'i relationships have led to the election of two third-term Provincial Assembly members through

141

support from the families of their in-laws: Yü Ch'en Yüeh-ying, representing her father-in-law Yü Teng-fa's family-led faction in Kao-hsiung County, and Chang Wen-hsien, representing his father-in-law Hu Lung-pao's family-led faction in Tainan County.

Nonkin Relationships and Factions

The inability of the small family, larger lineage, and/or ch'in-ch'i relationships alone to handle the demands of a modernizing society has resulted in individuals' searching for relationships with other groups that would enable them to maintain an effective security system. Morton H. Fried points out that it is not just the conditions of modernization that have forced the Chinese to seek aid from nonkin sources. Fried believes that his description, below, of nonkin relationships in the mainland Province of Anhwei, where he did research during 1947 and 1948, is generally applicable to traditional Chinese society as well.

> All elements of the population, rich and
> poor, rural and urban, peasant and gentry,
> engage in extensive non-kin relationships.
> The fields in which these relationships
> take place are numerous and diverse. No
> Chinese family of my acquaintanceship is, to
> any significant degree, self-sufficient.
> The poorest elements in the Chinese popu-
> lation, the beggars, are not only completely
> dependent upon outside society for their
> subsistence, but are frequently organized
> as a body, for the sake of increased efficiency.
> Likewise, the richest and most stable gentry
> families are attached to a myriad [of]
> non-related individuals. Some of these
> supply the rich family its subsistence,
> others aid it in the defense of its position.217

In this section, a number of traditional nonkin group relationships will be described in terms of (a) how these relationships are currently being utilized on Taiwan to cope with the pressures of modernization and (b) the frequent involvement of these relationships with the nontraditional factions and faction politicians.

142

Surnames and Clans

In the search for security-guaranteeing relationships, unrelated people with the same surname represent the next step beyond maternal relatives. Surname
relationships were important on Taiwan even before
such forces as Japanese colonial policy and post-1945
economic and political change began to undermine the
power of lineages. This was especially true in areas
in which lineage power never fully developed to begin
with.

Taiwan did have settlers "who move[d] with [their]
immediate famil[ies] or in the company of a number . . .
of patrilineal kinsmen," thus presaging among such
settlers the development of strong, united lineages.[218]
But it was more common for settlers to share the following characteristics: (a) came from lower-class backgrounds, (b) came to Taiwan "from nuclear or minimally
extended families," (c) had "little direct experience"
in the management of lineage organization or ancestor
cults, (d) had "no money to operate" a lineage, (e)
"lacked immediately known illustrious ancestors" around
which lineage ancestor cults could crystallize, (f)
had "arrived in Taiwan with few relatives on the island
with whom cooperation along lineage lines would have
been useful or possible," (g) often "intended to return
to Fukien later and would have seen no point in the
establishment of full lineage trappings" on the island,
and (h) often immigrated in formally constituted groups
composed of members from the same locality on the mainland under the leadership of landlords or other authority
figures.[219]

When settlers possessing these unfavorable characteristics for the development of lineages were met by
"competition for strategic resources" from entrenched
non-Chinese or other Chinese ethnic groups already established in the area and/or needed to cooperate "for
purposes of exploiting the environment," the tendency
not to develop large, localized lineages was decisively
reinforced. Instead, the need to cooperate for defense
and environmental exploitation stimulated the "unrelated
family and lineage fragments" to develop "associations
which crosscut kin groups."[220]

143

One important example of such cross-kin associations is the surname group. Given the comparative paucity of surnames in Chinese society, combined with the "polite fiction" that people with the same surname are ultimately in the same family and with the importance attached to family relationships, "identity of surname" has frequently been a basis for mutual support between otherwise unrelated Chinese.[221]

To rephrase this in terms of the analysis in Chapter 3 above, when a Chinese finds it necessary to establish a supportive-exchange relationship with individuals with whom he shares no clearly distinguishing traits, he places exaggerated emphasis on those less distinguishing traits that are shared (in this case, a common surname). The overemphasized trait then provides the intimacy that legitimizes the relationship in Chinese terms by ensuring that the relationship will not be felt as a crassly impersonal series of materialistic exchanges. Additionally, the overemphasized trait vouches for the likelihood that the relationship will successfully serve the interests of its parties.

Under the pressing needs imposed by competition for strategic resources and/or by the necessity to cooperate for purposes of exploiting the environment, therefore, surname (combined with such other shared traits as place of origin, ethnic group, place of current residence, and leadership of an authority figure who may have led the settlers to immigrate in a group to begin with) often formed the basis of new relationships.[222]

Such relationships, still built on the more basic blocks of family and lineage fragments (though perhaps not in themselves very formally organized),[223] were manifested by combinations of (a) villages predominantly populated by one surname group, (b) alliances between such villages, based on surname, for various purposes,[224] and (c) the combining of a number of (often extremely distantly) related and/or unrelated family and lineage fragments of the same surname into a formally constituted family-name association[225] (i.e., a clan, an association of individuals that "involves an agreement that kinship exists without specifying exactly how the parties to the relationship are in fact connected"[226]).

Burton Pasternak, in his analysis of why associations

144

that crosscut kin groups developed under certain circumstances on Taiwan but not under other circumstances,
stresses that such cross-kin associations as surname
groups only developed under the above-described cir-
cumstances--when settlers possessing the unfavorable
characteristics for the development of lineages listed
above were met with conditions that reinforced the tendency not to develop lineages. When settlers possessing
unfavorable characteristics for the development of
lineages were met with conditions favorable to the development of lineages, however, "partrilineal ideology"
was still bound to assert itself in the formation of
formally constituted lineages ("descent groups" in which
"one traces and specifies all connecting links in a gene-
alogical web").227

Conditions favorable to the development of lineages
occurred when unrelated family or lineage fragments
settled in an area in which competition for strategic
resources from entrenched non-Chinese or other Chinese
ethnic groups already established in the area and/or
the need for cooperation for purposes of exploiting the
environment was minimal.228   In such "an uncontested
environment," the lineage fragments "will show little
inclination toward consolidation" with other unrelated
lineage fragments in the area.229

Development of lineages will be especially encouraged, moreover, as eventual population growth causes
competition for strategic resources between the family
and lineage fragments within the settlers' community
and when "the production of agricultural surplus" stim-
ulates concern "with limiting access to [lineage] estates and, therefore, with distinguishing themselves
as a group from other" settlers in the area. "Patrilineal affiliation might then serve as a critical consideration in intravillage competition, and might, in
turn, reflect itself in the nature of intravillage conflict as well."230

According to Pasternak, even when settlers possessing unfavorable characteristics for the development of
lineages were met with conditions that reinforced the
tendency not to develop lineages, it was still common
for the "patrilineal ideology" to manifest itself eventually. This was demonstrated not only in the formation
of lineagelike clans or fictive lineages but also

145

in their decline in the face of the later development of genuine patrilineal lineages.

When conflict with ethnic groups that were origi-nally established in the area became less critical, when "the larger population potential of irrigated-rice agriculture has been realized, when population begins to press down upon available land and water resources"-- much as in the areas in which lineages developed from a combination of settlers with unfavorable characteris-tics and favorable local conditions--cooperation between unrelated people of the same surname became less impor-tant. Instead, people began to be more concerned with protecting their own property and wealth from the en-croachments of others within their own settlers' commu-nity.231 Therefore, genuine lineages developed as a method of restricting claims to given wealth by requir-ing "that all members be able to detail exactly how they are related to the founding ancestor, always a definite, historical person."232

As these tendencies began to manifest themselves in those areas in which lineage development was delayed, however, those areas came under the influences of such forces as Japanese colonial policy and post-1945 econom-ic and political change, forces that destroyed the viability of much more solidly developed lineages. Thus, this late manifestation of "patrilineal ideology" was soon "truncated."233

At the same time, for these same reasons, other-wise constituted surname groups were also threatened. Just as with lineages, surname groups based on old inter-ests--mainly territorial--became inadequate for the new needs of their individual members. As with lineages, they too became unstable, often segmenting, each seg-ment joining a different dyadic faction. Many smaller groups, however, apparently joined one or another fac-tion as a unit.234

Still, unlike formal lineages, which are legitimized and vouched for by a trait shared by a typically small set of specifically designated individuals, Chinese surname groups are legitimized and vouched for by a trait shared by some of the largest sets of individuals on earth (e.g., all people named Ch'en, Wang, or Li). Although the enlarged and more complex political world

146

now relevant to the individual's interests is likely to
cause many originally constituted surname groups to become less useful to both rank-and-file group members
and ambitious faction leaders, individuals who share
the original groups' surnames but are not group members
live all over Taiwan. Thus, opportunities are widely
available for rank-and-file group members and faction
politicians to promote their interests within the enlarged
and more complex world now relevant to their interests
by establishing and/or taking advantage of new supportive-exchange relationships legitimized and vouched for
by a shared surname trait.

     Under these circumstances, one would expect to find
new supportive-exchange relationships based on surnames
being formed as fast as old ones are being modified or
discarded. A striking example of this contrasts clans
with lineages. As formally constituted lineages are
declining, "Taiwan is experiencing a boom in clan organization."

> . . . people see the need of maintaining
> larger webs of kinship than families provide,
> especially under the changes of modern life
> which make nuclear families increasingly
> prevalent. Many of these people band togeth-
> er to establish new clans or seek to join
> existing ones. 235

     These new clans, it should be noted, are different
from Taiwan's original surname groups. The original
groups were primarily trait groups based on surname,
often reinforced by such other traits as common place
of origin, same Chinese ethnic group, and common place
of residence. Although all of these traits may have
served to bring the individuals into association, common
residence supplied the bulk of the shared interests.
These trait groups were based on supportive-exchange
relationships, but the relationships were primarily
between the individual and the group as a whole. Dyadic
supportive-exchange relationships existed within the
groups, but they were not the predominant means of binding the members together.

     The interests on which the newer clans are based
are much more eclectic--some still based on territory,
but others arising from the many other traits that indi-

viduals in a modernizing society find themselves in possession of. Moreover, the interests of clan members do not necessarily stem from shared traits. Some interests may, but many arise from the different traits possessed by the motley membership. Thus, many members are bound together by complementary, not shared, interests; and this binding will be much more in terms of dyadic supportive-exchange relationships, the interests served by each dyad in the clan being different from those being served by any other dyad.

Paradoxically, the importance of the one shared trait of surname may well be more stressed in the new clans than in the older surname groups. In the older surname groups, territory was at least as important as surname in generating mutual interests and supplying a trait to vouch for and legitimize the relationships involved. For the clans, however, the varied nature of the membership probably leaves surname as the only trait shared by all. It is, therefore, likely to be especially stressed for its value in legitimizing and vouching for the relationships of which the clan is composed. This will be the case even though the role of the surname in generating the shared interests on which the clan is based is probably nil.

"If Someone Comes from the Same County, You Support Him!"

In his discussion of dyadic factions, Ralph W. Nicholas notes that dyadic-faction leaders throughout the world recruit their followers "on diverse principles."[236] This observation is in accordance with the ideal-type definition of dyadic factions as being established without necessarily making reference to the sharing of distinguishing traits. Recruiting followers on diverse principles, the faction leader may or may not make reference to the principle of shared traits, depending on the efficacy of that principle in bringing individuals over to his side.

In a society such as Taiwan's, in which people are likely to view their security needs in terms of shared traits and in which they use shared traits as a necessary reference for the establishment of security-guaranteeing relationships, therefore, faction leaders recruiting on diverse principles pay particular attention to the shared traits of family, relatives, and surnames in establishing the supportive-exchange dyads on which their factions are based. The leaders offer to ensure a better security system for their recruits in exchange for whatever support the recruits can give in return--the whole relationship being legitimized and vouched for by the shared trait.

People viewing themselves in terms of residence in a given locality on Taiwan (the same people discussed above as viewing themselves in terms of belonging to specific families, having certain relatives, and bearing certain surnames) are also concerned with their security system. Because of the possibilities for the establishment of security-guaranteeing relationships arising from this residence trait, moreover, these people are also potential recruits for dyadic (as well as territorial trait) faction leaders.

This section deals with people viewing themselves in terms of their residence in a given locality, as well as the way this trait is related to Taiwan's factional politics.

Given the exigencies of early settlement on Taiwan, it was not necessary for individuals to share a common surname in order to form associations based on common interests. The "unrelated family and lineage fragments" that were stimulated by the need to cooperate for defense and environmental exploitation to develop associations that crosscut kin groups often did not share the same surname. Common residence was usually enough to bestow those interests necessary to form common-interest associations. [237] Common residence was also sufficient to legitimize the association and vouch for its probable efficacy in serving its members' interests.

Again, other traits may have been involved, especially in bringing the unrelated family and lineage fragments together in the first place. The members may have originally immigrated to Taiwan in a formally constituted group. They may have all come from the same locality on the mainland. They may have been held together by the leadership of a landlord or other authority figure. They may also have been members of the same Chinese ethnic subgroup.[238]

149

The dynamics of the development and decline of these common-interest associations follow closely those of the development and decline of surname groups. Indeed, but for the added factor of surname, the two are identical. General- and/or specific-purpose common-interest associations, with different degrees of consciously formal organization, were formed (a) between small groups of contiguous or noncontiguous neighbors, (b) between the members of virtually an entire village, and (c) as an alliance between the memberships of more than one village.[239]

As with surname groups, when competition with ethnic groups that were originally established in the area became less critical and when "the larger population potential of irrigated-rice agriculture has been realized; when population begins to press down upon available land and water resources," cooperation between unrelated family and lineage fragments became less important. Instead, people began to be more concerned with protecting their own property and wealth from the encroachments of others within their own settlers' community. Lineages, therefore, began to develop as a method of restricting claims to given wealth.[240]

Just as these tendencies began to manifest themselves in those areas in which lineage development was originally delayed, however, the influences of such forces as Japanese colonial policy and post-1945 economic and political change combined to truncate this late manifestation of patrilineal ideology.[241]

But for these same reasons, reasons that also threatened lineages and surname groups based on old interests, the solidarity of common-interest associations also began to break down. Often this was the direct result of Japanese colonial policy and/or the loss of associational assets as a result of the KMT's land reform.[242] In other cases, unless the common interest that bound the association together remained important to members after the post-1945 economic and political changes, groups of neighbors, village associations, and alliances of villages began to segment, with different segments being courted by different dyadic factions. When common interests that originally bound the association in question together remained important to members or when the members found new shared inter-

150

ests, the association remained united and, if relevant
to the interests in question, acted in local factional
politics as a trait faction.

The Breakdown of Territorial Solidarity

As with lineages and surname groups, examples of
the breakdown of territorially defined trait groups are
many. Bernard Gallin, in the following example, illus-
trates the growing disunity of the village he studied
under the impact of changing political conditions:

> The explanation given by the villagers and
> others in the area for this lack of unity was
> that a number of Hsin Hsing villagers voted
> along [dyadic] factional lines and so cast
> their ballots for another village's candidate
> rather than for their fellow villager . . .
>
> Because the peasants have so many new inter-
> ests that draw them away from the affairs
> of the village, they will vote with their
> [dyadic] factions according to their personal
> interests . . . The villager is thus drawn
> further away from identification with the
> village and its people into relationships
> which better serve his personal needs.243

In terms of village disunity in response to changing
economic conditions, Gallin continues as follows:

> The impact of these newly expanding contacts
> and communications with the outside has sub-
> jected the villagers to many new influences,
> including those from growing urban-indus-
> trialism in Taiwan. Such influences have
> resulted in an important turning away from
> the traditional identification with and
> loyalty to the village.244

Village unity and lineage unity were not necessarily
mutually exclusive. In regions where lineages displayed
a certain amount of development, they may or may not have
chosen to cooperate with one another in promoting village
unity. In cases in which lineages did promote village
unity, the decline of village and lineage unity were

151

closely related. This was not simply because they were both subject to the same political and economic conditions. In these cases, the decline of lineage unity actually had a direct effect on the weakening of local village organization. Where politically and economically influential lineages cooperated in the election of their village's main officials, for example, any decline in lineage unity resulted in a weakening of village unity because such village unity was based on lineage unity.245

The Continuation of Territorial Solidarity

Although the cohesiveness of territorial groups declined in the face of the power of nonterritorial dyadic factions, people on Taiwan still take their resident trait very seriously. This should not be a surprise. Despite some overidealized models of political modernization, locality has continued to be a defining interest, even in the most modern of polities. It is, therefore, to be expected that the breakdown of territorial solidarity in the face of more "functional" interests will always be limited. Issues affecting the vast majority of people in any one locality in a similar manner are bound to continue to arise and to arouse the unifying instincts of the inhabitants.

Evidence of the continued effect of geography is abundant at all levels on Taiwan. Within some village neighborhoods, for example, the traditional importance and continued influence of lineage solidarity plus its close relationship to geographical solidarity are clearly manifested.

> The traditional closeness of the tsu and
> smaller kinship groups is heightened by their
> geographical positioning in the villages.
> Each tsu organization or lesser kinship group
> of families lives mostly in its own separate
> neighborhood or compound in the village.246

In village neighborhoods in which lineages did not exert an overriding influence on solidarity, the importance of geography is still manifest in the continued prevalence of large numbers of common-interest associations of contiguous and noncontiguous neighbors.247

As for the larger area of an entire village, village

152

lineages and/or common-interest associations may provide
the context for cooperative and crosscutting interperson-
al relationships, tying villagers together in a unified
web. A striking example of a common-interest association of this nature was discovered by Burton Pasternak
in the village of Ta-t'ieh, in Taiwan's P'ing-tung
County. Virtually all families in this multisurname
village, and no outsiders, own stock in the financially
successful Make Prosperous Limited Shares Corporation.
The villagers receive benefits from the corporation
both as individual shareholders and through the corporation's grants to the village as a whole.[248]

External forces may also encourage villagers to draw
together in common interest. Crissman reports that the
villages he studied in Changhua County still present
a united front on issues involving them with the outside
world. As with lineages, the demands of dyadic faction
and locale are often in conflict. Just as dyadic-faction
leaders in lineage-faction conflict situations are wary
of urging lineage members to vote against their kin,
Crissman finds feeling for local area substantially
stronger than loyalty to dyadic faction in cases of
locale-faction conflict.[249] As a consequence, he notes
that all candidates in his area do well at home, no
matter what local dyadic-faction alignments dictate.[250]
Crissman and others even cite examples of recent physical battles sparked by intervillage disputes.[251]

A striking illustration of territorial favoritism and
solidarity on the rural district-township level is reported
by J. Bruce Jacobs. In the rural district Jacobs studied,
administrative arrangements, marketing patterns, relative
networks, and other socioeconomic factors divided the district's northern area from its southern part so completely
that virtually no distinguishing traits shared by individuals from both areas ever developed. With no shared
traits, there was little to generate mutual interests for,
vouch for, and legitimize supportive-exchange relationships capable of linking individuals in the north with
those in the south. As a consequence, parties to almost
all supportive-exchange relationships remained within the
same area, facilitating the establishment of mutually
opposed north and south factions.[252]

Finally, on the county level, out of the five assemblymen that Tainan County elected to the Provincial

Assembly's third term (1963-1968), three (and possibly a fourth) were identified with the river-north faction and one with the river-south faction. Moreover, the river-north faction controlled the county mayor's office and had almost half the votes (some being neutral) in the County Assembly.

New Territorial Trait Factions

Taiwan has both earlier and later types of territorial factions, each corresponding to a different stage of socioeconomic development. Examples of earlier types of territorial factions are politically active territorially based lineages, surname groups, and village associations, as well as the north-south factional division reported by J. Bruce Jacobs. According to the previous analysis--specifically for Taiwan and in a more general fashion for other developing political systems-- as the enlarged and increasingly complex world continues to impinge on these earlier-type territorial factions, their members will be infused with new traits. These new traits will provide the members with compelling new interests that can be protected and furthered best through the formation of new supportive-exchange relationships, often with partners not sharing the members' territorial trait.

Members of the earlier-type territorial faction, therefore, will be increasingly oriented toward the formation of these new nonterritorial supportive-exchange relationships. At the same time, the interests provided by the original trait of shared territory will become less important to the members in comparison to the interests provided by their newly acquired traits. Members of the earlier-type territorial faction, therefore, will become proportionately less oriented toward the formation or maintenance of supportive-exchange relationships with those sharing the original territorial trait.

These new traits may provide interests for the new nonterritorial supportive-exchange relationships because they and the interests they inspire are shared by the new partners. Additionally, or as an alternative, the partners may each possess different new traits that inspire different but complementary interests. Some of the new traits may also facilitate the formation of

154

new nonterritorial supportive-exchange relationships because they are shared by potential members and are seen as the type of traits capable of legitimizing and (more specifically in relation to Taiwan's Chinese society) vouching for the new relationship.

As for the original shared territorial trait's capability of providing interests for, vouching for, and legitimizing supportive-exchange relationships, because the interests it provides will become less important to the members of the earlier-type territorial faction, the members will form and maintain fewer supportive-exchange relationships with one another and thus find less use for the shared territorial trait as a legitimizer and voucher for their relationships.

Ultimately, members of the earlier-type territorial factions will increasingly abandon or modify their original territorial trait relationships and/or supplement them with the new, more eclectically based supportive-exchange relationships. (There are indications, however, that this process may be retarded by the continuing emotional ties with which the original relationships are infused plus the stubborn persistence of any long-standing habitual behavior.)[253]

In areas in which the decline of earlier-formed territorial and other trait factions is already advanced, weakened versions of both the earlier trait factions and the newer dyadic factions now share the same political arena. Specifically for Taiwan, the dyadic factions themselves, in turn, appear to have been instrumental in the formation of "newer" types of territorial factions, which have joined the dyadic factions and the earlier-type trait factions in the political arena. In the following paragraphs, the role of Taiwan's dyadic factions in the formation of these newer types of territorial factions plus the coexistence of the newer territorial factions, the dyadic factions, and weakened versions of the earlier trait factions on Taiwan will be explained.

Two central factors in any explanation of the formation of Taiwan's newer territorial trait factions are the boundaries of an election district and the specific issues involved in an election. The boundaries of an election district determine who is in the arena of competition and who is excluded.[254] If a district is comprised of only one town or if one town is dominant in a district, there will be little stimulus to remain united, and internal competition will easily develop. In an election district in which other areas can mount a credible threat, however, the stimulus will be to remain united. In a similar manner, an issue may arise that will affect everyone in a given area equally, whereas a second issue may divide an area along functional lines.

Examples of the effects of boundaries and issues are given by Crissman. He found the town of Erh-lin splitting internally over issues important only within the town itself but presenting a united front in its battles with other regions in the county. In a neighboring area, Crissman found that the three warring dyadic factions of Ch'en, Wu, and Lin put aside their usual alliances with the Ch'en and Lin factions of other areas of the county and joined forces to ensure one more seat for their area in the County Assembly when a redrawing of election district boundaries threw their area into serious competition with other areas of the enlarged district. 255

From these examples, a relationship between dyadic factions and locale may be hypothesized. In areas on which the enlarged and increasingly complex world has already heavily impinged, dyadic factions are the most salient conflict organizations in local politics and cut across territorial divisions. But, depending on the issue and the boundaries of the election district they are competing in, the dyadic factions comprising a localized factional system may well unite in an alliance from time to time, forming a temporary "territorial faction" against the outside world. Alternatively, because of a given issue or changes in election districts, certain localized components of two or more competing dyadic factions may, on occasion, withdraw from the dyadic factions, forming a temporary territorial faction.

This explanation is supported by Crissman's further analysis of the nature of factions in his area. Crissman saw that the dyadic factions in his area were based on geography, but the case was not that of one dyadic faction controlling a large contiguous area facing the area controlled by a second dyadic faction over a hostile border. Instead, from the rural district and township

councils to the representatives that each rural district
and township sent to the County Assembly, there was a
nearly equal power balance between the two dyadic factions in each rural district and township.

The support for each of these factions came from
cells of territory, each cell occupied by a territorial
trait group, often supplemented by such other traits
as family-lineage, surname, and relative networks. The
cells supporting each faction were interspersed among
one another, the cells of one faction just as likely
bordering on cells of the rival faction as bordering
on cells of its own faction.

Each cell had been recruited into one or the other
dyadic faction through a chain of jen-ch'ing supportive-
exchange relationships, vouched for, legitimized, and
deriving their interests from the trait of territory,
often in combination with such other traits as mentioned
above. At the lower levels, it was perhaps someone
with a large household, a doctor with many patients, or
an urban precinct or village headman who guaranteed the
votes of his family, relatives, and friends in return
for rewards to keep himself and his clients satisfied.
Above him rested a hierarchy of supportive-exchange dyads,
usually ending with one dyadic-faction leader in control
of the town or district hall and his rival in control
of the Farmers' Association. The control of these two
points provided much of the sustenance for the dyadic
factions and thus was an important condition of power.

With the control of these strategic points, the
rural district-township dyadic factions, already in a
kind of competitive two-party system, are also similar
to U.S. parties in that the local (rural district-township), not the central (county), dyadic faction has the
most power. One does read and hear of countywide dyadic
factions however.[256] These county factions came into
being because of the resources available through control
of the county mayor and the County Assembly. Thus, somewhat permanent alliances are formed by the rural district-
township dyadic factions. The result is that in Changhua
County, the rural district-township factions have almost
all identified with either the name of Ch'en or Lin and
are allied with their counterparts in other rural districts and townships, forming Changhua's Ch'en and Lin
factions.[257]

157

The above analysis of dyadic-faction organization explains normal dyadic factional alignments. It also explains what is occurring when rural district-township dyadic factions forsake their county allies to join temporary territorial factions. But does this analysis explain I-lan and Tainan, where territorial factions appear to be more permanent?[258]

It is possible that the more-permanent territorial factions are examples of earlier types of territorial factions that have not yet been modified by an enlarged and more complex world. There is evidence, however, that for areas such as Tainan, the persistence of earlier-formed territorial trait relationships has played a minor role. This evidence suggests that the territorial factions are of the "newer" type, largely formed by another product of the enlarged and more complex world--the dyadic faction.

According to this evidence, given an electoral situation (election district boundaries and issues) in which the interests of the local area appeared to be threatened, one dyadic faction, over a period of time, has managed to "unite the locale." Through such tactics as gaining control of all significant resource outlets (town hall, Farmers' Association, and other influential offices), depriving the opposition of access to them, and using them to attract support, together with the skillful making of "dumpling soup," dramatizing the need for unity against outside threats, and vote buying, the opposition has been absorbed and/or rendered ineffective.

When this same process took place in areas bordering on one another, perhaps encouraged by ambitious leaders of a potential countywide dyadic-faction alliance, the appearance of a large and permanent territorial faction was assured. Given its territorial nature, moreover, those on the outside were then encouraged to unite in self-defense, forming countervailing territorial factions.

Migratory Properties of Territorial Traits

In addition to the ability of the shared residence trait to vouch for and legitimize supportive-exchange relationships established by individuals in their home community, earlier shared residence in a home community can vouch for and legitimize supportive-exchange relationships even after the parties have moved to new areas of Taiwan. If the parties have moved their residences to the same new area, moreover, continued proximity and common interests arising from the similar situations in which the parties find themselves will reinforce the likelihood that the earlier shared residence trait will be called upon to vouch for and legitimize new supportive-exchange relationships.

The importance of earlier shared residence has already been presented as one factor in the formation of cross-kin cooperative associations among the original immigrants to Taiwan. Use of the trait of earlier shared residence to vouch for and legitimize supportive-exchange relationships is also currently prevalent now that Taiwan's modernization is causing rapid rural-to-urban migration. In recent times, for example, many individuals from Lu-kang Township have moved their residence to Taipei City. Partially through the relationships established with these individuals, a former Lu-kang resident, Huang Ch'i-cheng, was elected as one of Taipei City's six representatives to the Provincial Assembly. The factions into which Kao-hsiung City's politics are divided provide a second example. These three factions consist of the original residents, those who came from P'eng-hu County, and those who came from Tainan County.[259]

Fictive Territorial Traits

As the enlarged and more complex world continues to orient Taiwan's citizens toward supportive-exchange relationships with increasingly varied types of partners, the likelihood that the potential partners to a relationship will not share traits distinguishing enough to vouch for and legitimize their relationship will also increase. Faced with this problem, the partners may turn back to shared territorial traits for their vouching and legitimizing needs.

This surprising development may take place because the definition of the territory shared is flexible. Potential parties to a relationship may not live in the

same village, but given their pressing need to find
some shared trait with which to vouch for and legitimize
a potentially profitable supportive-exchange relationship, they may discover that current (or even previous)
shared residence in the same township, county, province,
etc., is sufficient.[260]

Of course, the larger the territorial unit shared,
the less likely that the territorial unit in itself will
provide shared interests to reinforce the supportive-
exchange relationship. Moreover, the larger the territorial unit shared, the more the shared territory will
be a fictive trait. Also, fictive traits, being less
distinguishing and less "real," will be weaker than other
traits in vouching for and legitimizing the relationship.

Ethnolinguistic Trait Groups and Factions

The Hakka people are the traditional movers in
China. According to population reports, about 1,000
years ago the Hakka people began to leave the K'ai-feng
area in northern China and move south. They established
villages bordering on, but separate from, those of the
original settlers in much of southern China. They
were known as Hakka, meaning "guest families." Like the
ancestors of other Taiwanese, the ancestors of Taiwan's
Hakkas emigrated to Taiwan during the seventeenth through
nineteenth centuries.

Blood flowed in battles between the other Taiwanese (usually referred to as Minnan people because they
speak the Minnan dialect of Amoy as opposed to the
Hakka dialect) and the Hakkas before the populations
settled down, the Hakkas generally being pushed into
less productive areas. Indeed, previous discussion of
the need for unrelated family and lineage fragments to
bypass the formation of lineages in favor of associations that crosscut kin groups when faced with competition for strategic resources from entrenched ethnic
groups already in the area is heavily based on examples
of Hakka versus Minnan competition. Thus, unlike territorial factions divided only because of geographical
residence, a long history of ethnic antagonism is added
on to territorial divisions in the regions divided between these two peoples.[261]

160

With the exception of this extra antagonism, however, in other respects regions divided between Hakka and other Taiwanese are host to political behavior much like that displayed by other territorial trait factions. For example, Ch'en Ch'ang-shou, at the time mayor of T'ao-yüan County, spoke of the "gentleman's agreement" between the Hakka and Minnan politicians of his county. If the mayor is Minnan, then the speaker of the County Assembly must be a Hakka. Further, the deputy speaker in such a case should then be a Minnan personage. If, however, the mayor is a Hakka, then the deputy speaker must also be a Hakka, and the speaker must be Minnan. Upon being told that the Cantonese person who was present during this discussion would thus be denied access to a political position, Mayor Ch'en denied any unfairness, replying, "As soon as he finds a way to increase the Cantonese population to the point where it will have a significant effect on the vote, we will change the agreement to account for their numbers."[262]

Of course, these ethnolinguistic divisions, very much like the territorial divisions discussed above, are not the sole determiners of political alignment. Although Minnan areas and Hakka areas often vote together as territorial trait factions, leaders of dyadic factions, "recruiting on diverse principles," have successfully brought Hakka and Minnan individuals together into their groups either on the basis of or even despite their language and territorial distinctiveness.[263]

"Friends Coincide with Factions . . . Common-
Interest Groups and Friendship--the Same!"

Given the exigencies of Taiwan's local politics, it is unlikely that ordinary citizens in need of security and faction leaders in need of followers will ignore the need-fulfilling qualities of friendship. The relationships already discussed included important elements of friendship. This section will focus on friendship itself, as it is related to Taiwan's local politics.

Eric R. Wolf, in his aritcle "Kinship, Friendship, and Patron-Client Relations in Complex Societies," distinguishes two kinds of friendship: (1) emotional friendship, which "involves a relation between an ego and an alter in which each satisfies some emotional need in his opposite number," and (2) instrumental friendship, in which the goal of "attaining access to resources--natural or social"--is vital to the relationship.[264]

It would be wrong to contend that emotional friendship does not exist among the Chinese. For example, Lucian W. Pye notes

> . . . the extraordinary importance that the Chinese attach to friendship. While in the West the suppression of sexuality has led to a great emphasis upon romantic love and to anxieties about the realization of and permanence of heterosexual relations, the Chinese have had almost exactly the same concern with friendship. Chinese poetry has stressed the value of friendship, the joys of relaxed companionship, and the sweet sorrows of separation.[265]

But, in regard to friendship among the Chinese, Pye goes on to note that the emotional element is not basic, but secondary:

> There is a high degree of propriety in Chinese culture in calculating the value of particular relationships and in describing them in terms of reliability and steadfastness. The measure of friendship does not have to be purely psychic satisfaction; it can be seen quite openly in material terms.
>
> . . . in modern times there has been considerable opportunism and calculation in the manner in which Chinese have sought to find the security of group association. This initial pragmatic approach to political loyalties apparently tends to strengthen rather than qualify the intensity of later idealistic and emotional commitments. This is possibly because the very style of relating choice and emotion is to limit the play of emotion until after decisions have been made, and to associate the demonstrations of emotion with the proclamation of loyalties--much as the American student decides with pragmatic calculation

162

what college he should attend and only later
manifests any sense of school spirit.[266]

According to Pye's hypothesis, the base of friendship in Chinese society is the calculation of advantage.
Chinese friendship, therefore, would be predominantly
instrumental.

It is clear, however, both from Pye's testimony
immediately above and from the discussion of jen-ch'ing
at the beginning of Part II, that although the emotional
element is not basic, it is still crucial. It is not
proper behavior simply to "calculate" human relations.
Proper behavior must be "personalized" (i.e., legitimized)
through the use of the concept of jen-ch'ing. Solomon
expands on this concept as follows:

> Chinese do indeed talk about the importance
> of "human feelings" or jen ch'ing in inter-
> personal relations, and stress how important
> it is to chiang [pay special attention to]
> jen ch'ing in dealings among friends. But
> the "emotions" that they seem to refer to
> by these oft-quoted phrases are those related
> to the interdependent quality of social life:
> the need to have an authoritative individual
> or friends who can be relied upon to give
> help or take responsibility in solving life's
> problems . . . In a Western vocabulary the
> emotions that they imply by their conception
> of mutual help are those of sympathy and a
> sense of responsibility for one's dependents,
> and not so much those of affection or pleasure.[267]

If these hypotheses concerning friendship among the
Chinese are accurate, the norms surrounding the institution of friendship in Chinese society are well suited
to the needs of individuals involved in Taiwan's local
politics. Indeed, one may hazard that the norms surrounding the institution of friendship in Chinese society
are so similar to the norms surrounding the supportive-
exchange relationships of which factions are universally
comprised that a Chinese friendship relationship is,
in fact, one type of supportive-exchange relationship.[268]

Both the more universal version of supportive-
exchange relationships and Chinese friendship relation-

163

ships, for example, are based on the calculation of mutual and/or complementary interests. Both relationships, moreover, need the existence of real or fictive shared traits to provide the intimacy necessary to legitimize what would otherwise seem a crassly impersonal series of materialistic exchanges. More specifically within Chinese society, both the Chinese version of supportive-exchange relationships and Chinese friendship relationships need the existence of real or fictive shared traits to vouch for the relationship's capacity to satisfy the interests of its parties.

The only difference between a supportive-exchange relationship and a Chinese friendship relationship concerns the shared trait of friendship. Unlike the more universal version of supportive-exchange relationships, Chinese friendship relationships by definition employ the shared trait of friendship to aid in legitimizing themselves. Also, unlike the specifically Chinese version of supportive-exchange relationships, Chinese friendship relationships by definition employ the shared trait of friendship to vouch for their efficacy.

The suitability of the institution of friendship to the needs of individuals involved in Taiwan's local political factions owes much to the friendship trait's capability of vouching for and legitimizing supportive-exchange relationships between more diverse kinds of individuals than any other trait yet mentioned. The traits of family, lineage, relatives, territory, and surname are all shared by limited numbers and kinds of specifically designated people. To be friends, however, no such objective limiting criteria need apply.

Therefore, not only can the trait of friendship be called upon to supplement supportive-exchange relationships already vouched for and legitimized by other shared traits, but also in the absence of other shared traits, potential parties to a supportive-exchange relationship can still discover that they are "friends," calling upon the shared trait of friendship to vouch for and legitimize their relationship. This independence of the friendship trait from limited numbers and kinds of specifically designated individuals, moreover, makes friendship even more suitable than any other trait to meet one's needs in the enlarged and more complex political world that exists on Taiwan today--a world that

164

increases the chances of mutually profitable exchanges between individuals who otherwise share no traits to legitimize and vouch for their relationship.

The suitability of friendship to the needs of individuals in Taiwan's local political factions, however, has limitations. Unlike the more distinguishing traits of family, lineage, relatives, and territory, for example, shared friendship in itself can provide no mutual interests to tie the related parties together. Successful friendship relationships are always based on independent mutual and/or complementary interests.

Furthermore, because the shared friendship trait is specifically created to vouch for and legitimize a new supportive-exchange relationship and does not exist prior to the new supportive-exchange relationship, it is a fictive shared trait. Thus, it is not particularly strong in its vouching and legitimizing role. Stronger friendship relationships are vouched for and legitimized by supplementary shared traits, such as the more distinguishing, real, and previously existing shared traits of lineage and territory. In this sense, friendship is even less of a distinguishing shared trait than surname or expanded definitions of territory.

Solomon notes that, in general, friendship among the Chinese becomes unstable when the statuses of the two parties begin to drift apart:

> . . . tension in friendship is rather similar
> to that which we observed in superior-sub-
> ordinate relations: the more powerful, or
> . . . the more resourceful, member of the
> relationship fears the demands for assistance
> which normative expectations of friendship
> place upon him. Hence there is a desire to
> keep the "friend" at some distance if there
> is not expectation of reciprocity.[269]

An important point about Taiwan's politics in relation to this finding is that given the faction-ridden environment of much of the countryside, together with the utility of friendship relationships and supportive-exchange relationships in filling the needs of individuals attempting to cope with this environment, the more powerful or more resourceful member of the relationship as well as his less endowed partner are both heavily motivated to maintain close ties. The powerful member is eager to use his power on behalf of his friend, because his friend is in possession of adequate resources (support at the polls) to reciprocate. In Taiwan's case, therefore, the expectation of reciprocity is high.[270]

Have Good Fortune, Together Share
Have Hardship, Together Bear

Thus far it has been shown that the shared traits of family, lineage, relatives, and territory may serve to legitimize, vouch for, and sometimes provide interests for supportive-exchange relationships. In the absence of these, or as a supplement to them, shared traits of surname, "expanded territory," language, and friendship may be pressed into service. In this section, one more shared trait capable of vouching for and legitimizing a supportive-exchange relationship--alone or as a supplement to other traits--will be presented.

> The next day in the peach garden, a black
> ox and a white horse were prepared for the
> sacrifice. The three men burnt incense,
> bowed, and spoke an oath thusly: "We, Liu
> Pei, Kuan Yü, Chang Fei, although of dif-
> ferent surnames, because of coming together
> as brothers, thus with one mind unite our
> strength, to save [one another] in distress
> and to aid [one another] in danger; above
> to serve the nation, below to soothe the
> black-haired masses. We do not seek the
> same year in the same month on the same day
> to be born. But we want the same year in the
> same month on the same day to die. Imperial
> Heaven, Goddess of Earth, bear witness to
> these intentions. He who turns his back
> on righteousness, he who forgets kindness,
> Heaven and man together kill." The oath
> finished, they bowed to Hsüan Te [Liu Pei]
> as the elder, Kuan Yü as second, and Chang
> Fei as the younger.[271]

This famous passage by Lo Kuan-chung from The Romance of the Three Kingdoms, a fourteenth-century novel considered one of the great works of Chinese literature, serves as a model for unrelated individuals on Taiwan, who, more or less according to ritual, artificially posit the existence of a state of brotherhood (and/or sisterhood) between one another, thus forming ceremonial or sworn brotherhoods.[272]

Although supportive-exchange relationships legitimized and vouched for by the primordial shared traits of family, lineage, and territory are declining under pressure from an enlarged and increasingly complex world, ceremonial brotherhoods (in similarity to clan associations and friendships), because of their independence from traits shared by limited numbers and kinds of specifically designated individuals, offer a flexible-- and appealingly traditional--trait capable of legitimizing and vouching for relationships involving the exchange of resources between individuals from a wide variety of social levels and circles.

Also in similarity to clan associations and friendships, however, the ceremonial brotherhood trait itself offers no mutual interests to aid in tying together a supportive-exchange relationship. Successful ceremonial brotherhoods, therefore, are always based on independent mutual and/or complementary interests. The ceremonial brotherhood trait serves as a purely fictive trait, invented to legitimize and vouch for the relationship. Even in this latter role, the fictive nature of ceremonial brotherhood makes it a weak trait. Stronger relationships are legitimized and vouched for by additional, more distinguishing, "real" traits.[273]

As with factions, some informants sought to play down the significance of ceremonial brotherhoods. For example,

> Ceremonial brothers is an old-fashioned
> method. It does not have great effect
> anymore. Especially for a provincial assem-
> blyman whose scope is great . . . [he]
> can't have enough to guarantee enough votes,
> and they are not necessarily reliable.

Such interviews seemed at first to provide evidence that ceremonial brotherhoods are indeed out of date, used only by some old politicians, and even then to little

avail. This thinking was further supported by a young
up-and-coming provincial assemblyman who disparaged the
significance of ceremonial brotherhoods while describing
his own "modern" organization. His organization is not
temporarily called into being a few weeks before the
elections; it is always in existence. It meets each
month. Each time it meets in a different district or
township, where the political worker responsible for
the host area makes all the preparations for the meeting.

Stephan Feuchtwang, a researcher who live in and
studied the village of Mountain Street, located in Taipei County, presented the first evidence to this author
that challenged the conclusion that ceremonial brotherhoods are unimportant on Taiwan. In China, he hypothesized, no relation can be informal or casual. It must
be formalized. If possible, it must be given a name and
have meetings. Thus, friends or individuals with common
interests often form brotherhoods. Previously, as in
The Romance of the Three Kindgoms, they would have a
ceremony, perhaps in a temple before the gods. But
for [some] young people, that is anachronistic. Still,
the basic relationship is the same. For example, there
is a group of young men from Mountain Street, some of
whom live and most of whom work in Taipei City. All
but one of them are unmarried, increasingly away from
home, and facing similar problems. They have established
such a brotherhood, which meets every three months for
a meal. The brother relationships are [often] what
constitutes friendship among young people now in Taiwan. 274

It was the youth of this group, conflicting with
the image of old-fashioned people and ineffectual ways,
plus Feuchtwang's suspicion that the above-mentioned
young up-and-coming provincial assemblyman's "modern"
organization sounded a good deal like the Mountain Street
brotherhood that sent this author back to the young
assemblyman for more questions.

Confronted with further questions, the assemblyman
reversed himself. Not only did the organization that
he originally described turn out to be a brotherhood, but
also his methods depend heavily upon such groups. He
belongs to a great many. They are mostly peer groups--
organizations of young men. He has many brothers, and

168

each brother has friends (and other brotherhoods) outside the assemblyman's brotherhoods. Thus, influence
spreads. The assemblyman further noted that he has so
many of these brotherhood meetings that he is usually
quite busy. Sometimes two are scheduled for the same
time. If one cannot be changed to another day, he
will try at least to have one meet a little earlier.
Thus, he can divide his time between the two more effi-
ciently. "They are satisfied with a little time."

Feuchtwang provides even more evidence of the
continued importance of brotherhoods in discussing
Candidate N and his visits to Mountain Street. Previously
it was noted that Candidate N came to Mountain Street only
four times during his election campaign (page 114).
Each time there happened to be a funeral ceremony in
which he participated and for which he contributed
money. Relevant here is that N learned of and arranged
participation in the funeral ceremonies through his
relations to ceremonial brothers living in Mountain Street.
Feuchtwang further indicates that, as with the young
provincial assemblyman above, ceremonial brotherhoods
play a very important part in Candidate N's political
tactics in general. [275] A provincial assemblyman who
competed against Candidate N in the election estimated
the number of ceremonial brothers N has at around 800.[276]
Similarly high numbers of ceremonial brothers are estimated for other active politicians on Taiwan.

Given its flexibility and its appealingly traditional quality, it would not be surprising to find faction leaders using ceremonial brotherhood to bind them
closer to their followers. In one case, for example,
an entire local faction was discovered to be organized
in terms of a ceremonial brotherhood.[277]

In addition to its usefulness as an internal binding agent, ceremonial brotherhood may also serve as a
binding agent between factions. Crissman and DeGlopper
speculate on the importance of brotherhood relationships
in tying leaders of different factions, all relatively
equal in power, into alliances.[278] In this case,
ceremonial brotherhood becomes a method of ameliorating
the problems that the Chinese allegedly have when dealing with status equals. Thus, Crissman writes,

169

These grand alliances are composed of equals--
men who are equivalent powers in their own
local regions, and thereby differ significantly from local factional alliances. The
latter are best viewed as opposed networks
of patron-client relationships. They have
recognized overall leaders . . . who control
or at least influence a body of less important
political figures. The careers of the latter
depend not only on their individual wealth
and the number of ordinary people who owe them
support, but also on the favor of the men at
the head of their factions, who can to a certain
extent control whether or not they will win
the elections they enter. There is a definite,
albeit fluid, status hierarchy within each of
the local alliances.

In the context of the county as a whole, on
the other hand, there are no recognized overall
factional leaders. The grand alliances are
formed on the basis of the self interest of
co-equals, and can be viewed as opposed sets
of networks based on friendship and temporary
advantage. The grand alliances are less stable
than the local factions because of changing
local interests and the lack of status differences
among the participants. Consequently, sworn
brotherhood is frequently employed within the
grand alliances in order to cement relationships
that otherwise lack structural strength. It
is also incompatible with the patron-client
relationships of which they are composed.279

More on factions and ceremonial brotherhoods comes
from a description of the relationship of liu-mangs
to politics. A liu-mang in Taiwan is not to be confused
with a t'ai-pao. A t'ai-pao is a Western type of juvenile
delinquent. He is likely to be a city boy, the son of
a middle- or upper-class family. He wears flashy, mod
clothes and goes around in a gang in search of fun and
trouble. A liu-mang also has his gang of fun- and
trouble-seekers. But this type of "young tough" fills
a position in the traditional social structure.

Arthur Wolf reports (in 1968) that in the Taipei Basin
there is a gang of liu-mangs in every village. They act

as an underground service fraternity. They often provide
the manpower for religious festivals, obtain contributions
for village temples, and make sure that fellow villagers
obtain jobs in Taipei County's coal fields without having
to pay the usual kickback. Crissman and DeGlopper also
noted such gangs in their areas in Taiwan.[280]

The religious festivals that the gangs participate
in are often--in part--friendly ritual conflicts between
village representatives. They involve ancient types of
weapons that the representatives spend much time training with before the festival. From time to time, these
friendly rituals turn into brawls between the two villages'
liu-mang gangs.[281]

Such festivals are not the only instances in which
the gangs are found involved with violence. "What
you want, they will do it." Thus, in addition to such
infamous acts as stealing girls and selling them into
prostitution, they also perform such services as protecting their village from the gangs of other villages and
beating up, or worse, one person or another whose behavior
is too much for the villagers at large.[282]

The importance of these liu-mang groups for this
section is that they are sworn brotherhoods[283] and that
they have connections to the upper--more respectable--
elements of society, including the type of politicians
who involve themselves with factions. Thus, Feuchtwang
notes that Candidate N was once a liu-mang and probably
still is close to them in Hsin-tien, his home township.[284]

In the village Wolf studied, if one wants votes,
he visits the brother of the deceased leader of the local
gang. This family had its beginnings in the gang. Now
it still has access to the gang, although the family
has since risen to a more respectable social status.
Money is channeled through this brother to the liu-mangs.
They, in turn, buy the votes.[285]

Crissman also speculated on the possible connection
between violence and the activities of liu-mang gangs
in his area. He noted such instances as the knifing
of a faction leader and the settling of debts with
people who failed to deliver the votes they promised
or who purposely cheated on the amount of money they
were given to buy votes with.[286] Thus, there is evidence

to suggest that sworn brotherhoods among young toughs, besides providing a sort of Mafia-type protection service for their more respectable fellow villagers, are also connected to local faction leaders, providing them with political services.

A final note concerning ceremonial brotherhoods is that they are not specific to Taiwan's or to Chinese society. Fictive brotherhood relationships akin to Taiwan's ceremonial brotherhoods exist in many societies. In all societies in which there are such fictive brotherhood relationships, their major function is to aid in legitimizing (i.e., adding warmth and intimacy to) supportive-exchange relationships that would otherwise be felt as crassly impersonal series of materialistic exchanges. (The additional function of vouching for the relationship's capacity to satisfy the interests of its parties is more specific to ceremonial brotherhoods in Chinese society.)

In not being specific to Taiwan's or to Chinese society, therefore, ceremonial brotherhoods are similar in their universality to factions, families and lineages, in-law relationships, relationships based on residence, and relationships based on ethnolinguistic traits. This chapter presented only two relationships that have few parallels in non-Chinese societies--those based on surnames and those based on a hypothesis of a specifically Chinese kind of friendship.

Chapter 6

THE PROVINCIAL ASSEMBLY'S LI AND HSÜ FACTIONS

The Generation of Factions within
the Provincial Assembly

It has been shown that Taiwan teems with supportive-exchange dyads linking politicians together into many local and countywide electoral factions. In terms of higher governmental levels, however, evidence indicates that supportive-exchange dyads linking politicians from different counties are not numerous enough to form cross-county or provincewide factions.

Factional organization at these higher levels is apparently hampered by governing elite hostility to independent large-scale political organization and by a lack of scarce resources to compete for in political arenas above the county level. Under heavier elite pressure and with fewer resources at stake, therefore, whatever factionalization exists in the Provincial Assembly is far less marked than the factionalization present in Taiwan's county and local assemblies.

Given this lack of factionalism at cross-county and provincewide levels, conflict within the Provincial Assembly is rarely more serious than in the following illustration:

> Within the Provincial Assembly, except for
> Speaker Hsieh Tung-min and a minority of
> other members, who, for reasons of health,
> never touch their mouths to glass, almost
> everyone is a famous general in the alcohol
> army. It has been said that the result of
> one alcohol battle between Li Chien-ho and
> Hsü Chin-te was that one man drank two dozen
> bottles of beer, the other finished seven
> bottles of Shao-hsing wine.[287]

The Provincial Assembly's "less marked" conflict, however, did become more serious in 1963, when one of the few scarce resources at stake in the Assembly arena became available for competition. Because of the availability of this scarce resource, the competition between Li Chien-

173

ho and Hsü Chin-te came to involve more than drinking.
In 1963, the members of the third term of the Taiwan
Provincial Assembly had just been elected, and the ques-
tion of who was to be deputy speaker was raised.

Although the deputy speakership has only minor formal
powers, these powers, combined with the office's prestige
and the informal power deriving from the halo effect of
this prestige, are not prizes to be ignored.[288] Attracted
by this combination of prestige and power, Li Chien-ho
and Hsü Chin-te began their competition. As if consciously following the faction-building principles described
above (on pages 148-149, for example), they began to
recruit assemblymen into their respective factions.

The reasons assemblymen joined these factions also
follow the faction-building principles described above.
The assemblymen are active politicians, individuals with
less concern for maintaining a minimum standard of living
than for name and for profit. Therefore, given that
Li Chien-ho and Hsü Chin-te ranked among Taiwan's wealth-
iest people, those who offered their votes to one of them
could expect a handsome repayment directly applicable to
this concern for name and profit. Further, for those who
supported the winner, his resulting better access to
resources made the attaining of an applicable repayment
even more likely.

With this in mind, it is interesting to review the
following quotations:

> Assemblyman X was on Hsü's side until Li
> Chien-ho got the money going and paid lots
> of attention to him.

> Assemblyman Y is with the deputy speaker.
> They are friends. The speaker helps him.
> Assemblyman Z is with the deputy speaker.
> [It is] not a matter of money--just friends.
> A is close to Li Chien-ho. A doesn't have
> much money.

> The main source of keeping their men together
> is money . . . C is the deputy speaker's.
> But naturally he doesn't follow him all the time.
> [You] have to have an appearance of independence.
> [You] follow only when it is important.

As has been noted, the faction leader in his quest
for supporters and the supporter in his search for aid
do not simply choose one another at random. The Chinese
have been socialized to identify certain traits that,
when shared with a prospective partner of a supportive-
exchange relationship, have traditionally been associated
with legitimizing the prospective relationship and vouching for its chances for success. Thus, in the Provincial
Assembly, the assemblymen look to these traits for their
organizing principles.

In this way, Li Chien-ho and Hsü Chin-te were not
brought together with their supporters by the simple
offering and needing of financial aid. Who will offer
money to whom and who will support whom are somewhat
predetermined by the specific traits that each member
shares with various individual fellow assemblymen. For
example, although the provincial assemblymen from Taipei
County spent much energy stealing each other's votes during
elections, they tended to unite behind Li Chien-ho because
they were from the same county and because three of them
had the same surname. Further, in at least one case,
support came to Hsü Chin-te from a former classmate.
Also, one assemblyman noted that because he had the same
surname as Hsü Chin-te, the Li faction did not approach
him for support. They feared his possible relation to
Hsü. In the end, Hsü approached him.

Explaining the existence of factions in terms of
competition for available resources seems to make sense
in that, after the contest was decided, when the assemblymen had little left to fight over, the factional alignments in the Assembly became less and less salient. In
1968, just before the election of the fourth term of the
Provincial Assembly, they were reported to be quite
unimportant.

The above description of the development of the
Assembly's two factions adheres to the principles of faction development presented in earlier discussions. But
additional principles suggest that the above description
is not complete. These additional principles suggest
that even if jen-ch'ing supportive-exchange relationships
are not continually of obvious use, once formed, they are
not to be let go lightly.

Provincial assemblymen, albeit one's colleagues, are

175

important individuals in their own right. Many have further importance through the filling of positions outside the Assembly itself. Although it might not be necessary for jen-ch'ing alignments within the Assembly to combat each other continuously, once such alignments are formed, given Chinese feelings about the need for a security system, it would be foolish to let them lapse.

This logic also applies to the more secure parties in such relationships. They too will be highly motivated to maintain their supporters behind them for use in as yet unforeseen battles. If this explanation is an accurate reflection of the thinking of members of the Assembly's two factions, it would aid in understanding why factional activity in the Assembly became diluted, but why the factions did not disappear.

This explanation, if correct, further aids in putting into perspective another group of facts supplied by informants, facts that indeed make the above description incomplete. According to these facts, the Li and Hsü factions did not first appear with the struggle for deputy speaker in 1963. The 1963 struggle was just one of many cases when the continuing diluted struggle between the two factions congealed. The actual beginnings of the two factions are to be found early in the history of the Provincial Assembly, in 1951, when its name had just been changed from the Taiwan Provincial Senate during its reorganization into the Taiwan Provisional Provincial Assembly. [289]

At this time, for the same types of reasons involved with the competition for deputy speaker in 1963, a struggle developed between the supporters of the speaker, Huang Ch'ao-ch'in, and the deputy speaker, Lin Ting-li. At that time, both Hsü Chin-te and Li Chien-ho were members of the Assembly. They were respectively recruited into the Huang and Lin factions. It has even been said that both Huang and Lin, after retirement from the Assembly, kept their fingers in the Assembly pie through successors such as Hsü and Li. [290]

Mildness of Conflict Level within
the Provincial Assembly

As was noted above, the factionalization within
the Provincial Assembly was "less marked" than the
factionalization present in Taiwan's county and local
assemblies:

> Previously Huang Ch'ao-ch'in opposed Lin
> Ting-li for speaker and Hsü supported Huang
> and Li Chien-ho supported Lin. From aid
> came human feeling, but no great hatred.

This mildness of Provincial Assembly factionalization is reflected in the number of members who abstained
from participation in the Assembly's factions. Interviews
reveal that only twenty-three members were in Li Chien-
ho's faction and only sixteen were in Hsü Chin-te's faction. Apparently the resources at stake were not sufficient to motivate the participation of the thirty-five
remaining assemblymen. Moreover, among the assemblymen
were those with the financial ability to create their own
factions, turning the competition for deputy speaker
into more than a two-person race. It seems, however,
that they did not view the prize as worth the investment.

The mildness of conflict between the Assembly's two
factions is paralleled by the general nature of the assemblymen's legislative behavior. According to informants,
any assemblyman, simply by asking, can obtain the support
of virtually any other assemblyman for a wide variety of
purposes. Three reasons are given for this. First,
there is the concern for face, which, according to the
assemblymen themselves, makes it difficult for one Chinese
to turn down a request from another Chinese. Second,
there is the assemblyman's recognition of the need for
reciprocity. Third, as noted above, the assemblymen
rarely see themselves as competing for scarce resources.

> Since our powers are few, it is the same to an
> assemblyman if he supports or doesn't support
> another assemblyman's resolutions. There is
> thus little conflict, since nothing much is
> at stake.
>
> Because much of the Assembly is not important,
> factions are not important, and members do not

177

take them so seriously.

This lack of competition for scarce resources, combined with the concern for face and reciprocity, has apparently created a situation of great laxity in terms of proposing and voting on Assembly resolutions. Below, Huang Ch'ao-ch'in discusses the problem:

> Sometimes a member would sign resolutions that were mutually conflicting, one to benefit the consumer, one to benefit the farmer, for example. Upon pointing out the illogic of the member's position, the member would reply that he could do nothing else. Both sides beseeched him . . . Many times everyone would sign a bill (up to forty members), and it would still not pass [because of obvious defects that would be noticed only later]. It was a problem of jen-ch'ing. Therefore it looked bad, and a limit of five undersigners was made.

Concerning the Assembly in 1968, a current member added

> . . . often on the second day they would reintroduce and rediscuss. The first day a member beseeches and receives friends' support, and they pass it. That night, those who understand get scared and convince them to change it, and it is taken up a second time the next day. It happens often.

With these examples of laxity in legislative behavior, the analysis of factionalization and conflict within the Provincial Assembly is almost completed. It remains only to balance the heavy emphasis this analysis has placed on material resources as motivating factors for factional conflict with testimony of informants asserting that nonmaterial factors are also involved in motivating factional conflict. This chapter, therefore, concludes with the statement of a provincial assemblyman that sums up the nature of these nonmaterial motivating factors.

> The speaker is a scholar and accepts all opinions, is very democratic, and thinks all ideas over. The deputy speaker is a big businessman. He is quick to decide and

178

reject other ideas, and he doesn't want to
listen all the time to new ideas. And in
previous sessions the difference of the two
[types] on this attitude encouraged the
formation of two factions.

PART III

MODERN-TYPE INTEREST GROUPS
AND THE PROVINCIAL ASSEMBLYMEN

In addition to groups centered around competition for local political resources, one is also likely to find in the galleries of the Provincial Assembly representatives from groups that are less a product of specific localities than a product of Taiwan's modernizing economy. Under the influence of such a modernizing economy, the political system of a society is affected in various ways.

One of these ways has already been introduced-- the rise of local dyadic factions, replacing the lineage and village groups as a major power to which local politicians must make reference. A second way that a modernizing economy affects the political system is through the tendency to divorce the politician from total dependence upon local groups, because the modernizing economy gives rise to new groups whose "modern" goals are not inevitably tied to a specific locality. These new groups, seeing that their own security systems are intimately related to the political system, search for aid among the local politicians. As a result, the politicians' choice of support groups is widened.

Part III introduces these new groups. It emphasizes the economic development approach to the study of Taiwan, supplemented by the confrontation, anthropological, and psychological approaches. Chapters 7-9 focus on the assemblyman's relationships to three types of modern businesses: those that are the assemblyman's personal property, those that hire an assemblyman to represent them, and those that must influence assemblymen indirectly because they cannot hire their own assemblyman.

Chapters 10 and 11 deal with the people's associations sponsored by Taiwan's governing elite. Chapter 10 explains how the governing elite tries to use the people's associations to categorize and control Taiwan's entire population. Chapter 11 explains the countervailing attempts of the members of the people's associations to use their associations to further their shared interests.

181

Chapter 7

PROTECTING "MODERN," BUT PERSONAL,
INTERESTS OF ASSEMBLYMEN

We are not supposed to be an assembly of
gentlemen who have no interests of any kind
and no associations of any kinds. . . . That is
ridiculous. That might happen in Heaven,
but not, happily, here.

--Winston Churchill, about the House
of Commons[291]

According to many political scientists, given the
effects of economic development, Taiwan's provincial and
local-level politics should be evolving toward a neat
differentiation of roles between lobbyists employed to
represent specific interests; political parties reconciling and integrating these interests with one another,
producing a limited number of policy alternatives; and
assemblymen, beholden to no specific interests, choosing
one or another of these policy alternatives.[292]

Despite rapid economic development, however, such
an idealized lobbyist-party-assemblyman system is still
rather underdeveloped in Taiwan. As the point was made
by an assemblyman, if one really wants to find lobbyists,
he must look to the assemblymen themselves. It is these
businessmen who, in the true fashion of the bougeois
revolution, have penetrated the legislature to make sure
that its decisions are favorable to them and, in many
cases, favorable also to their fellow entrepreneurs outside
the legislature.

This identification of the personal interests of
assemblymen with the modern economic sector is very common
in Taiwan. Below are some illustrations:

People who have money all know, the best method
for the protection of wealth is to participate
in political activity . . .

The goal of industrial and commercial giant
Li Ch'ing-yün in participating in political
activities is to establish a storm-safe harbor
for his enterprises.[293]

183

> There is a law that you [an assemblyman]
> are not supposed to vote on what you personally
> have an interest in [li-hai kuan-hsi], but
> the law is really not enforced very strictly.
> For example, over half of the Assembly members
> are either doctors, have husbands who are
> doctors, have medicine factories, or are
> pharmacists. I supported the government on
> not letting doctors sell medicine. In theory,
> all with li-hai kuan-hsi should not have
> participated in the vote. But then their
> would have not been a quorum. Therefore,
> they voted and defeated it.[294]

Conflict of Interest and Moral Judgements

Discussions with assemblymen about the self-inter-
ested activities of some of their colleagues revealed an
ambivalence concerning the morality of apparent conflicts
of interest:

> In relation to the Transportation Committee,
> one should recognize two ideas. One is that
> they know about it and therefore have the
> qualifications and should participate. The
> other is that they are protecting themselves.
> And who knows for sure what is really right?

> I am moral and walk the straight and narrow.
> I want to be a good assemblyman. But I am
> also an adviser and will help the company with
> the government. And the government is good
> to the company because of me.

When the Central Government decided to take back
control over the inspection of perishable exports from
the provincial government, the Assembly's opposition to
this decision provided further examples of attitudes
toward apparent conflicts of interest. Thus, while deny-
ing that he was on the payroll of the Federation of Banana
and Citrus Fruit Cooperatives, Assemblyman Huang Chan-an
explained that his opposition really stemmed from his
ownership of about 45 acres of land that produce perishable exports. Because of this ownership, he maintained,
he understood why the provincial government should retain
control of perishable export inspections. As for other

184

assemblymen, they explained their opposition as follows:

> . . . each owns a farm, a produce-finishing
> factory, or is involved in an enterprise selling
> agricultural produce abroad. Their reasoning
> is expressed very thoroughly: after the Bureau
> of Inspection is placed under the Ministry of
> Economics, the members of the [National] Legislative
> Yuan will not have the experience to oversee
> the affairs of inspection.[295]

The argument is not being made here that there are
no muckraking, "throw the rascals out" attitudes with
regard to conflict of interest on Taiwan. But there
does seem to be enough ambivalence toward activities on
behalf of special interests to leave the way open for
at least the eventual acceptance of the legitimacy of the
lobbyist role in Taiwan's political system. In view of
the nature of the ambivalence illustrated above, however,
it is more reasonable to expect the acceptance of a system
such as that described by Samuel Beer, in which it is not
only a right, but also virtually a requirement, that
interested parties take part in the making of decisions
that affect them.[296]

Entrepreneurial Faction
vs.
Conscientious Faction

An illustration of a muckraking, "throw the rascals
out" attitude was forcefully brought to the attention
of the author the first time he met Assemblyman Huang
Ch'i-cheng. Huang was raving in anger because his fac-
tory-owning colleagues had just defeated a resolution
designed to benefit retiring factory workers. Later,
in an interview, he noted that he was a member of an anti-
entrepreneurial faction in the Assembly.

The division of the members of the Provincial
Assembly referred to by Assemblyman Huang was also noted
by other informants. Two types of assemblymen were
portrayed. One was very busy with private enterprises
outside the Assembly, had little time to spend on such
Provincial Assembly responsibilities as attending meetings, did not care much about his Assembly responsibilities unless they affected his private interests, and did

185

little for the general welfare. The other had little or no outside interests, was able to devote most of his time to Assembly responsibilities, and was credited with being interested in and willing to do a good job for his constituents and for the general welfare.[297] As would be expected, most assemblymen saw themselves in the latter category.

Many saw this category as containing the more serious, more competent, and more effective assemblymen.[298]

> Assemblyman Wu Ch'üan-an does not have much money. He doesn't go to bars. He studies. He knows how to learn. Those with money do not have the time. Poor men have more time.

> If your outside enterprises are very important, you do not come much, and you cannot keep up with Assembly affairs. As a result, you cannot use the power over the budget as well. Therefore, those who come have power.

But, as with the ambivalence displayed with regard to possible conflicts of interest, here too words were spoken on behalf of the businessmen.

> Yes, there are the selfish ones who only come when things affect them or if their constituents especially push them to come because of an important matter concerning the locality. But then you have to understand, they have to make a living and cannot always come. They do not necessarily like this. Wu I-wei and Chang Fu do not have businesses and have nothing else to prevent them [from coming].[299]

Further words were spoken to indicate that the businessman does not lack weapons in his fight for effectiveness. Examples of the usefulness of money in politics have already been noted (pages 174-175). Money also buys secretaries to help one keep up with the Assembly's business. In addition, a number of assemblymen are recognized as influential in the Assembly not only because of their money but also because of the experience and understanding they have obtained from involvement in business activities.

The defense of businessmen goes further. Two rich businessmen even claimed that only a wealthy individual should become an assemblyman: "You should have an economic foundation. Too many members without it try to 'make it' through their influence as assemblymen."

Some members who were known for their low participation argued that this was a virtue: "Those like me, who do not speak much in the Assembly, have weight. Those who just criticize all the time do not have a great deal of power. I do not speak unless it is important." This is quite unlike Assemblyman Chang Fu, who proudly stated that statistically he talks in the Assembly more than anyone else. Nor does he feel that this give him less weight. He notes that, after he speaks, many people write to him about what he has said.

Concerning which faction is the most effective, it is difficult to come to a final judgement. Perhaps the following statement by a "conscientious" member is not too far from the truth:

> Both have power, members from outside with
> enterprises and members who come often. The
> latter do not have power from outside, but
> get power from knowing what is going on.
> Those who come win the sympathy of others.
> They make a good impression on the voter.
> The others are very specific. They only come
> to protect their own interests. Others have
> a grasp of everything. In my opinion, the
> conscientious members who always come can win
> most of the time, though not all the time,
> if there is a conflict between them and the
> others.

The "Grabby" Faction

Those members who enter the Assembly with no "economic foundation" but who are trying to "make it" through their influence as assemblymen may be envisioned as comprising a third faction. They do not yet have the credentials for membership in the entrepreneurial faction, nor are they content with concentrating on fulfilling their normative assemblyman's role as members of the conscientious faction.

It is these members who have the worst reputations among their colleagues, in the press, and in public opinion. Needless to say, no assemblyman admits to belonging to this "grabby" faction or defends the behavior of this faction's members. The opinion of the press concerning this faction is typified as follows:

> There are some provincial assemblymen who especially run about for private interests. Even if it is not his business, he puts his foot in it, causing the government to be rather troubled. Like selling Japanese beer, taking T'ang Jung [a publicly owned company] stocks and selling cheaply, using relatives' and friends' names to establish companies to make unlawful gains, struggling to obtain land and then get profit for nothing, etc., . . . you name it, they've done it.[300]

Although no assemblyman will admit to belonging to this faction, circumstantial evidence indicates the membership (or former membership) of a number of assemblymen. One individual, for example, was remembered by an official as presenting an impoverished appearance and as living in a slum when he was elected to the Assembly. Five years later, he was impeccably dressed and, according to a reporter, had just built a big new house from his dealings since election. Another assemblyman was found to have moved from a storefront walk-up on a crowded street to a walled-in home that compared with the homes of some of the biggest businessmen in the Assembly. The limousine in his driveway was also comparable.

188

Chapter 8

BUSINESS SENDS OUT A CANDIDATE OR HIRES A SUCCESSFUL CANDIDATE AFTER ELECTION

". . . a considerable number of MPs on both
sides of the Commons act as the paid political agents of outside bodies--whether trade
unions, churches, business companies or pressure
groups--lobbying Ministers on their behalf
and sometimes, when they rise to speak, reading
aloud almost verbatim, the brief they have
received from the body which retains their
services." These relations . . . only become
"unethical if [the MP] conceals their existence
when he speaks on their behalf. And the only
breach of Parliamentary privilege which can
occur is if the outside organization brings
improper pressure to bear on him, in order
to influence his vote."[301]

Assemblymen on Taiwan represent not only their own
business interests but also those of individuals who are
not members of the Assembly.[302] According to informants,
"many members are chosen directly by industries and the
like." Others receive periodic payments to look after
the affairs of interested parties. As a result--in similarity with legislatures throughout the world--the core
of each of the Assembly's relevant committees is staffed
by assemblymen representing their own interests together
with assemblymen representing outside parties. The outsiders "write comparatively reasonable resolutions and
interpellation questions" and in other ways guide the
actions of their agents in the Assembly.

The quotations that follow indicate something
more of the "flavor" of the relationship between interested outsiders and their agents within Taiwan's locally
elected assemblies.

There are those who feel that in order to
protect their interests, the banana farmers
hope to be able to capture a powerful seat
in the County Assembly. A powerful seat could
expend energy speaking for them, remedying and
making up for their past losses, and aiding

189

in their future profit and development. Looking at the situation from another viewpoint,
it seems that this time the fruit industry
circles are prepared to put all strength forth
in an all-out battle. If they are not able
to capture the nomination for speaker, they
will retreat and try for second best. They
will fight for deputy speaker.303

Huang Ch'en Sen, the wife of the former head
of the board of directors of the T'ai-hsi
Bus Company, Huang Ch'i-pa, has decided to come
out on her horse in contention for next term's
Provincial Assembly seat . . . As everyone
knows, Huang Ch'en Sen's coming out on her
horse was decided after the calling of a
meeting of the T'ai-hsi Bus Company's board
of directors. The main goal was for the interests of the said company, because Huang
Ch'en Sen is not very enthusiastic about
politics. 304

Representative of Oneself and of Others

One assemblyman can, of course, simultaneously
fill the roles of self-representative and representative
of outside parties. An interesting example of this is
the businessman who participates in politics in order to
protect his own business but whose business also happens to
employ many people and makes many additional people dependent on his employees' paychecks. Because his political
activity benefits his business, those related to his
business are also likely to benefit. The beneficiaries
and the businessman, realizing the importance of their
mutual political support, will strengthen and develop
their relationship.

Many provincial assemblymen were mentioned as representing both themselves and a large number of business
dependents. Two examples follow:

Lai Sen-lin and Li Chien-ho . . . not a matter
of money . . . [but] enterprises. Many
people rely on their enterprises to live.
Therefore they have that political base.
Others have money, but less people work for

190

them, and therefore they do not have a political base. Many people have money. Therefore it is not only money.

[Magazine praising a candidate running for
the Provincial Assembly, Lin Wei-k'uan]
In recent years, in managing his coal-mining
enterprises, he has built them into a large,
successful operation. This was of great
profit to the local economy, solving the
employment and livelihood problems of a
great many of the people living in the area.
Such people as the residents of the T'ou-fen
and San-wan region, who work in the coal
mines he manages, are his basic source of
votes.305

The benefits accruing to a political businessman
are so apparent that employees may themselves encourage
their boss to go into politics.

My boss is also going out to be a candidate.
We encouraged him to go. It was not the
Cab Drivers' Association, but the people
in his own company. We have no money. It
is very hard. The hearts of the people are
all important.

Double Representation and Modernization

According to some theorists of modernization, the
introduction into a nonmodern society of a modern struc-
ture--one that involves hiring and providing security to
individuals in accordance with criteria germane only
to the tasks that the individual is hired to perform--
will have a debilitating effect on that society's nonmodern authority structures. Previous to the introduction
of the modern structure, large numbers of dissatisfied
individuals had no alternative but to submit to the particular ethnic, regional, and/or kinship authority structure into which they were born. One who refused to submit could not be reborn into an alternative security-
guaranteeing structure. The recalcitrant person found
himself outside of society, risking a "solitary, poor,
nasty, brutish, and short" life. With the appearance
of a modern structure, however, the dissatisfied--but

191

task-competent--individual no longer has to submit to his particular nonmodern authority structure in order to be secure. Therefore, dissatisfied individuals rush to join the modern structure, leaving the nonmodern structures helplessly behind.306

Given conditions of insulation from the pervasive influence of nonmodern social values and the nonmodern authority structures that perpetuate them, it may indeed be possible to maintain in a nonmodern society a structure that hires and provides security in accordance with criteria germane only to the task that the individual is hired to perform. An example of such insulation may have been provided by the foreign concessions in China's old treaty ports. But it is also likely that, without proper insulation, nonmodern social values and nonmodern authority structures will subvert the modern structure.

These tendencies to subversion exist on Taiwan: "You have to get an introduction from a person with a high position, even to work in a factory."

This subversion, as with businessmen personally representing themselves in the Provincial Assembly, discounts any claim that one is dealing with "politically developed," "modern" behavior as these terms are currently defined by many political scientists. Indeed, one must go back to the discussion of factions, where patronage (in this case, a job in a politician's enterprises) was paid for in electoral support.

But such traditionalism is not necessarily irrational.307 Previously it was noted that, despite the congruence of traditional Chinese psychology and factional behavior (pages 107-108), in some country villages, any rational individual with the goal of security--whether his psychology was traditional or modern--would seek to join a faction. The objective situation would force him to.

In employer-employee relations too, the rational choice coincides with traditional behavior. The employee needs the security of an employer-patron and obtains it through the workings of traditional ethnic, regional, and/or kinship authority structures. Once employed, he has both the security of the original authority structures through which he obtained employment and the

192

security of a direct employer-patron, employee-client relationship. At the same time, he is probably not related to any other politician in any favorable way. Also, if his employer wins an election, the government will favor his enterprises, providing the employee with a third security guarantee.

This situation creates another obstacle to modernization. If the development of independent and powerful labor unions is defined as part of modernization, such a modern development will be greatly hampered by the apparent harmony of employer-patron and employee-client interests.

This harmony of interests between capital and labor is reflected in the activities of two provincial assemblymen. The first lists himself as an adviser to both the United Labor Union and the chamber of commerce of his city. The second lists previous positions as president of a county-united labor union, a vice-president of the province's United Labor Union, and president of a county chamber of commerce. Moreover, both assemblymen list themselves as director and/or chairman of the board for a number of employing companies.[308]

Of the latter assemblyman, in his campaign headquarters (the sign on the door announced a company for which the assemblyman listed himself as chairman of the board), an aide who said he was from the Bus Drivers' Association related that the assemblyman was originally a bus driver and had worked his way up to be a labor union leader. "And then his enterprises prospered. After they prospered, he also became close to businessmen. And just recently the drivers asked him to be an adviser."

In another interview, the assemblyman spoke for himself. Given his relations with both sides of the labor-capital complex, it is no wonder that he sounded like a "broker." According to Wahlke, a broker is a legislator who sees his role as that of a compromiser, arbitrator, coordinator, and integrator of the conflicting interests and demands of interest groups, constituencies, and executive agencies.[309] Speaking in his private home, with his factory next door, he related the following:

Between the businessman and labor, for example
over insurance, I am a middleman, and we
try to find a reasonable solution.

I have pretty good connections with commerce
and labor associations . . . many many of them.

I either attend or get reports on their
meetings. I spend time explaining what is
going on involving them [in the Assembly]
. . . not so much their representative as a
middleman between them.

Chapter 9

BUSINESS TRIES TO INFLUENCE UNRELATED ASSEMBLYMEN

The Need for a New Theory of
Associational Democracy

Recent theories concerning legislatures and their environments have denied the judgment that interest groups and the lobbying they do are corruptions of otherwise admirable political systems. Instead, these theories have striven to find a respectable place for interest groups within the democratic process. Early in the period of this striving, Alfred De Grazia wrote the following:

> So long as we suppress rather than educate
> the group formations of American life, we
> lower the quality of their membership and
> activities. We distort their operational
> code by forcing them to mold it absurdly to
> the main theory of the democratic state
> produced by the Enlightenment.
>
> . . . a major task lies before political
> science, the task of creating an ideological
> climate able to assimilate the diverse justi-
> fications and descriptions of interest group
> life into a new theory of associational
> democracy. 310

The results of this striving is that, at least within political science circles, the task has been successfully completed. A new ideological climate prevails, heavily influenced by a number of new theories of associational democracy. Through the writings of such political scientists as Samuel Beer, Harry Eckstein, and Gabriel Almond, interest groups have taken their place alongside legislatures, executives, courts, and political parties as crucial members of a healthy political system.

Reference was made above (page 183) to one of these new theories of associational democracy when it was noted that, according to the thinking of some political scientists, Taiwan's was not yet a modern (healthy) political system, since the incidence of overlapping membership

195

between interest groups and the Assembly was too high. According to this particular theory, interest groups and assemblies must be two relatively distinct structures, fulfilling two complementary, but distinct, functions for the political system. The two complementary, but distinct, functions are (a) interest articulation, "the process by which individuals and groups make demands upon the political decision makers," and (b) rule-making or legislation. Interest aggregation, "the function of converting demands into general policy alternatives," performed especially by political parties, should link the two.[311]

This particular theory of associational democracy argues that without a clear differentiation between (a) demand-making interest groups, (b) political parties converting demands into general policy alternatives, and (c) assemblies choosing between these general policy alternatives--among other dysfunctional outcomes--"the heavy load of raw, unstructured demands" may overwhelm "the decision-making structures by the sheer volume of demands, and thus [render the decision-makers] helpless to construct effective and consistent policy."[312]

The New Theories of Associational
Democracy on Taiwan

The very language used to discuss interest groups on Taiwan suggests that the new theories of associational democracy have not been accepted there as ideal forms of government. Taiwan's governing elite, along with many nonelite politicians, and rank-and-file citizens, still appear tied to the "main theory of the democratic state produced by the Enlightenment" when they use the phrase yüeh-shu-t'uan (a binding, disciplining, detaining, regulating, or restraining group) to describe interest groups. The words ya-li-t'uan (pressure group) and li-i-t'uan or li-hai-t'uan (interest group)--words that more closely translate the English terms--seem to be reserved for the use of American political science students struggling to find Chinese equivalents, and for no one else.

In general, this author left interviews with the impression that, as with the Enlightenment view, informants--in disagreement with many political scientists and in disagreement with the habits and customs of their own society--did not see as moral, competent, understandable, or democratic a group's defense of its own interests. Instead, reflecting the idealized views of the

196

governing elite, informants saw interest groups as social units that bring pressure to bear on governmental organs in order to further their own partial, selfish interests in disregard for the needs, if not the will, of all.

Even in terms of actual (as opposed to ideal) patterns of behavior, informants indicated nonacceptance of the new theories of associational democracy. This was especially true of the particular theory of associational democracy that stresses the need for differentiation between interest-articulation and rule-making structures. As the behavior of provincial assemblymen described in the previous two chapters demonstrates, informants favored the breaking down of the differentiation between interest-articulation and rule-making structures: "And if you have the means, you will become an assemblyman yourself, instead of beseeching assemblymen."

Of course, there are interest group representatives who do not have the means to become assemblymen. Nor can their interest groups hire assemblymen. For them the only alternative is to reluctantly accept the interest-articulation/rule-making differentiation; they must resort to lobbying.

> Lobbying . . . you can see a lot of entertaining. Assemblymen are always being asked out . . . because you cannot always support or hire your own man, or have a man whose interests parallel yours in the Assembly.

The rest of this chapter deals with these "reluctant" lobbyists.

The Nonexistence of Interest Groups?

As with previous discussions of factions and ceremonial brotherhoods, the question arises about whether these interest groups exist to any significant degree. Certainly Chapters 7 and 8 have given enough examples of businessmen-assemblymen and businessmen hiring assemblymen to suggest that there are large numbers of interested businessmen who fail either to become assemblymen or to hire assemblymen but who continue to seek other channels of influence. Moreover, the following chapter describes the organization of many categories of citizens into large governing-elite-sponsored people's associations, which appear as potentially powerful interest groups. Still, most assemblymen agreed with the Assembly staff member who noted the following:

Pressure groups . . . [are] not well developed
. . . [we] have people's associations all
over (like hotel owners, etc.), and they will
send their men to get help, usually when they
have a problem. They do not necessarily follow legislation all the time. Usually it is
a matter of one person from an industry going
to protect himself . . . not the industry
as a whole . . . and privately trying to
influence assemblymen. And his effect can be
very great. But this kind of influence on
Taiwan is small, though growing.

The following chapter analyzes why governing-elite-
sponsored people's associations are not very active on
behalf of their members. As far as other interested
parties are concerned--that is, those that are not formally organized into governing-elite-sponsored people's
associations--although the pressuring of assemblymen
takes place, the pressuring party (as the quote above
indicates) is more likely to be an individual or a small
group of business partners rather than a more or less
formally constituted associational interest group.

According to many political scientists, the associational interest group is the "modern" interest group,
especially found in, and geared to, modern society by
virtue of its specialized and sole mission of articu-
lating interests for interested parties whose own mis-
sions are, in turn, too specialized to permit them to
articulate their interests for themselves. Additional
modern aspects of associational interest groups include
their being based on the cooperation of all individuals
with similar interests arising from the sharing of a
given trait (i.e., peers); their striving to satisfy
these interests by promoting policies of benefit to all
these individuals, showing no favoritism (particularism)
to some over others; and their often becoming large
impersonal bureaucracies because of the number of individuals involved.[313]

This same situation of individuals and small partnerships crowding the channels of influence--with large,
formal associational interest groups appearing rarely--
was seen in the discussions of businessmen-assemblymen and
businessmen hiring assemblymen. That it also appears
here should not be a surprise. These individuals and

198

partnerships are simply the losers in the competition
to become assemblymen or to hire assemblymen.

Associational Interest Groups:
Preempted by People's Associations

Part of the explanation of why few large, formal
associational interest groups are found in the channels
of influence is because so many potential interest groups
have already been formed as governing-elite-sponsored
people's associations.

Associational Interest Groups:
Too Advanced for Today's Taiwan

An argument useful in explaining the lack of spontaneous formation of associational interest groups outside the framework of the people's associations (especially since the people's associations are not performing
in the expected role of interest groups) is that expectations are premature. Perhaps there is a lack of demand
for these or other organizations to perform as interest
groups because the private interests of Taiwan have not
yet developed far enough on the scale of modernization.

According to Gabriel A. Almond and G. Bingham Powell,
Jr., modernization, based on "industrial, technological,
and scientific revolutions" within the society, is associated with (a) the breakdown of "traditional patterns
of belief" and "traditional forms of family and social
life" and with (b) the development "of a large number of
special interests, which can be the basis for associational interest groups."[314] Perhaps Taiwan's industrial,
technological, and scientific revolutions have not yet
progressed to the point where the breakdown of traditional
patterns and forms and the development of special interests have created the need for "modern" associational
interest groups.

Associational Interest Groups:
Preempted by Adapting Traditional Groups

An alternative explanation for the lack of formation
of associational interest groups outside the framework

199

of governing-elite-sponsored people's associations somewhat contradicts Almond and Powell, however. The explanation grows out of the example of Japan. The success
of the industrial, technological, and scientific revolutions within Japanese society involved a definite trend
toward the formation of special interests and associational interest groups. But this trend was really a
cloak for the adaptation, not the breakdown, of traditional patterns of belief and traditional forms of
family and social life. Although some goals and techniques changed from those common to a traditional society
to those of an industrial society, the traditional
Japanese patterns of belief and forms of social life
proved very effective in attaining the new goals and in
using the new techniques.

Given the effectiveness of traditional patterns
and forms, the social life within modern Japan's special
interests and associational groups remained much the same
as the social life within groups oriented toward traditional goals. Some groups, goals, and techniques changed,
but most social relationships remained the same.[315]
This is to be expected, however. If traditional forms
can successfully cope with the exigencies of the modernization revolution, the lack of strain felt in utiliz-
ing them--added to prejudice for traditional forms and
prejudice against, and lack of knowledge about, alternative forms--would act to keep the traditional forms
prospering.

The suggestion here is that perhaps traditional
forms of human relationships on Taiwan, especially as
these forms have adapted to changing circumstances, are
coping well enough with the modernization revolution
(i.e., are giving adequate security to the various
categories of persons in the changing society, including
newly developing special interests) so that no need is
felt for the new forms of associational interest groups.

Perhaps, at this point on Taiwan, (a) the traditional
patron-client form, adapted to the relations between
employers and employees, businessmen and assemblymen,
and faction leaders and faction members, (b) the resurgence in almost unchanged form of the traditional relations between clan members and between ceremonial brothers, and (c) the continued existence, in weakened form,
of family-relative, locality, and ethnic networks, taken

together, are still strong enough to fulfill the functions of ensuring individual security systems.

Associational Interest Groups: Too Unattractive for Today's Taiwan

In addition to the argument that, at the present time, no need is felt on Taiwan for the new forms of associational interest groups, it can be further argued that those attempting to strengthen their security systems find the use of associational interest groups for this purpose positively unattractive. With the many changes that have taken place in Taiwan's society as a result of political change and economic development, traditional landlord-patrons, as well as family-relative, locality, and ethnic networks, have become weaker ensurers of the individual's security system.

Strongly motivated to restrengthen his security system, the individual is very much attracted by those traditional forms that are adapting successfully--such forms as patron-client, clan, and ceremonial brotherhood. Unexpectedly, from the point of view of much contemporary modernization theory, this attraction to traditional forms is reinforced by the unattractiveness of the associational interest-group alternative.

There are at least five reasons why protective associational interest groups based on the shared interests of employed, employing, or other categories of interested peers are unattractive to the security-seeking individual on Taiwan.

1. The potential members of an associational interest group probably still hold to the premodern perception that resources relevant to security are too scarce to be more or less equally shared among themselves in any satisfactory manner.

2. Cooperation and trust among peers, necessary for the formation and maintenance of an associational interest group based on shared interests, may be hard to obtain because of such factors as (a) Chinese, in their formative years, being explicitly taught that human relations are full of insecurity and danger, (b) the historical and often contemporary experience

201

of actual factional, ethnic, village, and lineage conflict and mutual suspicion at the local level, and (c)
the possible nonexplicit, subconscious socialization
hypothesized by Pye and Solomon, causing the Chinese to
doubt their ability to carry on nonconflictive relations
with their peers without the constant intervention of
"a strong and unified authority" to maintain harmony
among them. 316

3. The disinclination of the Chinese to rely on
large institutions (such as associational interest
groups) built around general, impersonal behavior--
a disinclination reinforced by the experience of the
particularistic favoritism displayed by the large bureaucratic organizations that they are familiar with on
Taiwan.317

4. The general policy of the governing elite on
Taiwan, as well as the individual behavior of the governing elite's bureaucrats, has been to use the resources
of the government to dispense rewards appropriate to
maintaining the loyalty of individual politicians and
their followers instead of dispensing rewards across
the board to all individuals in a given occupational,
business, or other standard interest category. At the
same time, the voter is already predisposed to support
politicians seeking personal followers, given the voter's
tendency to favor personal-dependency relationships over
collective action with his peers. In combination, governing elite, bureaucrat, and voter behavior tend to divide
potential members of associational interest groups as they
compete with each other to become followers of the reward-
dispensing politicians.318

5. The individual is predisposed to ignore associational interest groups composed of needy individuals
like himself but containing no resource-dispensing
individuals with whom he may establish a personal relationship. Moreover, a large associational interest group
is not likely to provide circumstances that promise
to bring the ordinary member into personal contact
with resource-dispensing individuals, even if such individuals are members. Sworn brotherhood groups and clans,
however, whose memberships may well cross class lines,
are often explicitly formed for the purpose of putting
resource-dispensing individuals in touch with a group
of potential followers.319

202

In view of these five reasons, with the progressive loss of the protection of landlord-patrons, as well as of family-relative, locality, and ethnic networks, the individual increasingly sees his needs in terms of his own particular problems, unrelated or even in opposition to others facing exactly the same problems he is facing.[320] Therefore, he falls back on the traditional expedient of crossing class lines, leaving his social peers to fend for themselves, as he seeks a personal, one-to-one dependency relationship with reward-dispensing individuals through some combination of such social forms as patron-client, clan, and/or ceremonial brotherhood.

Given the staying power and adaptability of such forms, it is even possible that as the modernization revolution progresses on Taiwan, these forms will continue to adapt with it and flourish. It is more likely, however, that there will be a limit to their adaptive capabilities and that they will be replaced by more "orthodox" modern interest groups. This process of replacement will be especially hastened as the developing economy begins to make citizens feel more secure about the availability of once-scarce resources, as large bureaucratic institutions begin to behave according to impersonal, general norms, as citizens begin to develop trust in the guarantees of these impersonally acting institutions, and as citizens begin to see their interests in occupational and class terms.[321]

Associational Interest Groups: Development Controlled by Political Leaders

Finally, in giving suggestions about why associational interest groups may be slow to develop, Almond and Powell hint at the content of Chapter 10's discussion of Taiwan's governing-elite-sponsored people's associations. Almond and Powell note that governing elites may attempt to control the development of new interests and associational interest groups. Perhaps the success of Taiwan's governing elite in this endeavor explains the slow development of new interests and associational interest groups there.[322]

The Lobbying Behavior of Interested Parties

As noted on page 197 above, when an interest-group representative on Taiwan could not support or hire his own assemblyman or have an individual whose interests parallelled his own in the Assembly, he was forced to become a "reluctant" lobbyist. He did not become a lobbyist because he admired an ideal propounded by some theory of associational democracy. This difference between the ideal of a theory and the specific reality of Taiwan is brought out in the following contrast between former Congressman Emanuel Celler's description of the ideal lobbyist in America and an official's description of how to be a real lobbyist on Taiwan.

A number of the modern lobbies operating in Washington are of the highest quality. With plenty of money to spend, they spend it on qualified analysts and advocates and provide Congressional committees with lucid briefs and technical documentation in support of their positions. Nothing is more informative and helpful to a legislative committee than to hear the views of competent, well-matched advocates on the opposite sides of a legislative issue . . .

This is not to say that it is necessary to maintain a costly and permanent organization in order to lobby effectively. Excellent presentations are constantly being made on behalf of relatively small lobbies . . . The effectiveness of such presentations lies in stating a position forcefully, clearly, and tersely--without frills. Congressmen are more appreciative than is generally known of lobbyists who respect their crowded schedules and keep representations to a minimum consistent with thoroughness. 323

First visit him and tell him who you are, etc., but do not ask him for what you need. First ask him out for entertainment [ch'ing-k'e].

In the normal town hall, if you want something, you ch'ing-k'e. For example, ask him and many important personages, and include an official

204

to prove it is not a plot. If it is successful,
he will be stoned, and the next day out--
so you can ask him. 324

Having laid the groundwork for an understanding of
lobbying behavior on Taiwan, this chapter will now conclude with a number of concrete examples.325

Besides the difficulty of finding provincial assemblymen taking advantage of the free suppers provided for
them during Assembly sessions because their schedules
are so crowded with entertainment provided by interested
parties, virtually every assemblyman interviewed referred
to the large number of individuals who come to request
aid (pai-t'o):

> Sunday . . . [is the] busiest day. From
> 6:00 in the morning until evening, there are
> petitioners representing groups and themselves
> · · · three living rooms full. And I am home
> all day listening to them.

> Getting title to land, taxes . . . [these are
> the] types of things they see me about. All
> sorts of people come. Representatives of groups
> and single farmers. And even from outside
> of Chia-i. Even people come with family
> quarrels. Wife and husband . . . kids won't
> listen to parents, and I have to lecture the
> kids.

> All sorts of people come to assemblymen.
> Trouble with, or not satisfied with, teach-
> ing or government job, retirement pay problems,
> formal petitions, etc.

> He is only around weekend mornings at a definite
> time. And people can be seen lining up while he
> is still sleeping.

> You are always on call. Sometimes in the
> middle of the night someone calls to get
> them bailed out of jail or paroled out.
> But that does not happen often. 326

These statements agree with this author's observations
of crowded parlors and frequent visitors in the homes

205

of the assemblymen he visited. The quiet and empty
living rooms of assemblymen who did not plan to run for
reelection also provided some confirmation for these
statements.

Concerning what actually goes on between the assemblyman and the petitioner, there are two schools of
thought, each probably containing part of the truth:

> I have no money, but I have enough to live
> on. I don't accept red envelopes [i.e.,
> gifts and bribes], or anything else . . .
> [I] don't go much to wine houses or drink
> much when there. I danced when I was 20
> years old. I don't go to dance halls now.

> Assemblyman Wu Ch'üan-an [quoted directly
> above]--someone comes to him and he writes
> it down. And then he brings it up [in the
> Assembly]. Right! Very diligent.

> Everyone sends money when they need help.
> No, not symbolic money, $1,000 NT, etc.,
> . . . for promotions, etc.

This continual contact between assemblyman and interested constituent is the substance of much of Taiwan's
local political activity. According to the Taiwan press
and the Assembly's records, during the 1966-1968 period,
this activity was exemplified by (a) Taipei County
assemblymen caught between the demands of KMT party
discipline to vote for a tax on meat and theater tickets
and the demands of butchers and theater owners packing
the Assembly's galleries to defeat the tax, "using absen-
teeism in order to hide themselves," and complaining that
if they voted for the tax, "tonight when returning home,
their stomachs would ache";327   (b) two owners of load-
ing and unloading companies from Kao-hsiung harbor losing
over $100,000 NT to provincial assemblymen in a midnight
game of political Mah-jongg in the Assembly dormitory; 328
and (c) the following protest, voiced on behalf of
Taiwan's small businessmen from the floor of the Provincial Assembly:

> As of now, businessmen fear the tax official
> as they fear a tiger. The tax official
> guards against the businessman as if against
> robbers and thieves. There is a mutual

struggle. In order to obtain complete collection, preventing loss of taxes, the Tax Bureau continuously makes new tax law explanatory rules, so many like the hairs of sheep . . . altogether there have been 12,803 explanatory tax rules. Among these, 58 percent have not been made public. Thus, businessmen are caused not to know what to follow, to break the law repeatedly, and to be heavily fined. Heads of big enterprises thus rely on those knowledgeable of tax laws to find loopholes and write false books. In many directions they duck taxes. Thus, there is the newly rising business of moonlighting tax officials, specializing in writing up false books. The small businessman, under his burden and in his annoyance, raises the sound of grumbling from all four corners. Thereupon a minority of tax officials who play with the law to obtain selfish ends have another crack to enter, putting forth with cleverness in large amounts. [329]

Chapter 10

GOALS OF PEOPLE'S ASSOCIATIONS
AND THE GOVERNING ELITE

Traditional Spontaneous Organizing
among the Chinese

The preceding chapter noted that large-scale,
"modern" associational interest groups are not forming
outside the framework of Taiwan's governing-elite-sponsored people's associations despite these associations'
ineffectiveness as interest groups. One important reason
cited for this was that small-scale, traditional, person-
to-person, authority-dependent relationships are still
more effective than relationships based on impersonality
and peer equality in meeting people's security needs.

Nevertheless, the importance of these relationships
does not explain the lack of formation of large-scale,
"traditional" interest groups in today's Taiwan. Many
large-scale interest groups--constructed by putting
together scores of small-scale, person-to-person, authority-dependent relationships--have existed throughout
Chinese history. This was in addition to such small
groups as families, lineages, friendships, business partnerships, and neighbors. Large-scale, traditional interest groups were especially prominent when these smaller
groups became inadequate in the face of a particularly
strong security threat.330 But even in the absence of such a
threat, many people in traditional China were organized
according to a myriad of categories into a number of nonfamil-
ial, often large, potentially interest-serving groups.331

To this historical evidence of the importance of
large-scale, traditional interest groups in Chinese society, Lucian Pye adds a contemporary observation:

> Whenever groups of Chinese are brought together
> they seem quickly to form themselves into
> structural organizations. In their overseas
> communities the Chinese have tended to sort
> themselves into their various associations,
> their huis and their tongs. It is entirely
> consistent with their culture that the Chinese
> prisoners of war in Korea did not become the
> apathetic mass of demoralized individuals

that prisoners usually are, but they quickly
and almost spontaneously became intensely
organized political groups; leaders emerged
overnight and the vast majority soon formed
themselves into solid hierarchical structures.

What we are hypothesizing, therefore, is that
in Chinese culture there is a spontaneous
tendency toward organization building.[332]

Expectations that a spontaneous tendency toward
organization building among the Chinese should have led
to the formation of large-scale, traditional interest
groups in today's Taiwan is heightened by Alexis de
Tocqueville's description of the link between such a
tendency and the liveliness of interest-group activity
in the United States:

Americans of all ages, all stations in life,
and all types of disposition are forever
forming associations. There are not only
commercial and industrial associations in
which all take part, but others of a thousand
different types—religious, moral, serious,
futile, very general and very limited, immensely
large and very minute. Americans combine to
give fetes, found seminaries, build churches,
distribute books, and send missionaries to the
antipodes; hospitals, prisons, and schools
take shape in that way. Finally, if they
want to proclaim a truth or propagate some
feeling by the encouragement of a great example,
they form an association.

I have come across several types of association in America of which, I confess,
I had not previously the slightest conception,
and I have often admired the extreme skill
they show in proposing a common object for the
exertions of very many and in inducing them
voluntarily to pursue it . . .

Thus the most democratic country in the
world now is that in which men have in our
time carried to the highest perfection the art
of pursuing in common the objects of common
desires and have applied this new technique

210

to the greatest number of purposes.[333]

Given the historical importance of interest-group
activity in Chinese society, taken together with the
insights of Pye and de Tocqueville, why does one not
find more spontaneously formed, large-scale, traditional
interest groups on Taiwan? Are there no faint echoes
of the great families of the Han dynasty, of the secret
societies of the Yüan--associations that, despite all
efforts of the imperial administration, grew into powerful administrative and military complexes and pursued
their goals to the point of toppling dynasties? [334]
The answer to these questions is found in the nature of
modern totalitarianism.

Totalitarian Opposition to Spontaneous Organizing

Spontaneous formations meet with a greater degree
of opposition on Taiwan than they ever encountered under
imperial regimes. Certainly the great families and secret
societies met with disapproval and attempts at suppression by the imperial regimes they grew up under.[335]
Moreover, imperial regimes attempted to enforce mutual-
responsibility systems, making entire families, neighborhoods, and guilds accountable for transgressions of
individuals.[336] These attempts at controlling spontaneity
were somewhat effective, given that the empire did
manage for long periods to ensure that no organization
became powerful enough to begin a serious civil war.
But the length of these periods had limits, and even
during these periods, the regimes were forced to accept
a great deal of less threatening spontaneity.[337]

In today's Taiwan, however, the type of opposition
that spontaneity meets with is the modern totalitarian
method of the governing elite, with its power to demand
much greater active support of the government and its
ability to tolerate much less opposition than the rulers
of empires. Thus the powerful Chinese tendency toward
spontaneous organization now runs into an even more powerful tendency toward suppression of spontaneity.

The totalitarian method used to combat spontaneity
includes the preemption of opportunities for spontaneous
organizing from below by organizing all citizens first,

211

under every conceivable designation, into groups sponsored by, and geared to, the support of the governing
elite. No room is left, or allowed, for organization
from below, whether the organizations be traditional
or modern-associational.

Groups organized spontaneously, by the people
themselves, will tend to be controlled by leaders who
derive power from their own success in organizing their
fellows and attaining their support. These leaders will
see their power based in the people they organized, not
in the governing elite, and will therefore not be readily amenable to governing elite control.

Groups sponsored by the governing elite, however,
will bring people together, but not because they are
following a leader who has convinced them that it is in
their private interests (not directly connected to any
citizenship role) to support him. People are brought
together through the orders of the governing elite as
citizens, to take direction from leaders who themselves
are not dependent for their positions on the group's
membership but on the governing elite itself--and behind
these leaders stand the legal sanctions of the police
and the courts.

Thus, the explanation for the lack of lobbying by
people's associations on Taiwan may not be that modern
interest groups have not yet been produced by Taiwan's
nonmodern economy nor that the people of Taiwan, although
organized on paper, have not yet developed the requisite
lobbying skills. (The Chinese seem quite capable of finding channels of influence when necessary, as previous
chapters have demonstrated.) Rather, the explanation
may lie in the organization of Taiwan's people's associations from above instead of from below.

Evidence supporting this explanation is abundant in
passages from governing-elite-sponsored publications that
are written to describe the elite's achievements in organizing Taiwan's population into occupational, commercial,
social, and labor associations. These passages display
a paternalistic attitude that presumes a need for heavy
elite guidance for associational activities. They further reveal the elite's intention to control the associations closely and to ensure their primary orientation
toward approved goals. Some examples follow:

212

Then it [the government] guided the people,
according to law, to organize associations.
. . . progressive personages of the various
circles were actively encouraged to organize
various classes of organizations.

. . . friendship societies, clubs, music
research societies, alumni associations,
etc. . . . After the relevant county or city
government (bureau) issues a permit and sends
out personnel to give guidance, an organizer
is chosen. . . . Nor may they seek donations
from outside the association, print and
distribute propaganda literature, or carry on
any other activities directed at outsiders.
If there comes into being one of the following
circumstances, the relevant county or city
government (bureau) may cancel the association's
registration and disband it: . . . the association destroys public order, or hurts the
public interest, or hurts good morals and
practices.

. . . each labor union [in addition to striving for the welfare of labor] aids to har-
monize the relations of capital and labor,
encourages cooperation in increasing production . . . honors and holds up for exemplifi-
cation "good men and good things," contributes
money to "respect the army and reward the troops,"
aids refugee fellow countrymen from the mainland,
and enthusiastically responds to the "Do
Not Forget Chü" movement.

[Cultural and academic associations] are to
research in specialized academic areas. Moreover, they should develop "oppose Communism,
resist tyranny" cultural propaganda work,
exposing the violent conduct of the Communist
bandits, deepening the knowledge of those within
and outside the country of the Communist bandits,
centralizing will and purpose, thus contributing
to the counterattack and the restoration of the
country.338

Evidence from interviews also supports the explanation that Taiwan's people's associations, organized from

213

above instead of from below, are weak supporters of their members' interests.

> Public associations are mostly very poor, and
> their offices are usually in an individual's
> home.

> Labor unions cannot strike. Their organiza-
> tions are weak. And after all, workers vote
> for the owner.

> Public associations do not become pressure
> groups . . . (a) Everyone has to join. They
> are not looked on as "our group." They see
> it more as a requirement than as protection.
> (b) Leaders . . . perhaps an honor and no
> salary. They are busy with their own affairs,
> not with association business. They are busy
> with their own livings. (c) Therefore, if
> people have problems involving their interests,
> they do not see the association as the proper
> channel and look for other ways or go to the
> government or assemblymen themselves.

Counterweights to Governing Elite Domination

Samuel H. Beer offers evidence in opposition
to the argument that groups organized or consciously
stimulated into being by political authorities tend to
become the puppets of such authorities. Beer observes
that in Great Britain--a model of "democratic" group
politics, with government, administration, interest groups,
electorate, and opposition all acting on and reacting to
each other in a framework of a truly democratic system--
the government often consciously stimulated the creation
of interest groups, and these groups did not become
puppets.

This evidence does not, in fact, negate the argument that has been made. The tendency to dominate does
have an effect. But a system as democratic as the
British system contains reverse tendencies, which act
as counterweights to heavy governmental domination.

Thus, in Great Britain, the government was motivated
to stimulate the creation of such groups by the need to

control the economy, and the resultant groups did partially serve to aid the government in formulating and
carrying out its policies.339   But, the counterweights
from British political culture and the prevailing power
structure kept the government from going too far.

For example, the British government itself was
"reluctant" to carry the policies of control to extremes.
Also, both the government and the people in general
shared the attitude that such interest groups had a
"right" to take part in policy making.   Moreover, this
attitude blended into a feeling that there are certain
rights that all groups have, one of these being the right
of noncooperation or obstruction.   Obstruction was a
legitimate, if unpleasant, possibility.   Finally, these
cultural factors existed in harmony with a reenforcing
power configuration.   Counterweight action was not only
legitimized in thought but also was a physical possibi-
lity.340

Chapter 11

PEOPLE'S ASSOCIATIONS AND TRADITIONAL
INTEREST-GROUP GOALS

Counterweights to Governing Elite
Domination on Taiwan

Despite governing elite domination of interest
groups, Taiwan is not a case of governing elite initiation and control in the absence of any counterweights
whatsoever. Besides the spontaneous Chinese tendency
toward organization building hypothesized above and the
more general counterweight of self-interest as opposed
to governing elite interest, counterweights similar to
those mentioned in Chapter 10 are also operating.

Government Reluctance to Go to Extremes

In Great Britain, Beer noticed a reluctance of the
government to press its control to extremes. On Taiwan,
there also seems to be a degree of reluctance. An individual on Taiwan is relatively free to be nonpolitical.
He is free to be silent about politics and to arrange
and rearrange his private life. (Such things as the
policeman's demanding that one's house have a flag hang-
ing outside on national holidays, the presence of a
military proctor in college dormitories, and pressure
in school and in the army to join the KMT qualify this
freedom to be sure.)

Taiwanese members of the KMT fighting for prestige
or economic advantages as members of local-level factions
remain well within the limits of the governing elite's
toleration. Even those who run against the KMT because
the KMT did not nominate a candidate from their faction
are easily tolerated by the governing elite. Indeed,
much of what has already been seen of local-level politics was left to the free play of factional ambitions.
The same laissez-faire policy holds for the activities
of people's associations.

Those who try the governing elite's tolerance,
usually politicians outside the KMT, are those who stray
from the path of prestige and economic goals and raise

217

issues such as expansion of civil rights or expansion
of elections to more important offices. They raise
issues of the right to criticize openly or challenge
openly in electoral contests officials who are guarding
the elite's basic policies. Even these politicians may
be tolerated, however, if they prove ineffectual in
spreading their views and in creating an organizational
base.

Just why the governing elite is so tolerant is a
matter for speculation. The understanding seems to be
that as long as behavior does not threaten its basic
policies, the elite will not interfere. Apparently
the elite is an accomplished player of the power game.
It knows exactly what it must control in order to reach
its goals. As long as it is attaining its goals, perhaps
it does not care to exercise more control over its
subjects. The more control the elite exercises, the
greater is the expenditure of time, energy, and other
resources that it must make. The elite sees the extra
amount of control as unnecessary for attaining its
goals. Therefore, it chooses more relaxed policies,
making fewer demands on its subjects and on itself.

Right of Participation in Policy-Making

Beer also noted the British attitude that interest
groups have a right to take part in the making of policies
that affect their interests. On Taiwan, there does seem
to be a preference for obtaining a consensus rather than
simply riding roughshod over a minority. Reenforcing
Bernard Gallin's contention (page 101 above) that consensus has always been highly valued in traditional
Chinese society, many of those interviewed seemed to
feel that almost everything should and, with enough
effort, could be worked out [hsieh-t'iao] to the satisfaction of everyone's interests.

> The KMT is the absolute majority and can
> always beat the nonparty in the Assembly.
> But there is much compromising [hsieh-t'iao].
> The Chinese way is to compromise. [You]
> do not have to beat them down. This happens
> all the time.

> The Provincial Assembly has been with the

218

government for a very long time and much
can be hsieh-t'iao and taken care of.

If an assemblyman wants a favor or has a conflict of interest, he can come to me and
hsieh-t'iao. [He does] not have to publicly
oppose. 341

An additional factor in this regard is the above-
noted ambivalence toward the individual who fights for
his own interests. (See pages 184-185 above.) A double
standard was involved--on the one hand, intolerant con-
demnation; on the other hand, tolerance of self-protec-
tion as the normal pattern of human behavior. This tolerance may also contribute to the view that it is legitimate for interested parties to participate in decisions
that affect them.

Further support for this view can be found in the
speculations of Pye and Solomon. Pye and Solomon postulated the existence of a need among the Chinese for
orderly relationships as a buttress against the fear of
anarchy. Perhaps this need for order encourages the seeking of agreement of all parties to a decision (at least
all parties capable of making trouble) to ensure that
all will accept it without creating a disturbance.

Further, in terms of the Pye-Solomon model of Chinese
political culture, given the pervasive sense of insecurity and the lack of confidence in the durability of
current protective relationships, it is possible that
many decision-makers will be motivated not to alienate
other people in the political arena. Given a turn of
events, the decision-maker may very quickly need these
other people as allies.342

Right of Noncooperation or Obstruction

Regarding British attitudes condoning a right of
noncooperation or obstruction, there is some evidence of
a similar attitude (at least concerning those questions
not affecting the elite's basic policies) on Taiwan.
In the late 1960s, one of the most mentioned examples
of condoning obstruction was the government's unwillingness to reconstruct the great estate of the Lin family
in Pan-ch'iao Township. Many felt that this great home

219

and grounds, abandoned by the original family, should be reconstructed and open to the public as a park and museum. Unfortunately, since the abandonment of the grounds, many squatters had moved in. They refused to go without compensation. It was even feared that if they were given compensation, other squatters would replace them, and the compensation cycle would never end.

The unwillingness of the government to take a firm hand in this matter seems to have as one element in it the recognition of the rights of the interested squatters to noncooperation and obstruction. Other examples are found in the widespread disbelief that merchants can be made to collect sales taxes for the government, as well as the unwillingness of the government to move against illegal shacks, set up often in the middle of main thoroughfares, until alternative housing is available. Such illegal shack dwellers have even been known to turn to violent obstruction of demolition crews.

Supportive Power Configuration

Regarding the finding that in Great Britain the power configuration supports the norms against enforcing control to extremes, there certainly appears to be no power on Taiwan that can successfully oppose the governing elite if the elite decides to enforce its control to extremes. It is likely, however, that the overuse of its power would cause so much resentment that after a string of pyrrhic victories, the regime would find its entire position endangered. This long-range view of Taiwan's power configuration may also have led the governing elite to follow a policy of restraint.

Counterweights and Noticeable Pressuring Activity of People's Associations

These counterweights explain why, although many perceive people's associations in Taiwan as being "not very active" in pressuring for their interests, these associations are active enough to be noticeable. The nature of the activity of people's associations will be clearer if it is categorized in the same manner as the lobbying activities of individual business firms. In terms of business firms, there were (a) assemblymen protecting their own businesses, (b) businesses sending out candidates to become assemblymen or hiring successful candidates after election, and (c) businesses trying to influence legislators they do not directly control.

Given the nature of people's associations, category (a) can be dropped--since people's associations are made up of many individuals who elect officers, and, unlike businesses, these associations do not belong to one person or one family. Therefore, only two categories of lobbying activities are relevant here: (a) associations sending out their own members to become assemblymen or hiring assemblymen otherwise elected, and (b) assemblymen as being pressured by associations to which the assemblymen are not related by employment or personal involvement.

Assemblymen as Representatives
of People's Associations

Becoming an Assemblyman, Instead
of Beseeching Assemblymen

As has already been noted, Taiwan does not display a neat differentiation of roles between (a) lobbyists employed to represent specific interests, (b) political parties reconciling and integrating these interests with one another, producing a limited number of policy alternatives, and (c) assemblymen, beholden to no specific interests, choosing one or another of these policy alternatives. Instead of a differentiation between lobbyist and assemblyman roles, much lobbying activity is found in the behavior of the assemblymen themselves. This was illustrated previously in descriptions of Taiwan's businessmen and their agents becoming assemblymen and using the power of that position to protect their business interests.

The same situation prevails for the lobbying of people's associations. As noted, the associations are not personal in the way that businesses can be personal. But associations do hire agents and designate officers to run in elections, and these agents and officers do become closely identified with the associations and their interests. Upon being elected, the association-assem-

221

blymen use the power of their Assembly positions to protect their associations, just as the business-assembly-
men use that power to protect their businesses.

People's Associations Support Candidates

In his book on the Provincial Assembly, Professor
Pao Ch'ing-chiu notes the importance of support from
at least some type of group for success in elections:

> Besides having the legal qualifications,
> it is necessary to have the support of a
> political party or other group; otherwise,
> even though one has registered for the elec-
> tion, his hope of succeeding will not be
> great.343

These groups are often people's associations. For
example, Hsü Hsiang-ch'eng, candidate for the Provincial Assembly,

> previously served as Miao-li County assem-
> blyman for the third and fourth terms.
> Currently he is serving as president of the
> Miao-li Fragrant Reed Oil Association . . .
> Recently, the members of the Fragrant Reed
> Oil Association, upon learning that he has
> already been nominated and registered for
> the election, all deeply celebrated on attain-
> ing the right man. Moreover, they mutually
> deliberated, wanting to support the needs
> of the campaign financially.344

According to the Provincial Assembly's records of
1968, 47 out of 70 assemblymen had belonged or then
belonged to at least one people's association. The
list of these groups on the next page gives an indication of the variety of associations supportive of local-
level electoral candidates.

Qualifications on People's Association
Support for Candidates

Certainly any association would be happy to have
members who become candidates for seats in Taiwan's

PEOPLE'S ASSOCIATIONS IN WHICH TAIWAN'S (1968)
PROVINCIAL ASSEMBLYMEN HAVE HELD MEMBERSHIP

Township or Rural-District-
wide Organizations

Women's Assoc.
Farmers' Assoc.
Irrigation Assoc.
Agricultural Assoc.
Sugarcane Products Assoc.

County or Citywide
Organizations

Cooks' Assoc.
Hotel Assoc.
Women's Assoc.
Drivers' Assoc.
Medical Assoc.
Farmers' Assoc.
Shippers' Assoc.
Butchers' Assoc.
Insurance Assoc.
Reporters' Assoc.
Fishermen's Assoc.
Dog Raisers' Assoc.
Auto Repair Assoc.
Pharmacists' Assoc.
New Medicine Assoc.
Movie Theater Assoc.
Chamber of Commerce
Import-Export Assoc.
General Labor Union
Jelly and Jam Assoc.
Customs Broker Assoc.
Coal Merchants' Assoc.
Silverware Shop Assoc.
Lumber Products Assoc.
Medical Industry Assoc.
Fragrant Reed Oil Assoc.
Three-Wheel Truck Union
All-China Pottery Assoc.
Fruit and Vegetable Assoc.
Real-Estate Brokers' Assoc.
Professional Barbers' Union
Professional Drivers' Union
Professional Printers' Union
Industrial Development Assoc.

Intermediate-Level Organizations

Regional Irrigation Assoc.
Ta-chia River Development Comm.
Stonegate Reservoir Encouragement Comm.

Province or Taiwan-wide Organizations

Women's Assoc.
Farmers' Assoc.
Butchers' Assoc.
Steamship Assoc.
Coal Mine Assoc.
Industrial Assoc.
Fishermen's Assoc.
Pharmacists' Assoc.
Tea Industry Assoc.
Tea Merchants' Assoc.
General Labor Union
Chamber of Commerce
Clock-Glasses Assoc.
Railroad Labor Union
Feather Export Assoc.
Rice Merchants' Assoc.
Marine Products Assoc.
Paper Producers' Assoc.
Dyeing Industry Assoc.
Irrigation Aid Society
Medicine Industry Assoc.
Medicine Production Assoc.
Shipping Contractors' Assoc.
Industry and Commerce Society
Cotton Weaving Industry Assoc.
Aborigine Area Construction Assoc.

Source: Chuan-chi, I, 1-18.

223

provincial and local assemblies. But the ability and willingness of associations to support candidates actively seem to vary widely from association to association. On occasion, a member-candidate may be given no support at all. A candidate may even find that he needs the association's backing far more than the association needs his candidacy.

The comment that follows, although probably too skeptical, is the type of evidence that cautions against assuming that strong associational support for candidates is the unqualified norm on Taiwan:

> Most of these men are using the organization's name for propaganda . . . [they are] not really sent by them to represent the Farmers' Association, etc. They do not have that kind of power. Similar with the Irrigation and the Fishermen's Association, etc. Chu Wan-ch'eng is really using the Provincial Farmers' Association. [With Ch'en Hua-tsung, the head of the Irrigation Association, it's] a little of being their representative and a little of using their name to get elected.

People's Association-Assemblymen Support People's Associations

Evidence that association-assemblymen protect and further the interests of the associations that aid their election campaigns is abundant. For example, just as business-oriented committees attract a large number of businessmen, the committee most closely related to a people's association (the Agriculture and Forestry Committee, closely related to the Farmers' Association) is heavily colonized by representatives from that association.345

Discussing his fellow members on the Agriculture and Forestry Committee, Assemblyman Liu Chin-yüeh, who was at the time the general manager of the Provincial Farmers' Association, noted that "all of these people are from the Farmers' Association system." During the interview, Liu repeatedly referred to the committee as "our committee."346

224

Nor are other relevant committees neglected. Assemblyman Chu Wan-ch'eng, who was at the time the president of the Provincial Farmers' Association, explained his membership on the Finance Committee as follows:

> I do not have to participate [in the Agriculture and Forestry Committee] because the general manager is already on it. Therefore the other person can go to another committee. And the Transportation Committee, etc., are not as related to agriculture and forestry matters as much as finance, especially because of the problem of taxes. Agricultural taxes are heavy.

In addition to descriptions of activity on behalf of the Farmers' Association, examples are available for such widely varying associations as those representing women and those representing coal mine owners.[347]

The Farmers' Association

The Farmers' Association appears to be the most active and independent of Taiwan's people's associations. Chapter 10 noted the attempts by the governing elite to shape the goals of the people's associations, making them support organizations instead of interest groups. This policy appears to have failed somewhat in terms of the Provincial Farmers' Association.

This activity and independence is demonstrated by the placement of buildings around the Provincial Assembly. One thinks of Washington, D.C., where government buildings and buildings housing interest-group representatives are strategically deployed around the Capitol Building, the target that the individuals in those buildings hope to reach. Government buildings are also strategically placed around the Provincial Assembly (40 minutes away in one direction, 5 minutes in the other). From these buildings, Mandarin-speaking individuals often ride to the Assembly to defend their programs and budgets. But unlike Washington, only one prominent nongovernmental group of buildings stands along the road to the legislature--the headquarters of the Provincial Farmers' Association. From the two largest offices in these buildings, two Taiwanese-speaking individuals often (1963-1968) ride to the Assembly not only to

225

defend their programs and budgets but also to vote on them with their fellow assemblymen.[348]

In addition to the province's two highest Farmers' Association officers being assemblymen, three other assemblymen listed themselves as officers in the association at one level or another (in 1963-1968). Ten more listed themselves as having previously been in the association. No other association had this many assemblymen, as can be seen in the following table:

ASSEMBLYMEN AS AFFILIATED WITH MAJOR
PEOPLE'S ASSOCIATIONS (1963-1968)

Assemblymen	Farmers' Assoc.	Fisher-men's Assoc.	Women's Assoc.	Chambers of Commerce	Labor Unions
Former members	10	2	4	3	4
Current members	5	3	3	4	2

Source: Chuan-chi, I, 1-18.

Only if all the business association-assemblymen are placed together under one category will the Farmers' Association-assemblymen be outnumbered. But coming from many different types of associations, the business representatives are rarely united.[349]

Perhaps the most surprising comment on the importance of the Farmers' Association on Taiwan was that made by a nonassociation-assemblyman concerning Assemblyman and Provincial Farmers' Association President Chu Wan-ch'eng: "Chu Wan-ch'eng is the most powerful individual next to the chairman [provincial governor] and the speaker of the Provincial Assembly in the province."

Some reasons for the activism and importance of the Provincial Farmers' Association were provided by General Manager Liu Chin-yüeh.

[There is a] very close relationship between
the Farmers' Association and the Assembly,
mainly because it involves provincewide
matters more than almost anything else does.
The problems of many of the public associations
do not go above the county or rural district-
township level. And also, their importance
in government policy is nothing like the
Farmers' Association's.

There are several possible explanations for the
activism and importance of the Farmers' Association.
On Taiwan, a large proportion of the population is still
in farm families (53 percent in 1967, 41 percent in
1975).350   The Farmers' Association not only reaches right
down into their villages organizationally but also, in
terms of the villagers' economic interests, is very close
to their pocketbooks.351   Only the Farmers' Association
has such a massive and firm base. More assemblymen are
businessmen than farmers, but the business community that
they are part of is smaller than the farming constituency.

To speculate further, no other part of the population is as firmly rooted in its home villages as are the
farmers. Emotionally and practically farmers take the
interests of their area as their own. Businessmen and
workers are more mobile, often returning to the farming
families from which they came for visits and to leave
behind a portion of the funds that they earned in the city.

Also, the farmer tends to have a stubborn conserv-
atism. Not in the nouveau proletarian's undefinable
position between city and countryside nor in the seasoned
proletarian's alienated condition, the farmer has his land
and his way of life. He can "feel" their value and is
willing to resist moves that threaten them--thus, his
natural "petit bourgeois" tendencies.

Further, given a tie to family tradition and traditional morality, not corrupted by the forced individual-
ism of the proletarian condition, he is willing not only
to struggle for what he has but also often to risk his
life so that his family and their descendants will benefit
from his sacrifice. (Even the Mencian idea of the right
of rebellion may have a part in this explanation, at
least for the Chinese farmer.)

227

Finally, it is probable on Taiwan that the farmers'
interests (after land reform) fall within the sphere
of activities that the governing elite sees as not necessary to control, thus giving room for the expression of
the above tendencies.

These tendencies may explain not only the activism
and independence of the Farmers' Association on Taiwan
but also such phenomena as kulak resistance to Stalin,
the general resistance of farmers to collectivism, Mao's
1927 observations of farmer activism in Hunan, farmers'
tendencies to revert to free-market capitalism, and
Communist China's troubles in relying on farmers' organizations for control over the population in the countryside. It appears that despite who originally sets up
and controls such an organization, the farmers have a
way of taking it over and using it to further their own
interests, as they define them.

The Labor Unions

It was noted previously that for many assemblymen
there is no contradiction between simultaneous represen-
tation of capital and labor. It was also noted that sometimes it is in the objective interest of the worker to
support his employer politically. In terms of this chapter,
information concerning this unexpected harmony between
capital and labor is also available.

Of the association-assemblymen who did not appear
to be strongly supporting their association's interests,
the labor union-assemblymen were conspicuous. For the
session of the assembly investigated, the efforts of the
labor union-assemblymen to aid labor unions were not
apparent in the interpellations they raised and were weak
in the resolutions they supported. Indeed, the best
prolabor showing was in their political platforms, written
for the 1963 elections.

If these three indicators are representative of their
actions for labor in general, the conclusion must be that
the labor union-assemblymen do not work very hard for
the interests of labor. A reason for this nonaction may
be found in the concurrent membership of two of the four
labor union-assemblymen in associations representing
employers. (A third is probably in a company union.)

Given these cross-memberships, the assemblymen might
have experienced a conflict of interest that lessened
their support for labor.[352]

More material concerning capital-labor relations
on Taiwan is found in KMT propaganda on behalf of candidates running for the Provincial Assembly. Labor union,
business association, and private business backgrounds
of KMT-nominated candidates are listed, along with descriptions of their devotion to both capital and labor.
No conflict between labor and capital is even hinted
at. Also, the possibility that the candidates have been
acting to aid their own businesses, and not simply working for the interests of the members of Taiwan's business
associations, is not explored.[353]

Assemblymen as Objects of Pressure from People's Associations Unrelated to Them

The topic of this section has previously been considered in discussions of the new theories of associational democracy (Chapter 9) and of people's associations
as governing elite-controlled bodies (Chapter 10). Here
it is only necessary to summarize the points already made.

1. The climate of opinion with regard to ideal
behavior is hostile to any form of lobbying, including
people's associations' lobbying assemblymen who are not
related to them by employment or personal involvement.

2. Perhaps Taiwan's economy has not yet developed
to the point where the lobbying of people's associations
is in demand nor to the point where more traditional
groups have lost their usefulness in protecting the individual.

3. Perhaps traditional groups have been able to
convert themselves to perform "modern" protective functions so that people's associations are not needed to give
the individual security.

4. Perhaps because of (a) the fear of scarce resources, (b) difficulties of cooperation among peers,
(c) a disinclination to rely on impersonal institutions,
and (d) support by governing elite policy, by the behavior
of individual bureaucrats, and by ordinary individuals

229

for person-to-person authority-dependent relationships, participation in protective associational interest groups based on the shared interests of peers is unattractive to the security-seeking individual on Taiwan.

5. Perhaps the governing elite has consciously prevented people's associations from becoming too active on behalf of the interests of their members.

6. Despite these restraints, there is evidence of pressure-group activities carried on by the members of people's associations.

7. These active people's association members, however, may actually be protecting themselves through membership in a more traditional group, with their concurrent membership in a people's association being incidental.

8. Alternatively, these members may be acting individually to protect their own interests through the traditional personalized technique of a one-to-one relationship with an assemblyman, with their membership in a people's association plus the benefits that other people's association members receive as a result of their efforts both being incidental.

9. If the people's association members are acting in concert, the climate of opinion with regard to actual behavior favors the more personalized method of penetrating the Assembly with one of their own agents rather than lobbying assemblymen who are not agents of the association.

10. With all the above restraints and alternatives, especially given the preference for the security of traditional personalized (as opposed to abstract formalized) relationships, as well as unfamiliarity with other possibilities, people's association lobbying of assemblymen who are not agents of the lobbyist's association is the least prevalent method of pressure-group activity carried on by the members of people's associations on Taiwan.

Given this summary, what remains for this section is to leave the reader with a little more feeling for the state of associational lobbying on Taiwan by quoting the perception of an assemblyman close to people's associations:

Originally public associations did not
really understand and did not know their
interests or how to defend them. Now they
are a little better and getting better.

Businessmen are always better and come out
more than other public associations, [with]
problems like taxes, importing, etc.

Carpenters . . . railroad laborers . . .
the Medical Doctors' Association, the Lawyers'
Association, other professional associations,
each came out once. And the Medicine Producers'
Association on one big issue . . .

[I] remember others coming out, but not more
than one time each. People's associations come
out seldom.

Assemblymen and Other Kinds
of Interest Groups

Besides business interests and people's associations,
all sorts of other interests impinge on the Provincial
Assembly. The types of interests are limited only by the
complexity of the society. Two major examples of nonbusiness and nonassociation interests are those of women and
of the descendants of Taiwan's original non-Chinese population, the aborigines.

Women are included in this section because the efforts
of the women's association-assemblywomen aid all women in
Taiwan, not just those women who are formally members of
the Taiwan Women's Association. [354]

For women and for aborigines, there are special voting
regulations to assure them of a minimal number of seats
in Taiwan's representative assemblies. For example, the
four 1972-1977 assemblymen who represented Taiwan's more
than 125,000 aborigines did not have to run against non-
aborigines. They had only aborigines as constituents.
Once elected, as one would expect, aborigine assemblymen
especially support aborigine interests. [355]

For women, if the population of an electoral district
exceeds a given figure, a woman, no matter how few her

231

votes, must be elected from that district.356 (Each district is assigned a specific number of seats according to its population. Each voter casts only one vote, and the specific number of candidates with the most votes are considered elected.) When only one woman is running, this regulation favoring women often results in the woman candidate's not campaigning at all or in her directing people who would normally vote for her to cast their ballots for her favorites among the male candidates.357

It was originally assumed that the ten women members of the 1963-1968 Provincial Assembly formed a group, perhaps in terms of issues in general, perhaps only in terms of women's interests in particular. This assumption was reinforced by observing the assemblywomen constantly congregating at each other's desks on the Assembly floor. Although some reporters denied that the assemblywomen could unite on anything ("as with other women, always backbiting"), subsequently collected data did show that they all supported interests concerning women to a greater degree than the average assembly member. Concerning other matters, however, the assemblywomen were shown to be less unified than their male colleagues.358

Examples of assemblymen being pressured or responding to pressure from nonbusiness and nonassociational interests other than aborigines and women conclude this section.

In relation to the local government regulations limiting the age of mayors . . . although of the arguments given in the dispute, everyone sounds reasonable, still actually there is another element existing. This other element is compounded of county and city mayors loath to leave their positions and provincial assemblymen preparing to satisfy their craving for county and city mayor positions. They do not want to see the passage of this bill. They, from within [the Assembly] and from without, have united together, their drums sending messages back and forth.359

The intention of this resolution [to encourage talented government workers to serve in rural areas] is good. But already there is very much good talent serving in rural districts

232

and townships. On the contrary, all over
come beseechings to provincial assemblymen
to think of a way to have them transferred
to Taipei City or Taichung City, etc., to serve.
And we assemblymen, in the end, really exhaust
strength, actively helping.[360]

Yesterday . . . one hundred people who practice
medicine without a license . . . upon seeing
the legislators leaving the chambers, one
after another, fell to their knees. Some
even kowtowed. All this made the legislators
feel very embarrassed.

. . . they stated that as soon as the [new]
physician law was put into effect, they would
immediately become criminals in the act of
practicing medicine without a license.[361]

Assemblymen as Individuals Who Attack as Well as Defend the Interests of Others

Given all the defending of interests described
throughout this study, it is not surprising that such
defense occasionally results in attacks on others.
In general, however, assemblymen strive to alienate as
few interest groups as possible. This is especially so
in their political platform statements. Rarely do political platform statements go further than to attack the
abstract targets of "corrupt people" and "selfish local
interests." In resolutions supported by assemblymen and
in the interpellations they raise, the list of targets
for attack grows. Still, abstract targets predominate.
Corrupt businessmen, corrupt and inefficient officials,
crooked politicians, and teachers who exploit students
come in for a heavy drubbing.

Leaving aside safe and popular targets and concentrating instead on less-abstract interests, one will
discover that the targets of these attacks are determined
by the assemblyman's personal-interest profile. For
example, those assemblymen attacking a specific local
area's interests are not referring to the area from which
their own votes come. This is certainly so for areas
competing for major port facilities, as their assemblyman debunks the qualifications of a rival port.

Similarly, the assemblyman attacking the interests of coal miners is probably a coal mine owner. Assemblymen who are licensed to practice as medical doctors oppose the right of unlicensed doctors to practice. Pharmacist-assemblymen speak out against the sale of inferior medicine. An assemblywoman who is trying to bar politicians with limited formal educations from office has both a regular medical degree and a Ph.D. Opponents of tax officials are likely to be big businessmen.

In general, attacks on the interests of others run the gamut from assemblymen attacking each other, through cases in which assemblymen attack outsiders in defense of their own interests, to cases in which the assemblymen more selflessly attack interests in terms of defending the general welfare.

On rare occasions, an assemblyman will attack another physically. [362] Almost as rarely, a verbal battle among assembly members will provoke an assemblywoman to demand an apology for a derogatory sexual reference.[363] More often, however, attacks on the interests of others are both reasoned and civil. For example,

> The government wants to break up all monopoly industry. Does this mean only to break up the glass industry monopoly? Or will all monopoly industry be broken up? If it is only partial, to open up the glass industry, this representative does not feel there is anything to be happy about. This is because glass products do not make up a large part of the people's livelihood . . . If you do not completely open up such industries that have a much closer relationship to the people's livelihood as the flour, cooking oil, etc., industries, but only choose to break up the glass industry monopoly, does this have much meaning? In recent years, general reaction toward the monopoly of the Yü Lung Motor Car Company has been great and vexed. Speaking truthfully, the protection of Yü Lung Motors is the protection of Japanese-produced automobiles. If the government wants to make clear its firm intentions to break up monopoly industry, it should . . . not allow Japanese-

234

produced goods to masquerade as national
products, even to the point of protecting
their monopoly and only choosing the glass
industry monopoly as a symbol of breaking up
monopolies. 364

PART IV

THE GENERAL MODEL OF A FLEDGLING
WESTERN-STYLE ELECTORAL DEMOCRACY [365]

This study has introduced much diverse information
relating to Taiwan's provincial and local-level political
system. The framework within which this information
was organized divided the environment of the provincial
assemblymen into (a) groups that center themselves around
support for or opposition to Taiwan's governing elite,
(b) groups that center themselves around competition for
local political resources, and (c) groups that have been
stimulated into existence by economic development.

In analyzing the assemblymen's relationships to
these groups, four approaches to the study of Taiwan
were initially used: (a) an approach that conceives of
Taiwan's politics as a confrontation between the governing elite and the Taiwanese, (b) an anthropological
approach that sees the Taiwanese as a complex group of
people, not simply a homogeneous mass opposed to the
governing elite, (c) an approach that stresses the effect
of economic development on political behavior, and (d)
an approach that stresses explanations based on psychological theories of Chinese political behavior.

Further along in the analysis, it became clear that
simply to place each piece of information introduced by
this study into one of three categories of groups and to
explain its significance in terms of one or more disparate approaches would not be as satisfying as linking
the data together within the framework of a comprehensive
model of Taiwan's political system--especially if this
comprehensive model was a general one that would provide
an explanatory description of a large number of historical
and contemporary political systems that share the characteristics of Taiwan's political system.

Upon further reflection, it became apparent that the
initial approaches were not so disparate after all.
Three of the four were channeling the data toward a model
of the type desired. The approach that conceives of
Taiwan's politics as a confrontation between the governing elite and the Taiwanese was channeling the data
toward Benjamin Schwartz's description of elite attitudes

237

in early modern China, as well as toward the contrast between the attitudes of governing elites and the attitudes of nonelite electoral politicians described in Myron Weiner's analysis of India and in James C. Scott's analysis of a number of third-world countries, including Ghana and Indonesia. The anthropological and economic development approaches were also channeling the data toward the analyses of Weiner and Scott, explaining the sociopolitical conditions giving rise to the attitudes of the nonelite electoral politicians they described.

Heartened because Schwartz, Weiner, and Scott had affirmed that their analyses were broadly applicable to historical and contemporary political behavior in many countries throughout the world, the author then restated their analyses in the form of what promised to be the desired comprehensive and general model. 366

The model that grew out of this restatement is one of a political system in a fledgling stage of Western-style democratic political development--a stage through which many well-established democratic political systems have passed, through which some less-established democratic political systems are now passing, and during which many less-established democratic political systems were truncated by power elites that found the characteristics of the democracies being established within their realms intolerable to bear.

The fledgling Western-style democratic political system delineated by the model includes three main aspects: (a) a relatively democratic subsystem composed of elections and elective offices involving at least some offices with at least some power; (b) a governing elite in control of at least the most powerful offices of the political system, whose control over these offices does not ultimately derive from competition within the subsystem's elections, and which has been socialized to measure the behavior of others (but not necessarily its own behavior) against extremely high standards of morality and competence; (c) nonelite politicians competing within the subsystem's elections and filling its offices, displaying what the governing elite perceives to be immoral and incompetent behavior offensive to its high standards.

The model describes how the governing elite has

238

become socialized to measure the behavior of others
(but not necessarily its own behavior) against extremely
high standards of morality and competence and why the
nonelite electoral politicians behave in a manner offensive to the elite's standards. It further describes
how the holding of these high standards leads the governing elite to lose patience with behavior that it perceives
as not living up to these standards and the elite's
tendency to replace such behavior with what it is convinced is its own, more democratic, though less electoral,
behavior.

According to the model, the governing elite in many
developing political systems, including Taiwan's, became
politically aware in an environment dominated by the
humiliation of their countries by the Western powers.
For the members of such elites, it became an urgent
task to restore "wealth and power" to their country,
thus erasing this humiliation and restoring their own
personal pride and self-esteem.

For such elites, the political system represented
by the word "democracy" was often seen as a major means
to the accomplishment of this end. But in order for a
"democratic" political system to serve as an effective
means, the elites were constrained to add to the definition of democracy elements not necessarily present in the
classical definitions of the term.

For example, for the faction of the Chinese governing elite that retreated to Taiwan, thus becoming Taiwan's
governing elite, one added element was the liberation of
the energies of the people. The "liberation" and
"freedom" of democracy would be the vehicle for liberat-
ing the energies of the people, energies that were assumed
to have been repressed by the old society. These energies
would provide the motive power behind the country's
resurgence to wealth and power.

A second added element was the channeling of the
energies of the people. The liberated energies of the
people could not be allowed to flow every which way,
creating conflict and chaos. They had to be channeled
in the direction of national resurgence.

A third added element was a nonconflictive policy-
making process. The prevention of conflict and the

239

channeling of energies would be accomplished through what was assumed to be--under the influence of Western thinking--a scientific policy-making process, involving the exchange of ideas in a nonconflictive, calm, rational manner. All parties would sincerely aid one another in the search for the "scientifically correct" method for solving whatever specific problem was under consideration.

In addition to the inclusion of elements of this nature in the definition of democracy, a second important influence on the attitudes of governing elites such as that on Taiwan came from the movements that elite members joined in order to make their desire for national wealth and power effective. These movements fostered a complex of values rooted in the necessities of a difficult struggle for ideological ends. Among these values were party loyalty, selflessness, the willingness to sacrifice for the general good, and the importance of duty and obligations over rights.

A cadre ethic also developed out of these movements. Through experience in their respective movements, the governing elite members came to believe that the movements' cadres (i.e., themselves), who struggled for so long, had been tested and proven to be especially qualified, in morality and knowledge, to be society's leaders.

For the governing elites, this cadre ethic is often held in combination with an expert ethic. The expert ethic was not a product of the movement experience. Rather, it was the result of the general recognition of the importance of "science" as an additional method for attaining wealth and power. According to this ethic, many government officials (again, the governing elite members), given experience and/or special schooling, are considered scientific experts. These experts are thought to be especially qualified to make decisions concerning social policy.

It is important to note here that it is not necessary for the believer in all of these values--nonconflictive policy-making, loyalty, selflessness, sacrifice, duty, and high qualifications from experience and schooling--actually to live up to them. The believer may consistently violate them. But his image of himself and the standards by which he judges others are defined by these values.

240

The second portion of the model explains why non-elite politicians competing within the framework of the subsystem of elections and elective offices are constrained by their environment to behave in ways that directly conflict with the values of the governing elites.

At the root of the behavior of nonelite electoral politicians is their desire to obtain votes in order to be elected to office. They desire election because of the great prestige, and often great power, that comes to elected officials. The power is especially attractive in countries such as Taiwan, where the economy is growing, creating many new interest groups that are seeking protection and conditions conducive to further development. Prestige is also important in such countries, since economic change, land reform (at least on Taiwan), the institution of elections, and other influences have undermined old bases of prestige but have left the desire for prestige intact. Elections remain as one of the few ways in which the individual can affirm, or reaffirm, prestigious status.

Votes in these countries come, in large measure, from rank-and-file citizens who are also feeling the effects of economic change, land reform, the institution of elections, etc. The major effect of these changes has been to undermine the strength of the groups and personages that previously gave security to these citizens. Landlord-patrons no longer have their original landed resource bases. Nor does the landlord's traditionally prestigious status continue to carry the same weight as before. Organized lineages have also lost their landed wealth and are beginning to lose their internal solidarity as lineage members divide along the lines of newly developing economic interests. At the same time, the developing economy and newly available elected offices are creating new groups and personages, with much more power than their traditional predecessors ever controlled.

Given the enfeeblement of his old protectors, the rank-and-file citizen, in an environment filled with new powers, faces the necessity of rebuilding his security system. Four circumstances appear to influence this strategy for rebuilding:

241

1. For various reasons (many of which were reviewed on pages 199-203 above), the use of horizontal peer-group organizations as building blocks for a new security system does not appear as an important alternative.

2. For many purposes (see pages 104-105, 108-109, and 202 [numbers 3 and 4] above), reliance on impersonal, formal-legal arrangements--of a governmental or nongovernmental nature--does not appear as attractive as reliance on personal, one-to-one, authority-dependent relationships.

3. Given that reliance on horizontal peer-group organizations and reliance on impersonal, formal-legal arrangements are not considered serious alternatives, by default, the rank-and-file citizen begins to conceive of his needs in terms of his own particular problems, unrelated to the problems of those outside his immediate circle.

4. The newly emerging nonelite electoral politicians are very anxious to solve the individual citizen's particular problems in exchange for his vote.

The resulting strategy according to which the citizen chooses to rebuild his security system increasingly causes electoral politics in the countries in question to take on the following characteristics:

1. Particularism: Nonelite electoral politicians are constrained to attract votes by satisfying the particularistic needs of individuals and small groups, in apparent disregard for the needs of the general community.

2. Corruption: Politicians are constrained to bend and break general rules (i.e., laws) in order to satisfy their voters' particularistic needs.

3. Divisiveness: Given great competition between electoral politicians and the necessity to obtain votes through personal relationships, politicians gather around themselves as many voters as possible, and mutually opposed factions form.

4. Lack of Principle and Lack of Party Loyalty: The focusing of the desires of both politicians and voters on personal security, wealth, and prestige causes both groups to form and break up relationships solely on the

basis of each relationship's current ability to further these desires.

5. <u>Lack of Comprehensive and Scientific Planning</u>: The ideas put forward to solve society's problems, in terms of what the governing elite believes are the comprehensive and scientific plans of experts, are chopped to pieces by the constant demands for particularistic consideration made by the constituents of the electoral politicians.

There are political scientists--and electoral politicians--who argue that despite these unsavory appearances, the above-described political system serves well the needs of the rank-and-file citizen living in a transitional society. After all, it is argued, electoral politicians in control of crucial resources are under extremely heavy pressure to expend these resources in helping rank-and-file citizens in exactly the manner that these citizens demand.

Moreover, given the above description of the effects that elections and a modernizing economy have on an originally traditional agricultural society, the political scientists argue that the development of these unsavory appearances is inevitable. Indeed, they are symptomatic of a transitional stage of development through which virtually all currently developed democracies have passed. Left alone, these unsavory appearances will diminish as the current transitional system is supplanted by more-developed stages.

As the developing economy causes citizens to feel more secure, as impersonal institutions prove their trustworthiness, and as citizens begin to see their interests in occupational and class terms, the argument continues, they will abandon their unilateral attempts to gain security by making particularistic deals with a patron and will pursue their interests through organizations that work for national, comprehensive-scientific policies designed to affect all citizens in a given category in the same way.

But for the governing elite, this transitional political system, with its particularism, corruption, divisiveness, lack of principle, lack of loyalty, and rejection of the elite's own "expert" leadership, is so com-

pletely opposed to the elite's conception of democracy
as being dedicated to the general good, honesty, unity,
principle, loyalty, and scientific planning that it is
difficult for it to heed such arguments. (It is doubtful that the elite would even tolerate the more-developed
stages that the transitional system is to be supplanted
by, since these more-developed stages suggest occupational and class organizations freely competing for their own
conceptions of their interests in disregard for the
elite's conceptions of the good of the whole political
body.)

This elite abhorrence of the electoral system exists
even though the elite is probably heavily involved in the
system--including in its "unsavory" characteristics.
Even if--as on Taiwan--the subsystem of elections and
elective offices does not involve the most powerful
offices of the political system, the elite must ensure
continuing legitimacy by having its supporters win the
great majority of those less powerful offices that are
up for election.

To ensure such victory at the polls, the elite
must make deals with those nonelite electoral politicians
who are already at the hub of networks of personal relationships that make them potentially powerful vote-
getters. Moreover, part of the deal must be that the
elite will enable the politician to deliver the particularistic (and perhaps corrupt) favors that so offend
the elite's general-good morality and scientific-planning
sensibilities. Further, in order not to become totally
dependent on one or another of these politicians, the
elite itself is forced to encourage and imitate the divisiveness and lack of principle it so much abhors.

Faced with such an abhorrent electoral system--and
perhaps egged on by their own complicity in the system,
tarnishing their superior image of themselves--the governing elites of many countries simply suppressed it. In
its place, they opted for one or another sort of "nonelectoral democracy," based on what the elite assumed to
be its own superior ability to determine the will and the
needs of the people.

As an example closely adhering to the general model,
this tendency to suppress the electoral system also
exists among the governing elite on Taiwan. In the par-

ticular case of Taiwan, however, a number of constraints are likely to act as a rare check on this tendency.

With all its unseemliness, the electoral system has brought tangible rewards to the rank-and-file citizens of Taiwan. Nonelite electoral politicians have also benefited. Moreover, the system has tied these politicians close to the citizens and has made them leaders of opinion and action. If the governing elite tried to do away with this system, it would be very difficult to convince the citizens and the politicians that any substitute would be more in their interests.

The problem is compounded because the governing elite is identified as a nonelected group, which did not even originate in the majority community. To repress the real elected leaders of the majority community and claim that somehow it is a better representative than they would be very difficult for the majority to accept.

Even constraints such as the above, however, have not always discouraged other governing elites from doing away with electoral systems. The reason why the feelings of the majority community and its leaders are so important for Taiwan's elite stems from the recent widespread rejection of this elite by the world's other governing elites, along with the communities they govern. Taiwan's elite could probably not survive if its own majority community joined this general withdrawal of legitimacy.

Indeed, one of the only remaining supporters of the Taiwan elite, the United States, is far more tolerant of imperfect democracy and would likely become less supportive of the Taiwan elite if the latter did away with its fledgling democratic system.

Thus, despite its distaste for the subsystem of elections and elective offices, Taiwan's governing elite can only deepen its own complicity in electoral politics--even committing itself slowly to including increasingly important offices within the electoral subsystem--if it is to have a chance at remaining the governing elite of Taiwan.

FOOTNOTES

1. See Matthews; Clapp; and Wahlke et al.
2. The term "mountain people" derives from the Fukienese-Taiwanese designation of the Chinese mainland as the "t'ang mountains" (personal communication, J. Bruce Jacobs). Sources for the following discussion are Kerr; Formosa Today; Mendel (1970); Tardio; Feng Tsao-min; Goddard (1958); Goddard (1966); China Yearbook (1967-1968); "The Month in Free China"; F. C. Lu; and Fitch.
3. Mendel (1970), 78-79; Mendel (1974), 147; Martin M. C. Yang, 235; and Appleton (1970b), 39-43, 47, 53, 56.
4. Mendel (1970), 2, 81; and Long, 60.
5. Mendel (1970), 1, 28, 49, 93; Mendel (1974), 155, footnote 2; Kerr, 367; and Crissman, 22.
6. "Tuo-shao Jen 'Yü T'ui Pu Te'"; Mendel (1970), 49-51, 112; Mancall, 20-23; Wang Kuo-yüan; and "Cheng-fu Jen-shih Kuan-tao Shu-t'ung . . ."
7. Kerr, 385.
8. "Veterans Adjust to Taiwan Life"; and Durdin (1973).
9. Martin M. C. Yang, 453.
10. "Veterans Adjust to Taiwan Life"; Durdin (1973); and Mendel (1970), 58.
11. Mancall, 24-25; and Appleton (1970b), 43.
12. It has been said that Chiang K'ai-shek's son has been co-opting numerous young Taiwanese administrators in order to correct this imbalance. Indeed, the percentage of Taiwanese in important decision-making posts has been increasing. Still, there is a long way to go before the Taiwanese can feel that their people have general decision-making power.

    For example, of the 79 top Central Government officials listed in the Government Directory of the 1976 China Yearbook, only 13 are Taiwanese. (Ninety-two government officials are actually listed, but sources lack information on 13 of these.) In the 1972-1973 China Yearbook, the figures are 8 Taiwanese out of 75, with information lacking for 14. In the 1967-1968 China Yearbook, the figures are 2 our of 54, with 15 unknown. This represents a considerable increase--from 3.7 percent to 11 percent to 16.5 percent.

    The picture appears better with regard to high positions in the provincial government. Although the figures for 1967-1968 have the Taiwanese dramatically outnumbered, in 1973 the Taiwanese were maintaining a slight numerical edge.

    For an indication of how far behind in representation in the KMT-sponsored national government the Taiwanese began, note that of the original 2,490 delegates representing terri-

247

torial units (as opposed to certain occupational groups and
women's groups) to be chosen for the National Assembly in
1947, only 19 were to be Taiwanese. The figures for the
Control Yuan, scheduled to be chosen in 1948, were 5 out of
233. For information on the numbers of delegates actually
chosen and the status of these delegates today, see the
discussion below of the Central Government.

In terms of ordinary civil servants, according to information published by Sheldon Appleton in 1970 (see citation
below), in the national government, most of the personnel
were mainlanders. On lower levels, almost 40 percent of
Taiwan's provincial, county, and city government employees,
including school officials and employees of government-
operated business enterprises, were mainlanders.

Sources for this footnote are China Yearbook (1967-
1968), 12, 90, 162, 444-623, 710-712; China Yearbook (1972-
1973), 544-729, 842-846; China Yearbook (1976), 73, 530-668,
745-749; Fu Ch'i-hsüeh, 231-232; Chung-yang Jih-pao (Air
Mail Edition), May 30, 1972, June 8, 1972, November 16,
1973; Jacobs (1971); Jacobs (1973); Sun Chia-ch'i; Mendel
(1970), 93-95; and Appleton (1970b), 42-43.

13. Mendel (1970), 32-37; and Kerr, 254-310.
14. By 1974 it had become popular on Taiwan to argue that the social
     separation between mainlanders and Taiwanese was slowly
     disappearing or that, indeed, it had already disappeared.
     The 1971-1972 international challenges to Taiwan's independ-
     ence were cited as an important cause of this increasing
     unity. (Interviews in Taiwan, summer, 1974; and statement
     by Minister Ch'en Tai-chu of the Nationalist Embassy, quoted
     in Mendel [1974], 154.) This argument is supported by the
     author's own impressions, after spending the summer of 1974
     on Taiwan. Sheldon Appleton, however, offers evidence to the
     contrary, leaving the author unable to arrive at a conclusion
     in this matter. See Appleton (1970b), 39-44, 56; Appleton
     (1973), 795; and Appleton (1974), 55.
15. Pro-Taiwanese claim that under Japan, Taiwan was modernized,
     in both material and educational terms, to a level far above
     that attained by the mainland provinces. Moreover, whatever
     the Taiwanese may have previously thought of the Japanese,
     They now tend to look back on their rule with respect, if
     not nostalgia. In contrast, however, because of continued
     Japanese aggression toward China, especially because of the
     behavior of the Japanese on the mainland during World War
     II and perhaps even because the Japanese upset the Sinocentric
     universe of the Chinese by violently destroying the China-
     as-big-brother/Japan-as-little-brother relationship of the
     premodern Far East, the Japanese are feared and detested by

248

most mainlanders on Taiwan today. The idea that a Chinese from Taiwan may say something good about Japanese colonial policy or that he may prefer to use Japanese rather than Mandarin as his language of literary expression drives the mainlanders crazy. On these points, see Mendel (1970), 16-28, 40, 42, 56, 62, 64-89; Tardio, 170-180; Crissman, 15; and "I-t'ang Ch'i K'o Yung Jih-yü Fa-yen!" The dichotomy between mainlanders and Taiwanese, with respect to their opinions concerning the Japanese, has carried over into Taiwan's younger generations, as attested to in Appleton (1973), 759, footnote 12; and in Appleton (1974), 55.

16. Kerr, 114-117, 419; Tardio, 109-143, 163-204; Mendel (1970), 40, 52, 57, 62, 64-88, 106; Martin M. C. Yang, 15; Mancall, 24; and "Yang Chin-hu Ch'u-ch'i Chih-sheng Ch'en Wu-chang."

17. Actually, before they left the mainland, the KMT supporters were dedicated to overthrowing ancient tradition in order to establish a modern republican nation. Indeed, many of these same mainlanders were quite iconoclastic before they came to Taiwan. See Mancall, 28.

18. Mendel (1970), 127. Mendel notes that under the Japanese, the Taiwanese had had "a ten-year experience with the mechanics of local elections" before the Nationalists came to the island. The Chinese did not bring local self-government to Taiwan. They only expanded the preexisting system. Even given this expansion, Mendel quotes the following: "The Japanese police did not interfere in our city elections, and there was no dominant party like the KMT today. We Formosan candidates were treated more fairly by the prewar Japanese parties than the mainlander Chinese KMT leader treat us now."

19. Huang Fu-tai, 15.

20. One method used to gather mainland votes is to rely on the influence of traditional "associations of fellow provincials" (t'ung-hsiang hui). These associations have long served to bring together Chinese from the same province or smaller area who are living together in a faraway place.

21. Also see Hsia Tsung-han, 66; and "Hsüan-chü Chien-t'ao Tsuo-t'an-hui," 29.

22. "Chung-li Liang-hsiung Chiao-chu Shih-chang Pao-tsuo."

23. On how the lines of power run and why Chiang K'ai-shek's son has become so powerful, see Sun Chia-ch'i; and Mendel (1970), 95.

24. Mendel (1970), 84; and Mancall, 5-17.

25. Signs saying "Don't forget what happened at Chü" (Wu Wang Tsai Chü) are all over Taiwan.

26. Sources for the KMT's history and ideology are listed in footnote 2 above.

27. The China Reader: Republican China, 89; Isaacs, 103-104;

Mendel (1970), 92; China Yearbook (1976), 71-72; and Chung-
yang Jih-pao (Air Mail Edition), November 12-16, 1973.
28. China Yearbook (1967-1968), 114.
29. China Yearbook (1967-1968), 119, 137; and China Yearbook
(1972-1973), 42-43.
30. China Yearbook (1976), 87-88, 101, 114.
31. China Yearbook (1967-1968), 180; and China Yearbook (1972-
1973), 125-126.
32. Chuan-chi, II, 2535.
33. China Yearbook (1972-1973), 10, 144, 181, 748; and Chung-
yang Jih-pao (Air Mail Edition), December 21-22, 30, 1969,
December 23-27, 1972, February 16, 1973, December 21, 1975.
34. See, for example, China Yearbook (1967-1968), 2-3.
35. China Yearbook (1967-1968), 2-3, 7-11, 13, 331-377, 714-
718.
36. Chung-yang Jih-pao (Air Mail Edition), April 15, 1971. Of
course, since the 1971-1972 advent of "ping-pong" diplomacy,
U.S. President Nixon's visit to mainland China, the expulsion of Taiwan's government from the United Nations, and the
mass withdrawl of formal diplomatic recognition from Taiwan's
government, this task of legitimization through proof of
international recognition has become much more difficult.
That Taiwan's government is still diligently discovering and
reporting evidence of international recognition for itself,
however, can be seen by reading the first page of the following editions of Chung-yang Jih-pao (Air Mail Edition):
March 27, 28, 29, April 23, 28, 1974.
37. China Yearbook (1967-1968), 633-635.
38. Fu Ch'i-hsüeh, 362-373, 381-411.
39. For example, see "T'ai-wan Sheng Ko Hsien Hsiang Chen . . . ,"
Articles 37, 39.
40. Liu Yen-fu, 33-34. Liu's statements "first plan for the
existence of the nation" and "just at this time of desperate
need to unify strength . . . to increase democracy and promote
self-government means for the local area to splinter its
strength" stand in great contrast to the following statement
by a representative of Ta-hsüeh Tsa-chih, a liberal magazine
now popular on Taiwan: "At the present time, the first thing
we must wrest forth is our existence. But existence, above
all, depends on unity. We believe the utility of democratic
politics is not only to urge forward true and substantial
unity, but is the correct line for the furture development of
the nation." ("Hsüan-chü Chien-t'ao Tsuo-t'an-hui," 33.)
41. China Yearbook (1967-1968), 170. Also see "T'ai-wan Sheng
I-hui Tsu-chih Kuei-ch'eng," Article 1; and "T'ai-wan Sheng
Ko Hsien Shih Shih-shih . . . ," Article 1.
42. China Yearbook (1975), 147. Also see "T'ai-wan Sheng I-

hui Tsu-chih Kuei-ch'eng," Article 3.

43. See "T'ai-wan Sheng I-hui Tsu-chih Kuei-ch'eng," Articles
    3, 29-31.

44. See "T'ai-wan Sheng Ko Hsien Shih Shih-shih . . . ," Articles
    17, 20, 21, 25, and Chapter 6; and "T'ai-wan Sheng Ko Hsien
    Shih Ts'un Li Min . . . ," Chapter 3, especially Articles
    2-5.

45. "T'ai-wan Sheng Ko Hsien Shih Shih-shih . . . ," Article 41.

46. China Yearbook (1967-1968), 634.

47. Although this author fears to footnote his sources with regard
    to secret police activities on Taiwan, he does dare to foot-
    note Mendel, who has published much convincing evidence in
    this regard. See Mendel (1970), 51, 54, 88-121; and Mendel
    (1974), 148. Other evidence of secret police activities may
    be found in Kerr; Formosa Today; Sun Chia-ch'i; "T'ai-wan
    Ching-hsüan-te Mi-mi Wen-chien"; and Fessler.

48. Indeed, one might contend that as long as such an atmosphere
    of suspicion exists, the government may as well save the money
    needed to support a secret police establishment. The atmos-
    phere of suspicion itself will keep the population docile and
    frightened. As many sociologists have pointed out, the
    belief that something exists is just as important for human
    behavior--and sometimes more important--than the fact of the
    thing's existence. Sheldon Appleton agrees with this observa-
    tion as it relates to Taiwan. See Appleton (1970a), 911
    and footnote 1.

49. For these and other examples, see articles in Ti-fang Tzu-chih,
    Number 60-61 (April 19, 1963), 15-30. The widespread use
    of Taiwan's closely controlled press to support KMT candidates
    and disparage the opposition was continuing as late as 1972, as
    indicated in "Hsüan-chü Chien-t'ao Tsuo-t'an-hui," 18, 24,
    27; and "Taiwan Warns Candidates on Mudslinging."

50. Hsia Tsung-han, 66. Some informants contended that KMT
    support is not always automatic: "You do not really get
    them all, often only half. Others are not interested.
    It is possible that a party member will receive an instruc-
    tion, but though he will vote as he should, his wife will
    vote as to cancel his vote."

51. Crissman, 19, 33, 43.

52. Also see Gallin (1968), 387; and Crissman, 33.

53. "Man-t'an Cheng-chih yü Tao-te."

54. "T'ai-chung Shih Tang-pu . . ."; and Chang Tsuo-chin.

55. For indications that the KMT has continued practicing these
    types of election-controlling activities, at least through
    the period of 1972, see "Hsüan-chü Chien-t'ao Tsuo-t'an-hui."

56. In relation to this election, see "T'ao-hsien Fu-i-chang
    Hsüan-chü . . ."; and "T'ao-hsien Hsia-chieh Cheng-fu-i-

251

chang Hsüan-chü . . ." In relation to attempting to control elections in general, see "I Te Wei Hsien."

57. Sun I-ch'i.
58. Also see Hsiang Chün.
59. For point-by-point documentation of this analysis concerning the KMT's role as mediator between Taiwanese electoral factions, as well as for extensive explanatory footnotes, see Lerman (1976)—an earlier version of this section.
60. The three major sources of this concept of Chinese political psychology are Pye; Solomon (1969); and Solomon (1971), especially 28-153.
61. Jordan presented these ideas at an April 26-29, 1968, meeting of field researchers in Taichung, Taiwan. Note that more like Pye, and less like Solomon, Jordan presented his ideas only as speculative hypotheses, yet to be tested and refined.
62. This description of DeGlopper's ideas is based on his presentation at an April 26-29, 1968, meeting of field researchers in Taichung, Taiwan.
63. Solomon (1969), 302-303.
64. Solomon (1969), 305-306.
65. For example, see Pye, 188-193.
66. The Statement in parentheses stems from the author's extension of DeGlopper's analysis. It should not be attributed to DeGlopper.
67. The discussion beginning "If the party has publicly lost face" and concluding "if one does feel shamed" is the author's extension of DeGlopper's analysis. It should not be attributed to DeGlopper.
68. The statement in parentheses stems from the author's extension of DeGlopper's analysis. It should not be attributed to DeGlopper.
69. For an interesting discussion of why it is important to reach a compromise within which everyone's face is saved, see Gallin (1966a), 267-269.
70. Except where noted (footnotes 66-68), this discussion is based on DeGlopper's presentation at an April 26-29, 1968, meeting of field researchers in Taichung, Taiwan.
71. The discussion in the latter six paragraphs combines conclusions from the author's 1966-1968 Taiwan research with those of DeGlopper's presentation.
72. "Hsin-chu Hsien-chang . . ."
73. Pao Ch'ing-chiu, 37.
74. Also see Crissman, 43.
75. For other examples of censorship, see "T'ai-wan Sheng Hsin-chu Hsien . . ."; and "T'ai-wan Sheng T'ai-pei Shih . . ." Censorship was still a practice in 1972, as reported in "Taiwan Warns Candidates on Mudslinging."

76. "Hsüan-chü Chien-t'ao Tsuo-t'an-hui" and "Taiwan Warns Candidates on Mudslinging" indicate that the government, like the party, has continued to use such election-controlling activities.

77. Wu-ti. The formal law, which does not appear as restrictive as the cartoon implies, indicating that the government may be stretching the law in its attempts to control electoral behavior, reads as follows: "The political platforms expressed by candidates may not consist of the following: (1) oppose the constitution, (2) damage the national interest, (3) oppose the 'resist Communism, fight Russia' national policy, (4) use false evidence to calumniate the government or to bring charges against any group, (5) purposely slander other candidates." "T'ai-wan Sheng Fang-hai Hsüan-chü . . .," Article 20.

78. Kuo Tzu-ming.

79. Pao Ch'ing-chiu, 108. Also see Mu Jung-ts'ui (1967c), 18; and Crissman, 24.

80. See also Chuan-chi, I, 324, resolutions 3046 and 3047.

81. Mu Jung-ts'ui (1967c).

82. Lerman (1977), 1408, footnote 2.

83. Lerman (1977), 1409, footnote 5.

84. Pao Ch'ing-chiu, 67-68.

85. Mendel (1970), 65. Also see Martin M. C. Yang, 15; and Lerman (1977), 1410, footnote 10. Faith in the expertise of government officials may have been stimulated by Sun Yat-sen himself. See Tan, 129-130; and Sun Yat-sen, 158-159.

86. Pao Ch'ing-chiu, 100, 67, and 69, respectively. Continuity is apparent between the distress of current KMT government officials and Sun Yat-sen's own attempts to free government experts from the hands of ill-informed laypeople. Sun hoped to alleviate the problem by dividing political power into sovereign rights (ch'üan), to be exercised by the mass of ordinary citizens, and administrative capability (neng), to be exercised by government experts. Such a division, Sun thought, would permit the mass of citizens to maintain control over the government's basic policies while permitting the government experts to implement these policies without undue interference from the nonexpert masses. See Tan, 129-130; and Sun Yat-sen, 158-159. Note that although such a model is still to be successfully instituted in Taiwan or China, the British appear to have been behaving in accordance with its precepts for years. See Beer, 91-102; Eckstein, 157-161; and Ike, 19.

87. Pao Ch'ing-chiu, 69. The confusion of government officials caused, on the one hand, by their textbook learning that democracy aids in unifying a nation (thus serving to bring it

wealth and power), but, on the other hand, by their actual experiencing the apparently divisive results of election campaigns is reflected in a <u>New York Times</u> article describing government officials attempting to shape the 1972 elections according to their textbook ideal: "Government officials say that a primary purpose of holding the election is to promote national unity and that any use of invective that is likely to breed bitterness and divisiveness, is deplorable." ("Taiwan Warns Candidates on Mudslinging.") That elections are supposed to "unite the population" is also argued by Tao Pai-chuan in "Nationalist Aide Asks First Elections on Taiwan." For further documentation of the points to be made in this section with regard to the attitudes of provincial government officials, see also footnotes 15 and 16 above.

88. The attitudes being described here are much the same as those that informed the KMT's concepts regarding the necessity for a period of political tutelage before the institution of constitutional government in China. According to the KMT's own interpretation, however, the period of political tutelage for China ended with the implementation of the 1946 constitution. Why these attitudes continue to result in effective restraints on the people and their representatives, even after the institution of constitutional government, has been explained on pages 23-28 above. For this footnote, see Fairbank (1971), 216; Tan, 118; and <u>China Yearbook</u> (1972-1973), 93, 137, 139, 145.

89. Pao Ch'ing-chiu, 107; and Liu Yen-fu, 34. If Pye and Solomon are correct (see pages 38-50 above), this faith in governmental authority may also result from Chinese political psychology.

90. Pao Ch'ing-chiu, 69 (see also 50-51, 68). Additionally, see Lerman (1972), 115, footnote 152.

91. Pao Ch'ing-chiu, 69. Similarly, measures must be taken with regard to political abuse of the Assembly's interpellation power: "Although the Provincial Assembly has not had such an obvious example, but . . . ," Pao Ch'ing-chiu, 74. For more concerning "preventing the calamity that has not yet happened," see Pao Ch'ing-chiu, 52, 99; Chien Ho; Lerman (1972), 118, footnote 155; and "I-t'ang Ch'i K'o Yung Jih-yü Fa-yen!" For additional mainlander plans to improve the political system, see Yang I-feng, 177-179; and Ch'en Li-fu (1971b), 14.

92. Agriculture and Forestry, Finance, Transportation, Civil Affairs, Reconstruction, and Education.

93. <u>Chuan-chi</u>, II, 2520-2586.

94. This statement was made by a former speaker of the Assembly while he was chairing a meeting. <u>Chuan-chi</u>, II, 2411.

95. Note that Hsieh (Tung-min) was finally allowed to retire,

but only to be given other middleman positions: first Taiwanese governor ever to be appointed for Taiwan Province
(1972-1978) and Vice-President of the Republic of China
(1978-   ). See Chung-yang Jih-pao (Air Mail Edition), May
30, 1972, and May 21, 1978.

96. Note that statistical analysis tends to confirm the strong
supportive role of the mainlander assemblymen. See Lerman
(1972), 125-127.

97. "T'ai-wan Sheng San-chieh Sheng I-yüan . . .," 20.

98. "Wang Sung Ch'iung-ying . . ."

99. "Wang Sung Ch'iung-ying . . ."

100. "Wang Sung Ch'iung-ying . . ."

101. Statistical evidence supports this conclusion. See Lerman
(1972), 135-136.

102. For further details concerning supportive non-KMT assemblymen,
see Lerman (1972), 139-140.

103. With regard to the size of the KMT's vote, see Mendel (1970),
99, 101-104, 109, 111; and Crissman, 34. Crissman offers
evidence to support the author's informants in the following
passage: "The dual society found in the large Taiwanese cities
where mainlanders are dominant economically, socially, and
politically, does not extend into rural areas such as south-
western Changhua, where there are very few mainlanders.
Taiwanese peasants are of course aware that ultimate authority
on the island rests with the Nationalist Army and the Taiwan
Garrison Command and that their Provincial Assembly has no
power to pass laws or set budgets, but there is little overt
hostility to the Nationalist regime in the countryside.
The standard of living has risen considerably since local
control was consolidated and things settled down after 1950.
The Nationalists are generally given credit . . ." Crissman,
20.
    In terms of the geographical distribution of mainlanders
on Taiwan, also see Appleton (1970b), 39-42. That students,
among others, do not credit the government with Taiwan's economic success is noted in Appleton (1974), 60; and Mendel
(1974), 147; as well as in sources quoted in footnote 15 above.
Further evidence on the concentration of antiparty votes in
the cities is offered in "A Curious Thing Is Happening in
Taiwan."

104. Mendel (1974), 148.

105. The expectation of success or failure as a general factor in
determining the willingness of individuals to participate in
a given activity is applied to political passivity in Taiwan
by Appleton (1974), 59. The importance of the KMT's "economic
lure" is stressed by Mendel (1974), 147, as well as by Appleton
(1974), 59. Local political factions and the KMT's patronage

255

are discussed in Parts II and III below.

106. Note that according to Douglas Mendel, the revolutionary
potential of the Taiwanese is so low that "the situation"
would have to be extremely "different" to motivate them to
take revolutionary action. See Mendel (1970), 244-245.
This assessment is supported by Mendel (1974), 148-149, 154;
Appleton (1970a), 910-923; Appleton (1970b), 53-59; and by
ex-CIA agent William M. Bueler and "other specialists on
China," as reported by Halloran.

Appleton's 1972-1973 findings, however, raise the possibility that a slow growth in the revolutionary potential of
students on Taiwan is indeed under way. According to Appleton,
this growth is being nourished by Western influences, which
are promoting the popularization of democratic--in addition
to already popularized acquisitive--values. See Appleton
(1973), especially 755-760; and Appleton (1974), 52-62.

Moreover, in light of the early 1970's downturn in the
KMT's fortunes, both Bueler and Appleton (1974), 59, list
a number of circumstances that might compel Taiwanese revolutionary activity, despite how distasteful such activity
may be for them. For Mendel, (1974), 154, however, this
remains a very remote possibility.

Finally, Appleton, in agreement with the assertion of
the author's informant, notes that whatever current attitudes
may be, "they are certainly subject to rapid change under
the pressure of dramatic events." (1974), 57.

107. Appleton (1970a), 911; Appleton (1970b), 38; and Appleton
(1974), 52.

108. According to Mendel, the Formosans clearly prefer freedom
"in theory." Despite his having to rely on the Japanese
and English languages--probably biasing his sample against
the KMT--and having to collect much of his sample in sur-
reptitious and unorthodox ways, his is a most convincing
attempt to obtain a general sample of Taiwanese opinion on
politically sensitive subjects. See Mendel (1970), 4-8,
96-97, 107-111; and Mendel (1974), 148-149. Bueler (see
Halloran), using similar techniques, independently came to
the same conclusion.

109. For example, Chuan-chi, II, 2536.

110. Lerman (1972), 470-491.

111. This is where Mendel places most of the Taiwanese.

112. For a balanced, if relatively out-of-date, view of the conflict in Taiwanese minds between political versus cultural and
political independence, see Meisner.

113. Concerning the nonencouragement of critical and creative
thinking, see Mendel (1970), 47-52; Tardio, 92-95, 205-
302; and Appleton (1970a), 911.

114. In this regard, besides what has already been written above concerning factions, Mendel notes "Despite differences of emphasis and attitude among segments of Formosans described below, and the socio-economic divisions separating them, all appeared to share an overriding sense of political frustration against mainlander rule. The common bond may be more negative than positive, however, as is natural in anti-colonial nationalism." Mendel (1970), 97.

115. Mendel argues that opinions from this portion of the spectrum may well cloak demands for independence. Mendel (1970), 86, 96.

116. Chuan-chi, II, 2574.

117. Chuan-chi, II, 2534. See also page 2579. This "antiexpert" opinion is shared by many of the foreign authors mentioned in footnote 16 above. For example, Felix Tardio writes as follows: "Any local adaptations in their buildings made by the Taiwan natives over the years to deal with sun, wind, rain, or humidity, as well as their use of local materials and method have been completely ignored and not even attempted to be understood by the mainland Chinese Architects with their 'obviously-superior' knowledge of green tiled roofs and 2,000 year-old twisting dragons.

    "The Chinese Nationalists brought with them, . . . 3-- Little or no understanding of method or efficient organization, 4--Out-dated systems of Architecture, education, Art, and Design, 5--A great number of ambitious men of government and military rank, who in general understood little of Art, Design, Culture, or Architecture, and with the driving desire to gain personal prestige, and to scheme, cut throats and compromise all values, 6--The sentimentality--and misconception--that Architecture could only be Old Chinese styles of the past from which they were free to pick, pluck, and choose, 7--No craftsmen or men who knew how to build or make things well, 8-- No Artists or men of artistic talent or feeling, 9--No understanding of the Physical Environment, 10--American Aid." Tardio, 196-197.

118. Even the contention that the people are too uneducated for democracy was denied by one nonparty assemblyman.

119. T'ai-wan Sheng I-hui Ti-san-chieh Ti-pa-tz'u Ta-hui I-yüan Chih-hsün . . ., 286.

120. Chuan-chi, II, 2525-2526. Also page 2551; and T'ai-wan Sheng I-hui Ti-san-chieh Ti-pa-tz'u Ta-hui I-yüan Chih-hsün . . ., 124. Liu Yen-fu argues that the Taiwan Provincial Assembly is indeed not a representative of the will of the people because (a) in actual fact, many assemblymen work for their own selfish will and not for the will of the people, and (b)

according to the Chinese constitution, the will of the people
is expressed directly by the people over the five branches of
government through their political powers of election, recall,
initiation, and referendum. Each one of these branches
exercises one of the five governmental functions of administration. legislation, adjudication, examination, and inspection, under the direction of the will of the people. These
functions are "equal within a cooperative division of labor."
No one branch has more authority than any other branch.
They are all simply servants of the people in their differing
areas. Thus, it is silly to speak of the Assembly with its
legislative function as somehow expressing the will of the
people more than any other branch. Liu Yen-fu, 43-44.

121. Chuan-chi, II, 2551-2552.
122. T'ai-wan Sheng I-hui Ti-san-chieh Ti-pa-tz'u Ta-hui I-yüan
     Chih-hsün . . ., 239. Statistical analysis supports the
     conclusion that the nonparty assemblymen form a core of oppo-
     sition within the Assembly. In terms of twenty-two out of
     twenty-four indicators, the nonparty assemblymen had higher
     opposition ratings than the average assemblymen. See Lerman
     (1972), 161-162.
123. This would be the position of Mendel and Bueler.
124. Oka.
125. Durdin (1971). Acquaintances and letters arriving from Taiwan
     at the time supported these reports. Also see Appleton (1973),
     755-760; and Appleton (1974), 52-62.
126. Jacobs (1973), 111; Jacobs (1974), 22-23; Mendel (1974),
     151-155; "A Curious Thing Is Happening in Taiwan;" and articles
     in The New York Times between October 11, 1971, and October
     27, 1973.
127. Martin M. C. Yang, 486.
128. "Yang Chin-hu Ch'u-ch'i Chih-sheng Ch'en Wu-chang."
129. Campaign leaflet for Hsieh A-shu.
130. Chuan-chi, II, 2569.
131. Chuan-chi, II, 2574.
132. T'ai-wan Sheng I-hui Ti-san-chieh Ti-pa-tz'u Ta-hui I-yüan
     Chih-hsün . . ., 189. Although this is an admittedly prej-
     udiced category, interview and other evidence suggests that
     it may indeed be an important area of KMT strength. See, for
     example, Mendel (1974), 147.
133. "Yang Chin-hu Ch'u-ch'i Chih-sheng Ch'en Wu-chang."
134. For a history of the KMT's suppression of the attempt to form
     an opposition party, see Mancall, 38; and Israel, 61-62. Also
     see Mendel (1970), 114-117. Part of the early 1970s KMT
     policy of accommodation with desires for more democracy has
     been a tendency to allow a slight increase in organized opposi-
     tion, as indicated in "Critics Form Bloc in Taipei Election"

and in two additional articles in <u>The New York Times</u>:
November 5, 1972, p. 20, and November 12, 1972, p. 9.
135. Hung Ch'un-mu.
136. Crissman, 18, 31-32.
137. Chao Chün-wu (1967a), 25.
138. Crissman, 35-36; and Gallin (1968), 368. Also see below,
pages 101-109, 133-172.
139. Ch'en Ming-t'ieh, 15.
140. Gallin (1968), 385.
141. Nicholas, 27, 44.
142. For the term primordial, see Scott (1972), 91. For corporate,
see Scott (1972), 91, 97; Landé, 104, 107, 109, 120; Nicholas,
28, 45; and Nathan, 38, 39, 42, 43. For ascriptive, see
Scott (1972), 91; and Nathan, 37. For collective, see Landé,
121. For categorical, see Scott (1972), 97. For trait, see
Landé, 121, 122. For the two definitions, see Landé, 121,
122.
143. For the following discussion on factions, the author has relied
primarily upon Landé, 104-105, 120-126. He has also consulted
Scott (1972), 91-97, 109-110; Nathan, 37-45; Nicholas, 27-29,
41-43, 45-46; and Crissman, 55.
144. On this point, for Taiwan, see Martin M. C. Yang, 436-437.
For patron-client relationships throughout the world, see
Scott (1972), 94; and Eric R. Wolf (1966a), 13.
145. Nathan, 39-40, and Crissman, 30, prefer to limit the definition to higher-level individuals.
146. Solomon (1969), 280.
147. Solomon (1969), 279, 284-285; DeGlopper; and interview with
Donald R. DeGlopper, February 10, 1968. Pasternak (1972),
152, notes the practice of "simply inventing common ancestors
to serve the purpose at hand." For evidence, Pasternak cites
Hsiao Kung-chuan, 352-354.
148. Crissman, 30-31. In terms of factions in Changhua County,
also see Gallin (1968), 391, 395. For Tainan County, see
Jordan, 9, 21-22, 136. In more general terms, see Nicholas,
26.
149. Gallin (1968), 395-396.
150. Lawrence W. Crissman at an April 26-29, 1968, meeting of
field researchers in Taichung, Taiwan.
151. Gallin (1968), 390.
152. Gallin (1967), 81. Also see Martin M. C. Yang, 400-401.
153. Martin M. C. Yang, 458, 464-465. Also see Lerman (1972),
201-202, footnote 22.
154. "Hsin-ying Ko-chia Yin-hang . . ."
155. Crissman, 35-36. "Hsin-ying Ko-chia Yin-hang . . ." reports
similar practices in Tainan County. Based on research in
Changhua County, Gallin notes that a "few packs of cigarettes

or some bath towels and soap" may substitute for cash in the vote-buying transaction. See Gallin (1968), 386.

156. Lockard, 220.
157. Lawrence W. Crissman at an April 26-29, 1968, meeting of field researchers in Taichung, Taiwan.
158. For examples, see "Sheng I-t'an Lao-chiang Li Chien-ho . . ." and Pai Chün.
159. Interview with Stephen Feuchtwang, February 21, 1968.
160. Lawrence W. Crissman at an April 26-29, 1968, meeting of field researchers in Taichung, Taiwan; and Crissman, 17-18, 31.
161. See pages 106-107 above; and Crissman, 8, 30, 35, 37-38, 42, 47, 53-54, 56-57.
162. Interview with Lawrence W. Crissman, March 22, 1968. Also Crissman, 30.
163. Interview with Lawrence W. Crissman, March 22, 1968.
164. Lawrence W. Crissman and others at an April 26-29, 1968, meeting of field researchers in Taichung, Taiwan.
165. Gallin (1968), 395.
166. Responsibilities of the Farmers' Association include the transportation, selling, storage, and finishing work necessary for farm products; the buying up and selling to the farmers of farm tools and other necessities of farm life; the managing of the market for selling crops; farm and crop insurance; irrigation; welfare and emergency aid; mediation in local disputes; and credit and banking facilities. T'aiwan Sheng Ti-fang Tzu-chih Chih-yao, 897, 898.
      Responsibilities of the township and rural district halls (also county-subordinate city halls) include matters of establishing, running, guiding, and overseeing of primary and social education; matters of sanitation and health; matters of transportation, irrigation, farming and forestry, and fishing and animal raising; matters of public facilities and public enterprises; rural district, township, or county-subordinate city cooperative enterprises; guidance in agricultural and industrial technology; fiscal matters of the rural district, township, or county-subordinate city; and matters of public welfare, charitable institutions, and disaster prevention. (Fu Ch'i-hsüeh, 398.)
167. Interview with Lawrence W. Crissman, March 22, 1968.
168. All but the mayor of Taipei since July 1, 1967. See Chuanchi, II, 2581.
169. Chuan-chi, I, 34, 109.
170. See page 117 above.
171. For example, see Lerman (1972), 155, 476-483.
172. "Chiang-tzu-ts'ui Chü-min Tai-piao . . ." and "Chiang-tzuts'ui Tu-shih Chi-hua . . ."

173. "Kuo Yü-hsin . . ."
174. "Sheng I-t'an Lao-chiang Li Chien-ho . . ."
175. Newsweek, June 9, 1969, 78.
176. Arthur P. Wolf at an April 26-29, 1968, meeting of field
researchers in Taichung, Taiwan. In regard to identification,
also see Crissman, 27.
177. Confucian Analects, Bk. XV, Ch. XIX. Translation from Mathews,
1096.
178. Arthur P. Wolf at an April 26-29, 1968, meeting of field
researchers in Taichung, Taiwan.
179. Lawrence W. Crissman at an April 26-29, 1968, meeting of
field researchers in Taichung, Taiwan.
180. Lawrence W. Crissman at an April 26-29, 1968, meeting of field
researchers in Taichung, Taiwan; Crissman, 26; Martin M. C.
Yang, 354, 359, 485-487; and Gallin (1968), 387-388.
181. Interview with Pao Ch'ing-chiu, January 15, 1968. Note that
the hypotheses that the Chinese have a strong need for identification with groups and a strong need for prestige are supported by Lucian Pye's speculations: "A host of Chinese
behavior characteristics, ranging from their intense concern
for form, ritual, and etiquette to their deep anxieties about
social and situational ambiguity and uncertainty, their sensi-
tivity to status issues, their dread of social confusion and
political disorder, and their constant search for belonging,
for identification with groups, and for the security of success and power--all fit together in a common pattern and in
varying degrees are related to the control of aggression,"
Pye, 33.
182. Lerman (1977), 1416, footnotes 35-36.
183. "Chüeh Pu Jung Chu 'Hsüan' Hai Kung."
184. Interview with Lawrence W. Crissman, March 22, 1968. Also
see pages 106-107, 112-113, and 116-117 above.
185. Chuan-chi, I, 465-468.
186. Ch'en Ch'i-fu et al.
187. "Pu Ts'uo Yüan-tzu T'ang . . ." Also see Tsung Hsin et al.
188. "Chia Hsien I-yüan Hsüan-chü . . ."
189. "Chia Hsien I-yüan Hsüan-chü . . ."
190. Presentations of Donald R. DeGlopper and Lawrence W. Crissman
at an April 26-29, 1968, meeting of field researchers in
Taichung, Taiwan, and additional interview with DeGlopper,
February 10, 1968. Also see stories in Lien-ho Pao, January
5 and 20, 1968 (Taichung edition); January 5, 1968 (Kao-hsiung);
January 7, 1968 (Taipei County and Hua-lien); March 3, 1968
(general edition); all on local news page 7.
191. Chao Chün-wu (1967c), 25.
192. Ho Fan (1967a).

261

193. Lerman (1972), 249-250; and Business Directory of Taiwan.
194. See above, footnotes 12 and 126.
195. This would be the case especially for those who are willing to solidify KMT support among their followers.
196. Reports at an April 26-29, 1968, meeting of field researchers in Taichung, Taiwan. In this regard, also see Mendel (1970), 95.
197. Ning K'o.
198. See Martin M. C. Yang, 363-422; and Crissman, 4, 27-29.
199. Large lineages were not universal on Taiwan, and, traditionally, other social relationships were also important for the security system of many individuals. For example, Jordan, 12-20, 104-114, introduces the importance of surname groups and god-worshipping groups in southern Taiwan. Martin M. C. Yang, 420-424, 437-444, notes the importance of landlord-tenant relationships alongside of and/or in combination with lineage relationships in many areas of traditional Taiwan. Pasternak (1969), 551-561; and Pasternak (1972) argue that under given conditions security was guaranteed by localized associations that crosscut kin groups and/or by fictive descent groups.
    That large lineages did offer security in many of Taiwan's communities is indicated by Martin M. C. Yang, 420-424, 437-444; Fried (1973), 365-366; Rohsenow, 477; Margery Wolf, 11; and Gallin (1968), 379.
200. Interview with Lawrence W. Crissman, March 22, 1968. Election results in Lien-ho Pao, January 22, 1968, indicate that 2,000 to 4,000 votes are often sufficient to elect one to local office.
201. Gallin (1968), 380-381; Pasternak (1969), 560; and Fried (1973), 365-366.
202. Gallin (1968), 387. The bracketed date "1950" has been substituted for Gallin's original date of 1959. J. Bruce Jacobs (1975), 232, calls attention to the necessity to change this date. The need for correction is confirmed by T'ai-wan Sheng Ti-fang Tzu-chih Chih-yao, 580.
203. Gallin (1968), 387-388.
204. Gallin (1968), 386.
205. Lerman (1977), 1415, footnote 32.
206. Lerman (1977), 1416, footnote 34.
207. Gallin (1968), 394.
208. Gallin (1968), 394.
209. Gallin (1968), 392-393, 397. See also Crissman, 27-28. The bracketed word "lineage" has been substituted for Gallin's original word, "clan."
210. See pages 104-105 above; and Jacobs (1976), 80-83.

211. Also see Crissman, 27.
212. Nicholas, 29.
213. Nicholas, 29.
214. Gallin (1968), 380, 396.
215. Gallin (1968), 380-381.
216. Birth control programs have often had to overcome the feel-
     ing among populations that the more children one has, the
     more help there would be on the farm, especially in old age.
     According to the above analysis, besides specific economic
     help on the farm, many children can also hold out the promise
     of a web of profitable ch'in-ch'i relationships.
217. Fried (1953), 218-219, as well as 123, 124, and 220-222.
     Indeed, the central importance of nonkin relationships at
     all levels of traditional and modern Chinese society is the
     main theme of the entire book. Fried also discusses this
     theme in his 1973 article, page 369. More narrowly, Lucian
     W. Pye notes that "although the family has traditionally been
     the prime unit of social organization, most Chinese families
     have not had adequate resources to meet crisis situations,
     and it has been commonly recognized that when 'times are hard'
     and 'conditions uncertain,' everyone will have to look out-
     side the family for possible means of help. In traditional
     China, disorder and natural calamities always brought a rise
     in memberships of secret societies, bandit bands, and other
     forms of fraternal and quasi-political association." Pye,
     180.
218. Pasternak (1969), 558. See also Pasternak (1972), 141.
219. Quotations taken from Jordan, 16-18. Jordan's characteriza-
     tion is supported by Pasternak (1969), 553-555, 557-558,
     561; and Pasternak (1972), 141, 146, 151-152.
220. Pasternak (1969), 554-555, 559; and Pasternak (1972), 139-
     140, 142-147, 149, 152, 159.
221. Jordan, 17-18; and Fried (1973), 364.
222. Jordan, 18; and Pasternak (1969), 558-559.
223. Jordan, 19; Pasternak (1969), 559; and Pasternak (1972),
     75-77, 140, 144-145, 150-153.
224. Jordan, 18-21; and Crissman, 4, 27-28.
225. Pasternak (1969), 559; and Pasternak (1972), 19, 75-77, 139-
     140, 144-145, 150-153.
226. Fried (1973), 363.
227. For the use of the term "patrilineal ideology," see Pasternak
     (1969), 560; and Pasternak (1972), 146. For definitions of
     lineage, see Pasternak (1969), 556; and Fried (1973), 362.
228. Pasternak (1969), 554; and Pasternak (1972), 18-19, 146-149.
229. Pasternak (1969), 555. Here Pasternak is quoting from
     Marshall D. Sahlins, 1961, "The Segmentary Lineage: An Organ-
     ization of Predatory Expansion," American Anthropologist,
     63, p. 326, to describe the general condition he illustrates

in his discussion of the Taiwanese village of Chung-she.
230. Pasternak (1969), 555-556, 561. See also Pasternak (1972), 140, 148, 153, 159; and Eric R. Wolf (1966a), 4-5. Concern with limiting access to lineage estates will also be displayed as sublineages limit access to their estates by other sublineages within their overall lineage. See Pasternak (1969), 556; and Pasternak (1972), 148, 153, 156.
231. Pasternak (1969), 555-556, 561.
232. Fried (1973), 365.
233. Pasternak (1969), 560; Pasternak (1972), 135-136, 146; Fried (1966), 293; and pages 133-139 above.
234. Crissman, 27-28; and Pasternak (1969), 560.
235. Fried (1973), 364, 366. For additional analysis of Taiwan's "boom in clan organization," see Fried (1966).
236. Nicholas, 27-29.
237. Pasternak (1969), 554-555, 559; and Pasternak (1972), 139-140, 142-147, 149, 152, 159.
238. Pasternak (1969), 558.
239. Pasternak (1969), 559; and Pasternak (1972), 26-36, 108-109, 137-146.
240. Pasternak (1969), 555-556, 561; and Fried (1973), 365.
241. Pasternak (1969), 560; Pasternak (1972), 135-136; 146; Fried (1966), 293; and pages 133-139 above.
242. Pasternak (1972), 108.
243. Gallin (1968), 395-396.
244. Gallin (1968), 381.
245. Gallin (1968), 380, 384-385.
246. Gallin (1968), 380. Also see Pasternak (1972), 7, 14-15, 91, 121, 124-125; and Martin M. C. Yang, 424.
247. Pasternak (1972), 100-108, 125.
248. Pasternak (1972), 95-103, 125.
249. Lawrence W. Crissman at an April 26-29, 1968, meeting of field researchers in Taichung, Taiwan. Also Crissman, 28, 52; and interview with Crissman, March 22, 1968.
250. Interview with Lawrence W. Crissman, March 22, 1968.
251. Donald R. DeGlopper at an April 26-29, 1968, meeting of field researchers in Taichung, Taiwan; Pasternak (1972), 103-105; and Crissman, 21, 23.
252. See Jacobs (1976), especially 83-84, 96.
253. Jacobs (1976), 84-86.
254. Jacobs (1976), 90.
255. Interviews with Lawrence W. Crissman, April 26-29, 1968, and March 22, 1968; and Crissman, 52-53.
256. For example, Chang Ping-cheng; T'ai-wan Sheng I-hui Ti-san-chieh Ti-pa-tz'u Ta-hui I-yüan Chih-hsün . . ., 179; and page 170 below, including footnote 279.
257. Interviews with Lawrence W. Crissman, April 26-29, 1968, and

March 22, 1968; and Crissman, 55-61.

258. Ch'en Ming-t'ieh, 15.
259. Chao Chün-wu (1967e), 25.
260. Jacobs (1976), 82.
261. The counties that contain large Hakka populations are T'ao-
yüan, where approximately one-half of the population is Hakka;
Miao-li with two-thirds Hakka; Hsin-chu with two thirds; Taichung with one-half; Hua-lien with one-half; and P'ing-tung
with one-half.
   Note that the Minnan Taiwanese are also divided by origin,
mainly into those with ancestors from Ch'üan-chou and those
with ancestors from Chang-chou. These divisions may also be
significant in Taiwan today, but the author has no evidence
that this is so.
262. Also see Chao Chün-wu (1967b), 26, and (1967g), 25.
263. For example, see Chao Chün-wu (1967f), 25.
264. Eric R. Wolf (1966a), 10, 12.
265. Pye, 103.
266. Pye, 172, 180-181.
267. Solomon (1969), 301.
268. James C. Scott unhesitatingly refers to the patron-client
relationship as a special case of a largely instrumental friendship. Referring to the Chinese case, Morton H. Fried identifies patron-client relationships by the Chinese term kan-ch'ing.
Fried would rather reserve the word friendship for those relationships that generally maintain "a tacit assumption of
equality." Eric R. Wolf appears to agree with Fried, noting
that "when instrumental friendship reaches a maximum point
of imbalance so that one partner is clearly superior to the
other in his capacity to grant goods and services, we approch
the critical point where friendships give way to the patron-
client tie." Wolf does allow, however, that Juilian A. Pitt-
Rivers' term "lop-sided friendship" is apt. See Scott (1972),
92; Fried (1953), 103; and Eric R. Wolf (1966a), 16.
269. Solomon (1969), 299-300.
270. See. for example, Gallin and Gallin, 96-97.
271. Lo Kuan-chung, 6.
272. For a discussion of ceremonial brotherhood groups in traditional Chinese society and on Taiwan today, see Gallin and
Gallin. For interesting notes on ceremonial brotherhoods
in traditional China, see Fried (1953), 61, 203-206. Concerning Taiwan specifically, also see Gallin (1966b), 172-
173.
273. Gallin and Gallin, 96; and Jacobs (1976), 83.
274. Gallin and Gallin, 91, and Gallin (1966), 172, encouraged
the author to add the bracketed qualifications to Feuchtwang's
description.

275. Interview with Stephen Feuchtwang, February 21, 1968.
276. Note that N was 30 years old at the time of the election, also quite young. T'ai-pei Hsien . . .
277. Interview with Stephen Feuchtwang, February 21, 1968.
278. Discussions with Lawrence W. Crissman, March 22, 1968, and with Donald R. DeGlopper, April 26-29, 1968.
279. Crissman, 56. Note that in this quotation, besides supporting the argument that brotherhoods are used to ameliorate the problem of status equals cooperating with one another, Crissman also contends that brotherhoods cannot include status nonequals and that countywide factions cannot have recognized overall leaders. Concerning these latter two contentions, the author must disagree with Crissman.

     That brotherhoods can include status nonequals is supported by Fried (1953), 205; Gallin and Gallin, 90, 92, 93-94; and by the translation from The Romance of the Three Kingdoms on page 166 above.

     That countywide factions may have recognized overall leaders is exemplified by the following articles: T'ang Yin-yü; Yen Chang-hsün (1967b); Chao Chün-wu (1967f), (1967g), (1967h); "Kao-hsiung Hsien-chang T'i-ming . . ."; "T'ai-chung Hsien-chang T'i-ming . . ."; and "T'ai-chung Hsien-chang Hsüan-chü . . ."

     Reports from Changhua County, from which Crissman takes his evidence, indicate agreement with Crissman that Changhua has no countywide factional system consisting of two or three "opposed networks of patron-client relationships . . . [with] recognized overall leaders." Changhua's four "factions" are indeed alliances of many much smaller, quite independent patron-client networks. See Chao Chün-wu (1967a), 26; and Shih T'u. The sources noted in the paragraph above, however, indicate that the factional systems of Chia-i, Miao-li, Kao-hsiung, and Taichung counties do include countywide patron-client networks with overall leaders.
280. Arthur P. Wolf, Lawrence W. Crissman, and Donald R. DeGlopper at an April 26-29, 1968, meeting of field researchers in Taichung, Taiwan. Also see Crissman, 36-37.
281. Arthur P. Wolf at an April 26-29, 1968, meeting of field researchers in Taichung, Taiwan. The presentations of DeGlopper and Jordan also provided evidence for this point.
282. Arthur P. Wolf, April 26-29, 1968, oral presentation.
283. Arthur P. Wolf, April 26-29, 1968, oral presentation.
284. Interview with Stephen Feuchtwang, February 21, 1968.
285. Arthur P. Wolf, April 26-29, 1968, oral presentation.
286. Lawrence W. Crissman at an April 26-29, 1968, meeting of field researchers in Taichung, Taiwan. Also Crissman, 36-37.

287. Mu Jung-ts'ui (1967b), 8.
288. Pao Ch'ing-chiu, 87-88. Also above pages 24-28, 90-96.
289. <u>T'ai-wan Sheng Ti-fang Tzu-chih Chih-yao</u>, 283.
290. To obtain further evidence concerning factions within the
      Provincial Assembly, data were gathered on (a) superior-
      subordinate relations between politicians within private
      business firms and within publicly owned firms and (b)
      cooperation between assemblymen in introducing joint resolu-
      tions for consideration by the Assembly. The superior-
      subordinate data did support the contention that the pre-
      vious faction leaders had maintained relationships with
      current members of the Assembly. The data, however, con-
      tradicted the contention that two factions existed within
      the Assembly during the later part (1966-1968) of its third
      term. Instead, both former faction leaders, one current
      faction leader, a number of allegedly current (1968) faction
      members, at least one independent assemblyman, and a number
      of former electoral officeholders of all sorts were found
      to be entangled in a web of connections. If the analysis
      is extended to relations that existed in the past, a number
      of other provincial assemblymen, including the other cur-
      rent faction leader, enter the web.
          The data on cooperation in introducing joint resolu-
      tions were used because the Provincial Assembly's votes
      are almost always unanimous and are rarely recorded and
      because of testimony that one of the manifestations of
      factional conflict was each faction's trying to sabotage
      the resolutions introduced by its opponents. This data
      also gave no support for the contention that factions were
      salient during the later part of the Assembly's third term.
          Despite nonsupport for the hypothesis that a Li fac-
      tion and a Hsü faction existed in the later part of the
      Provincial Assembly's third term, the data on cooperation
      in introducing joint resolutions do suggest the existence
      of a number of other groups. A listing of some of these
      groups follows, along with their average rates of coopera-
      tion between group members (in comparison with 1.75, the
      average rate of cooperation between any two assemblymen):
      I-lan County representatives, 2 individuals cooperating 5
      times; T'ao-yüan County representatives, 3 individuals
      cooperating on the average of 6 times per pair; Hsin-chu
      County, 2 individuals, 2 times, Changhua County, 5 indi-
      viduals, averaging 2.1 times per pair; Yün-lin County,
      4, 1.9; Chia-i, 4, 7.17; Chi-lung City, 2, 6; Taichung City,
      2, 3; aborigines' representatives, 3, 4.67; and represent-
      atives of small, out-of-the-way, backward counties, 3,
      2.67. Representatives of the remaining 10 counties and

267

cities had below-average rates of cooperation.

Mainlanders from areas from which no Taiwanese ethnic groups originated were above average, 4 individuals cooperating 2.5 times; Taiwanese who had lived on the mainland were below average, 7, 1.67. Mainlanders from areas from which no Taiwanese ethnic groups originated combined with Taiwanese who had lived on the mainland were also below average, 11, 1.67; but a selected group of "hard core" Taiwanese who had lived on the mainland were above average, 4, 2; and mainalnders from areas from which no Taiwanese ethnic groups originated combined with these "hard core" Taiwanese who had lived on the mainland were also above average, 8, 2.2.

Hakka assemblymen were above average, 8, 1.93; nonparty assemblymen were below average, 9, 0.89; even a "hard core" of nonparty assemblymen were below average, 6, 1.73. Committee chairman were above average, 6, 2.6; but of the committees, only the small Education Committee had an above-average rate, 6, 3.6. Interaction among women was below average, 10, 0.96; and no youth faction was evidenced, 14, 0.58.

For sources and more details concerning the substance of this footnote, see Lerman (1972), 322-334.

291. Winston Churchill, as quoted in Beer, 77. Beer is quoting from Report, Committee of Privileges, H. C. No. 118 (1946-47), Minutes of Evidence, p. 8.

292. Actually, many "developed" American state legislatures do not display this neat differentiation of roles. Nor is this differentiation displayed by the "classic" British parliamentary system. (See page 189 below.) Gabriel A. Almond, although more flexible than in his earlier work, still clearly feels that in order to develop into a political system with a high degree of capabilities, a relatively strict differentiation between the roles of lobbyist and legislator is essential. See Almond (1956), 36-37, 40-42; Almond (1960), 35-36, 40; and Almond and Powell, 90-91, 97, 105-109, 259, 261, 265, 271. On this point, also see The Emerging Nations . . ., 72, 87-90.

293. Mu Jung-ts'ui (1967a), 14, 15.

294. In order to obtain a less impressionistic picture of the relationship between the economic interests of provincial assemblymen and their behavior in the Assembly, the author gather together relevant statistics for analysis. Unfortunately, complete information on the economic interests of the assemblymen could not be obtained. Statistics on Assembly behavior were also incomplete. Therefore, the resulting statistical analysis can be taken only as additional impres-

268

sionistic evidence--evidence that supports the not surprising
conclusion that, in addition to other interests, the assemblymen do tend to protect their personal economic interests.
During the Assembly's third term (1963-1968), the following were primary among the personal interests of the assemblymen: banks, cooperatives, mining, chemicals and medicines,
insurance, textiles, sea products, forestry, trucking, travel
agencies, hotel, paper, port facilities, canning, food processing, bus companies, trading companies, construction, tires,
and tea. Sources for this footnote are reported in Lerman
(1972), 350-358.

295. Ying Chen-kuo.
296. Beer, 329-331.
297. Note that it is not apparent from the records that businessmen participated that much less than average members. Indeed,
the average attendance of assemblymen with more than one
business position outside the Assembly was 68.8 percent
of all regular meetings and 68.1 percent of all committee
meetings (in comparison to the average assemblyman's attendance of 66 percent of all regular meetings and 68.8 percent
of committee meetings). Records checked are for the third-
term Assembly's Eighth Session, November 14, 1966-March 3,
1967. For the source of this information, see Lerman (1972),
357-358.
298. Competence in the Assembly was associated both with subject-
matter expertise and with understanding of Assembly procedure
and customs. This type of expertise and understanding was
categorized in Wahlke et al., 165-169, 193-215, 247.
299. Note that the Assembly position is officially a nonpaying job.
Pao Ch'ing-chiu, 49-52.
300. "Hsien-shih-chang Sheng I-yüan . . ."
301. Beer, 24. For the source of this quotation from Labor MP
R. H. S. Crossman, Beer cites Andrew Roth, The Business
Background of Members of Parliament (London, 1963?), p. xv.
302. Whether this group of business representatives is growing
in proportion to the self-representatives is a question worthy
of future research. A growth in the proportion of representatives of business people based outside the Assembly may
demonstrate a trend toward role differentiation and thus,
according to many theorists, political development. See,
for example, Almond and Powell, 22, 49, 306-310. Care must
be taken, however, to keep the analysis comparative. Just
how far role differentiation has actually gone in the so-
called politically developed countries must also be ascertained.
303. Wang Ya-tung.
304. Wang Chien-chih.
305. "T'ai-wan Sheng San-chieh Sheng I-yüan . . .," 17.

306. Levy (1953), 164-166, 175-176; and Levy (1966), II, 395, 757.
307. Levy (1952), 423.
308. Chuan-chi, I, 16 and 5, respectively.
309. Wahlke et al., 256.
310. De Grazia, 120, 122.
311. Almond and Powell, 73, 98, 102-103, 132.
312. Almond and Powell, 105-107.
313. Almond and Powell, 78-79.
314. Almond and Powell, 91-97.
315. Levy (1953), 178-197; Lockwood; Osborn; Benedict; and Reischauer, 53-177.
316. For point (a), see pages 39-41 and 105-106 above; for point (b), see pages 38-39, 105-106 and 133-161 above; for point (c), see pages 42-44 above.
317. See page 104-105 above; and Gallin and Gallin, 95-96.
318. See pages 50-51 and 55 above; and Gallin and Gallin, 95-96.
319. See pages 146-148 and 166-168 above; and Gallin and Gallin, 96.
320. For manifestations of this situation throughout the developing world, see Scott (1969), 1143-1145, 1148, 1150; and Weiner, 209-213, 220.
321. Lerman (1977), 1420, footnote 51.
322. Almond and Powell, 97.
323. Celler, 7. Celler also makes it clear that less-than-ideal behavior is still to be had in Washington.
324. Interview at an April 26-29, 1968, meeting of field researchers in Taichung, Taiwan. In the area he studied in mainland China during the period of KMT rule, Morton H. Fried found a similar pattern of lobbying activities: "dinners are served, invitations are freely passed, and gifts and favors are granted. Sometimes, of course, bribery is the resort, but graft rarely passes in an abrupt or direct manner, instead, the passage of a bribe will simply be one element in a lengthy and complicated transaction." Fried (1953), 153.
325. Based on incomplete data, the author compared provincial assemblymen from counties and cities noted for given economic interests with average assemblymen in terms of their propensity to support resolutions, raise interpellations, and make political platform statements on behalf of these interests. The author's assumption was that the economic interests in the various counties and cities have given rise to interest groups that lobby their local representative to the provincial assembly. Therefore, the resolutions, interpellations, and political platforms of the "lobbied" representatives should be more supportive of the interests in question than those of the average assemblyman. In most cases, the data supported the hypothesis, although

the propensity to serve local economic interests was usually greater by very small amounts. The interests studied were lumber, paper, port facilities, food processing, coal-mining companies, coal miners, pineapple, tobacco, banana, sugar, labor in general, and business in general. Sources for this footnote are reported in Lerman (1972), 394-397. Note that the data in question also lend support to the argument for the continued cohesiveness of territorial groups presented on pages 148-160 above.

326. The last two paragraphs come from an interview with a city assemblyman concerning himself and a provincial assembly-man. Crissman refers to the "perpetual open house" maintained by "major political figures." Crissman, 32.

327. Yen Chang-hsün (1967a).

328. Mu Jung-ts'ui (1967b), 8.

329. T'ai-wan Sheng I-hui Ti-san-chieh Ti-pa-tz'u Ta-hui I-yüan Chih-hsün . . ., 247-248.

330. Pye, 180.

331. Fried (1973), 354-376; Fried (1953), 218-219; Gallin and Gallin, 89-90; Levy (1953), 166, 169, 172; Schurmann, 368; and Van Gulik, 98-100, 220.

332. Pye, 172-173.

333. De Tocqueville, 485, 486. In opposition to the stress on hierarchy and authority-dependent relationships as a base for large-scale interest groups in Chinese society, however, de Tocqueville ends this passage with the question "Is that just an accident, or is there really some necessary connection between associations and equality?"

334. Hsü Cho-yün; Yang Lien-sheng; Reischauer and Fairbank, 124-125, 129-130; and C. K. Yang (1961), 218-229.

335. Hsü Cho-yün, 2, 3; Fairbank (1971), 94-95; and Reischauer and Fairbank, 96.

336. Reischauer and Fairbank, 28, 159, 206, 213-214, 374; Fairbank (1971), 39, 152, 235; and Ch'u T'ung-tsu, 151-152.

337. Fairbank (1972); Reischauer and Fairbank, 96; and Van Gulik, 220.

338. T'ai-wan Sheng Ti-fang Tzu-chih Chih-yao, 869, 879-880, 891, and 876, respectively.

339. Beer, 294, 325, 337.

340. Beer, 296-297, 326-332, 337.

341. Note that two major proponents of the power of hsieh-t'iao are very rich. This leads the cynic to speculate that to them hsieh-t'iao is identified with buying off opposition. Indeed, it was suggested above that one of the main factors holding Taiwan together is such widespread buying off (co-optation). See Part I, pages 50-51, 55, and 67-68, and Part II above.

271

342. Pye, 178-184.
343. Pao Ch'ing-chiu, 35.
344. "T'ai-wan Sheng San-chieh Sheng I-yüan . . .," 17.
345. Lerman (1972), 355-357, 359-360.
346. A checking of this statement against the associational
     affiliations listed by the assemblymen themselves makes the
     general manager's statement appear exaggerated. If the
     affiliations listed by the assemblymen are correct, the rate
     of participation on the Agriculture and Forestry Committee
     is higher for Farmers' Association assemblymen than for
     other assemblymen. But certainly not all committee
     members are in the Farmers' Association. It is possible,
     however, that the general manager's information is more
     accurate than the assemblymen's listings. Sources for this
     footnote are <u>Chuan-chi</u>, I, 1-18; and Lerman (1972), 425-
     426.
347. For an assemblywoman representing women's groups, see "Fu-
     nü Ling-hsiu, Ch'en Lin Hsüeh-hsia." For a coal mine owners'
     association-assemblyman, see Pai Chün.
        As for business-assemblymen, here too information was
     gathered on the number of resolutions supported, interpella-
     tions raised, and platform promises made by interested assem-
     blymen on behalf of their interests. In general, the numbers
     support the contention that the association-assemblymen aid
     their particular association to a greater degree than do
     the average assemblymen. This was especially true for
     assemblymen who reported themselves as current or former
     members of the Farmers' Association, the Women's Association,
     the Fishermen's Association, commercial-industrial associa-
     tions, coal mine owners' associations, and pharmacist-medicine
     company associations. See Lerman (1972), 427-429, 439-442.
348. After the period of the author's research, a law was passed
     that no longer allowed the general managers of people's
     associations to hold concurrently the position of assem-
     blyman. With the passage of this law, the president of the
     Provincial Farmers' Association began to ride alone.
349. ". . . [I] do not see a great conflict between industry and
     agriculture, but I see it between specific business interests,"
     one assemblyman noted.
350. <u>China Yearbook</u> (1967-1968), 108; and <u>China Yearbook</u> (1976),
     130, 165.
351. See pages 106-107, 117 (including footnote 166), and 127
     above.
352. <u>Chuan-chi</u>, I, 5, 6, 11, 14, 16.
353. Possible conflicts between labor and/or capital and the
     government are also ignored. See "Kung-shang Pao-mu, Ch'en
     Hsin-fa"; and "Kung-yeh Chü-tzu, Li Ch'ing-yün."

354. Lerman (1972), 448-449.
355. Lerman (1972), 449.
356. Pao Ch'ing-chiu, 32.
357. See, for example, Yü Ying-chih.
358. Lerman (1972), 451.
359. Kung-sun Ch'ou.
360. Chuan-chi, II, 2328.
361. "Chin Pai Wu-chao Hsing-i Jen-yüan . . ."
362. For example, "Hsiang Ta-chia I-yüan Chin I Yen."
363. Chuan-chi, II, 2408, 2410.
364. T'ai-wan Sheng I-hui Ti-san-chieh Ti-pa-tz'u Ta-hui I-yüan Chih-hsün . . ., 165. Also see Chuan-chi, I, resolutions 3061 and 4029, on pp. 336-337 and 371, respectively.
365. Evidence for this chapter derives from the above study. For point-by-point documentation, as well as for extensive explanatory footnotes, see the lengthier version of this chapter, Lerman, (1977).
366. Schwartz (1964), 285, 288; Weiner, 227-228; Scott (1969), 1142; and Scott (1972), 91.

BIBLIOGRAPHY

ALMOND, GABRIEL A. 1956. "Comparative Political Systems." Polit-
itical Behavior. ed. H. Eulau, S. J. Eldersveld, and M. Janowitz.
Glencoe, Ill.: The Free Press, 34-42.
_____. 1960. "Introduction: A Functional Approach to Compara-
tive Politics." The Politics of Developing Areas. ed. G. A.
Almond and J. S. Coleman. Princeton: Princeton University Press,
3-64.
ALMOND, GABRIEL A., and POWELL, G. BINGHAM, JR. 1966. Comparative Politics: A Developmental Approach. Boston: Little, Brown
and Company.
APPLETON, SHELDON. 1970a. "The Political Socialization of Taiwan's
College Students." Asian Survey, X, 10, October, 910-923.
_____. 1970b. "Taiwanese and Mainlanders on Taiwan: A Survey
of Student Attitudes." The China Quarterly, 44, October-December,
38-65.
_____. 1973. "Regime Support among Taiwan High School Students."
Asian Survey, XIII, 8, August, 750-760.
_____. 1974. "The Prospects for Student Activism on Taiwan."
Taiwan's Future? ed. Y. H. Jo. Hong Kong: Union Research Insti-
tute for the Center for Asian Studies-Arizona State University,
52-62.
BEER, SAMUEL. 1966. British Politics in a Collectivist Age.
New York: Alfred A. Knopf.
BENEDICT, RUTH. 1946. The Chrysanthemum and the Sword. Boston:
Houghton Mifflin Company.
BUSINESS DIRECTORY OF TAIWAN. 1967-1968. Taipei: E. T. Tsu.
CELLER, EMANUEL. 1958. "Pressure Groups in Congress." Unofficial
Government: Pressure Groups and Lobbies. The Annals of the
American Academy of Political and Social Science, CCCXIX, September,
1-9.
CHAFFEE, FREDERICK H., et al. 1969. Area Handbook for the Republic
of China. DA Pam 550-63. Washington, D.C.: Foreign Area Studies,
The American University.
CHANG PING-CHENG. 1968. "Miao-li Hsien Hsia-chieh Fu-i-chang
Hsüan-chü, Luo Huang Hsiao-lan Hui Tang-hsüan Ma?" [Miao-li
County's Election for Next Term's Deputy Speaker, Will Luo Huang
Hsiao-lan Be Elected?]. Lien-ho Pao (Miao-li local area edition),
20 February, 7.
CHANG TSUO-CHIN. 1968. "Kuo-min-tang Chung-yang Chüeh-pu Ku-hsi
Wei-chi Ching-hsüan-che" [KMT Central Committee Definitely Not
to Treat Leniently Those Who Compete in Elections against Party
Discipline]. Lien-ho Pao (Taichung local area edition), 28 March,
7.
CHAO CHÜN-WU. 1967a. "Chang-hua Hsien I-yüan I-chang Hsüan-chü

Hsin Ch'ü-shih" [New Developments in the Changhua County Assemblymen and Assembly Speaker Elections]. <u>Liao-wang Chou-k'an</u>, 34,
4 November, 25-26.

_____. 1967b. "Chien-t'ao I-lan Hsien Pen-chieh I-hui-te Te
Shih" [Reviewing the Achievements and Failures of the Current
Term of the I-lan County Assembly]. <u>Liao-wang Chou-k'an</u>, 23,
19 August, 25-26.

_____. 1967c. "Chien-t'ao T'ao-yüan Hsien I-hui-te Kung Kuo
Te Shih" [Reviewing the Merits, Demerits, Achievements, and
Failures of the T'ao-yüan County Assembly]. <u>Liao-wang Chou-k'an</u>,
30, 10 July, 25-26.

_____. 1967d. "Ching-chu I-lan Hsien-chang, Ch'ün Hsiung Yüeh-
yüeh Yü Shih" [I-lan County Mayoralty Race, Herd of Heroes Jump-
ing at the Chance]. <u>Liao-wang Chou-k'an</u>, 22, 12 August, 25-26.

_____. 1967e. "Chüeh-chu Shih-chang, Kao-shih Ch'ün Hsiung
Ping-ch'i" [The Race for Mayor, Kao-hsiung City's Herd of Heroes
Are Off and Running]. <u>Liao-wang Chou-k'an</u>, 19, 22 July, 25-26.

_____. 1967f. "Miao-li Hsien I-chang Hsüan-chü Ch'u-lu"
[Early Intimations concerning the Miao-li County Assembly Speaker
Electoral Situation]. <u>Liao-wang Chou-k'an</u>, 32, 21 October, 25-26.

_____. 1967g. "Miao-li Hsien Shih-li Jen-shih Chiang Chu-lu Sheng
I-yüan" [Powerful Personages of Miao-li County to Compete for
Provincial Assembly Seats]. <u>Liao-wang Chou-k'an</u>, 33, 28 October,
25-26.

_____. 1967h. "Miao-li Hsien-chang Hsüan-chü, Liu Huang Liang
P'ai Ta Chüeh-chan" [Miao-li County Mayoralty Election, a Great
Decisive Battle between the Liu and Huang Factions]. <u>Liao-wang
Chou-k'an</u>, 31, 14 October, 25-26.

_____. 1967i. "T'ao-yüan Hsien Hsien-chang, Sheng I-yüan T'i-
ming Ta-shih" [General Nominating Situation for T'ao-yüan County
Mayor and Provincial Assemblymen]. <u>Liao-wang Chou-k'an</u>, 29, 30
September, 25-26.

CH'EN CHIH-P'ING. 1972. <u>Chung-kuo Wen-hua yü Jen-lei Ho-p'ing</u>
[China's Culture and the Peace of Mankind]. Taipei: Chiao-yü-
pu Wen-hua-chü.

CH'EN CH'I-FU et al. 1968. "Ch'en Chou Lai-fu Shan Ts'uo Yüan-
tzu" [Ch'en Chou Lai-fu Makes Good Dumplings]. <u>Lien-ho Pao</u> (Kao-
hsiung local area edition), 12 January, 7.

CH'EN LI-FU. 1971a. <u>Jen-hsing Ch'iang-sang-chih Wei-chi yü Chung-
hua Wen-hua Fu-hsing-chih Yao I</u> [The Crisis of the Decline of
Human Nature and the Essential Meaning of China's Cultural Ren-
aissance]. Taipei: Chiao-yü-pu Wen-hua-chü.

_____. 1971b. <u>Kuo-fu-chih Ch'uang-chien yü Chung-hua Wen-hua-
chih Pi-jan Fu-hsing</u> [Creative Insights of the Father of Our
Country and the Inevitable Renaissance of China's Culture].
Taipei: Chiao-yü-pu Wen-hua-chü.

CH'EN MING-T'IEH. 1968. "Ch'e-ti Hsiao-ch'u Hsüan-chü P'ai-hsi

276

Fen-cheng" [Thoroughly Do Away with the Tangled Wrangling of
Electoral Factions]. Ti-fang Tzu-chih, 176, 15 February, 15-16.
CH'EN PI-CHAO (PETER). 1973. "In Search of Chinese National Char-
acter Via Child Training." World Politics, 25, July, 608-635.
CHENG LUN [Correct Opinion]. 1968.
"CHENG-FU JEN-SHIH KUAN-TAO SHU-T'UNG, HSIN CH'EN TAI HSIEH JIH-
CH'Ü HUO-P'O" [To Run Smoothly Government Personnel Administration,
Policy of Hiring the Young and Retiring the Old Increasingly
Firm]. 1975. Chung-yang Jih-pao (Air Mail Edition), 26 June, 1.
"CHIA-HSIEN I-YÜAN HSÜAN-CHÜ TI-I HSÜAN-CH'Ü, CH'UAN YU JEN TS'UO
YÜAN-TZU T'ANG, CHIEN-CH'A-TSU CHIN-HSING TIAO-CH'A" [Chia-i
Assembly Elections, First Election District Rumors: People Are
Making Dumpling Soup, Overseeing Committee Investigating]. 1968.
Lien-ho Pao (Chia-i local area edition), 9 January, 7.
CHIANG FU-TS'UNG. 1971. T'ien Jen Ho I-te Wen-hua [The Culture
That Unites Heaven and Mankind]. Taipei: Chiao-yü-pu Wen-hua-chü.
CHIANG KUEI. 1966. Pai-chin Hai-an [Seashore of White Gold].
Nan-t'ou: Sheng Cheng-fu Hsin-wen-ch'u.
"CHIANG-TZU-TS'UI CHÜ-MIN TAI-PIAO, TSUO HSIANG PEI-HSIEN-FU CH'ING-
YÜAN" [Representatives of Chiang-tzu-ts'ui Residents, Yesterday
Petitioned the Taipei County Government]. 1968. Lien-ho Pao
(Taipei County local area edition), 27 March, 7.
"CHIANG-TZU-TS'UI TU-SHIH CHI-HUA, YING CHIN TSAO KUNG-PU SHIH-
SHIH" [The Chiang-tzu-ts'ui City Plan Must Be Promulgated and
Carried Out as Soon as Possible]. 1968. Lien-ho Pao (Taipei
County local area edition), 29 March, 7.
CHIEN HO. 1971. "Ch'i Kao I Chao" [One Move Smarter]. Chung-
yang Jih-pao (Air Mail Edition), 14 Spetember, 4.
"CHIN PAI WU-CHAO HSING-I JEN-YÜAN, TSUO HSIANG LI-WEI K'OU-T'OU
CH'ING-YÜAN" [Almost 100 Persons Who Practice Medicine without
a License, Yesterday Kowtowed to and Petitioned the Members of
the Legislative Yuan]. 1967. Lien-ho Pao, 24 May, 4.
THE CHINA READER: REPUBLICAN CHINA. 1967. ed. F. Schurmann and
O. Schell, New York: Random House, Vintage Books.
CHINA YEARBOOK. 1967-1968. ed. W. Liu and Lin Shu-ting. Taipei:
China Publishing Company.
_____. 1972-1973. ed. Lin Shu-ting and Shih Hwa-chang. Taipei:
China Publishing Company.
_____. 1975. ed. Chen Chen-tzu and Shih Hwa-chang. Taipei:
China Publishing Company.
_____. 1976. ed. Chen Chen-tzu and Shih Hwa-chang. Taipei:
China Publishing Company.
"CH'ING SHENG-FU TU-TAO FEI-LIAO CH'ANG, CHIANG-TI FEI-LIAO SHENG-
CH'AN CHIA-KO" [Request Provincial Government Supervise Fertilizer
Factories, Lower the Price of Fertilizer Production]. 1967.
Lien-ho Pao, 5 August, 2.
CH'U T'UNG-TSU. 1962. Local Government in China under the Ch'ing.

Stanford, Calif,: Stanford University Press.
CHUAN-CHI (i.e., T'ai-wan Sheng I-hui Ti-san-chieh Ti-pa-tz'u Ta-Hui Chuan-chi) [Records of the Taiwan Provincial Assembly, Third Term, Eighth Plenary Session]. 1967. 5 vols. Wu-feng: Taiwan Sheng I-hui Mi-shu-ch'u.
CHUNG-KUO JEN-SHIH HSING-CHENG [China's Personnel Administration]. 1973.
"CHUNG-LI LIANG HSIUNG CHÜEH-CHU SHIH-CHANG PAO-TSUO" [Two Powerful Chung-li City Personages Contend for the Mayor's Treasured Chair]. 1968. Lien-ho Pao (T'ao-yüan local area edition), 12 January, 7.
CHUNG-YANG JIH-PAO [Central Daily News]. 1967-1975.
"CHÜEH PU JUNG CHU 'HSÜAN' HAI KUNG" [Aiding in Election Campaigns Must Not Be Allowed to Interfere with Public Responsibilities]. 1968. Lien-ho Pao (Tainan local area edition), 12 January, 7.
"CHÜEH-I CHIANG-TI FEI-LIAO HUAN-KU PI-LÜ" [Resolves to Lower Fertilizer-Rice Exchange Rate]. 1967. Lien-ho Pao, 27 May, 2.
CLAPP, CHARLES L. 1964. The Congressman: His Work as He Sees It. Garden City, N.Y.: Doubleday and Company, Anchor Books.
CREEL, H. G. 1953. Chinese Thought from Confucius to Mao Tse-tung. Chicago: University of Chicago Press, Mentor Books.
CRISSMAN, LAWRENCE W. 1969. "Each for His Own: Taiwanese Political Response to KMT Local Administration." Unpublished paper presented at the London-Cornell Project for East and Southeast Asian Studies Conference, Ste. Adele-en-haut, Quebec, 24-29 August.
"CRITICS FROM BLOC IN TAIPEI ELECTION." 1973. The New York Times, 25 November, 9.
"A CURIOUS THING IS HAPPENING IN TAIWAN." 1972. The Christian Science Monitor, 19 December, 7.
DE GRAZIA, ALFRED. 1958. "Nature and Prospects of Political Interest Groups." Unofficial Government: Pressure Groups and Lobbies. The Annals of the American Academy of Political and Social Science, CCCXIX, September, 113-122.
DE TOCQUEVILLE, ALEXIS. 1966. Democracy in America. ed. J. P. Mayer and M. Lerner. trans. G. Lawrence. New York: Harper & Row.
DEGLOPPER, DONALD R. 1966. "The Origins and Resolution of Conflict in Traditional Chinese Society." Unpublished M.A. thesis, University of London.
DURDIN, TILLMAN. 1971. "Taiwan's Setback Spurs Reformers." The New York Times, 31 October, 21.
_____. 1973. "Veterans' Work Group Helps Taiwan." The New York Times, 7 July, 27.
ECKSTEIN, HARRY. 1960. Pressure Group Politics: The Case of the British Medical Association. Stanford, Calif.: Stanford University Press.
THE EMERGING NATIONS: THEIR GROWTH AND UNITED STATES POLICY. 1961. ed. M. F. Millikan and D. L. M. Blackmer. Boston: Little, Brown

and Company.

FAIRBANK, JOHN KING. 1971. The United States and China. 3d. ed.
Cambridge, Mass.: Harvard University Press.

_____. 1972. "Taipei Can Coexist with Peking." The New York
Times, 19 February, 31.

FEI HSIAO-TUNG. 1953. China's Gentry. ed. M. P. Redfield. Chicago:
University of Chicago Press, Phoenix Books.

FENG TSAO-MIN. 1966. T'ai-wan Li-shih Pai-chiang [One Hundred
Lessons of Taiwan History]. Taipei: Ch'ing-wen Ch'u-pan-she.

FESSLER, LOREN. 1972. "Taiwan Independence Advocate, Peng Ming-
min: Part II: Plotting, Prison, Escape." Fieldstaff Reports.
East Asia Series. XIX, 4. Hanover, N.H.: American Universities
Field Staff, Inc.

FITCH, GERALDINE. 1966. "Formosa Betrayed." Review of Formosa
Betrayed, by George H. Kerr. Free China Review, XVI, 3, March,
74-75.

FORMOSA TODAY. 1964. ed. M. Mancall. New York: Frederick A.
Praeger.

FREEDMAN, MAURICE. 1966. Chinese Lineage and Society: Fukien
and Kwangtung. London: The Athlone Press.

FRIED, MORTON H. 1953. Fabric of Chinese Society. New York:
Frederick A. Praeger.

_____. 1966. "Some Political Aspects of Clanship in a Modern
Chinese City." Political Anthropology. ed. M. J. Swartz, A. Tuden,
and V. W. Turner. Chicago: Aldine Publishing Company, 285-300.

_____. 1973. "China: An Anthropological Overview." An Introduc-
tion to Chinese Civilization. ed. J. T. Meskill. Lexington, Mass.:
D. C. Heath and Company, 341-378.

FU CH'I-HSÜEH. 1964. Chung-kuo Cheng-fu [China's Government].
Taipei: T'ai-ta Fa-hsüeh-yüan Shih-wu-tsu.

"FU-NÜ LING-HSIU, CH'EN LIN HSÜEH-HSIA" [Women's Leader, Ch'en Lin
Hsüeh-hsia]. 1963. Ti-fang Tzu-chih, 60-61, 19 April, 28-29.

GALLIN, BERNARD. 1963a. "A Case for Intervention in the Field."
Practical Anthropology, X, 2, March-April, 57-65.

_____. 1963b. "Land Reform in Taiwan: Its Effect on Rural Social
Organization and Leadership." Human Organization, XXII, 2, Summer,
109-112.

_____. 1964. "Rural Development in Taiwan: The Role of the
Government." Rural Sociology, XXIX, 3, September, 313-323.

_____. 1966a. "Conflict Resolution in Changing Chinese Society:
A Taiwanese Study." Political Anthropology. ed. M. J. Swartz, A.
Tuden, and V. W. Turner. Chicago: Aldine Publishing Company,
265-273.

_____. 1966b. Hsin Hsing, Taiwan: A Chinese Village in Change.
Berkeley: University of California Press.

_____. 1967. "Mediation in Changing Chinese Society in Rural
Taiwan." Traditional and Modern Legal Institutions in Asia and

279

Africa. ed. D. Buxbaum. Leiden: Brill, 77-90.

_____. 1968. "Political Factionalism and Its Impact on Chinese Village Social Organization in Taiwan." Local-Level Politics. ed. M. J. Swartz. Chicago: Aldine Publishing Company, 377-400.

GALLIN, BERNARD, and GALLIN, RITA S. 1977. "Sociopolitical Power and Sworn Brother Groups in Chinese Society: A Taiwanese Case." The Anthropology of Power. ed. R. N. Adams and R. D. Fogelson. New York: Academic Press, 89-97.

GODDARD, W. G. 1958. Formosa (Taiwan). Taipei: China Publishing Company.

_____. 1966. Formosa: A Study in Chinese History. East Lansing: Michigan State University Press.

HALLORAN, RICHARD. 1972. "Ex-Agent Sees 'Revolutionary Potential' on Taiwan." The New York Times, 12 March, 3.

HO FAN. 1967a. "Hsiang Pei-hsien I-hui K'ang-i" [Protest against the Taipei County Assembly]. Lien-ho Pao (Taipei City edition), 8 June, 7.

_____. 1967b. "I-yÜan-te Ch'iu Po" [The Assemblymen's Flirtatious Glances]. Lien-ho Pao (Hsin-chu County local area edition), 22 May, 7.

HO MING-CHUNG. 1971. Chung-hua Wen-hua Tui Shih-chieh Wen-hua-te Kung-hsien [Chinese Culture's Contribution to World Culture]. Taipei: Chiao-yÜ-pu Wen-hua-chÜ.

HSIA TSUNG-HAN. 1973. "T'ai-wan HsÜan-ChÜ Ch'ien-p'ing" [An Abridged Analysis of Taiwan's Elections]. Ming-pao YÜeh-k'an, 92, August, 59-66.

HSIANG CHÜN. 1966. "Pao-shih Yang YÜ-ch'eng Tao-pi Li-chien Ch'i-wen" [To Release Yang YÜ-ch'eng on Bail, Strange Tale of an Article Sowing Dissension]. Shih-tzu Lun-t'an, 287, 1 March, 3.

"HSIANG TA-CHIA I-YÜAN CHIN I YEN" [A Word of Advice for Fisticuff-Prone Assemblymen]. 1968. Lien-ho Pao, 6 January, 7.

HSIAO KUNG-CHUAN. 1960. Rural China: Imperial Control in the Nineteenth Century. Seattle: University of Washington Press.

"HSIEH-CHU NUNG-MIN K'UO-TA SHENG-CH'AN, CH'ING TUO CHÜ-PAN CH'ANG-CH'I TAI-K'UAN" [Aid Farmers to Enlarge Production, Request Increased Initiation of Long-Term Loans]. 1968. Lien-ho Pao, 29 January, 2.

"HSIEN-SHIH-CHANG SHENG I-YÜAN T'I-MING MU-HOU CH'UN-CH'IU" [Report from behind the Scenes concerning Nominations for County-City Mayors and Provincial Assemblymen]. 1968. Tzu-chih, 178, 16 March, 3.

"HSIN-CHU HSIEN-CHANG LIU HSIEH-HSÜN CH'IAO YING HSÜAN-CHAN, YIN-HUO TE-FU; CHU YÜ-YING LIANG CHAO SHIH TS'UO, MAN P'AN CHIEH SHU" [Hsin-chu County Mayor Liu Hsieh-hsÜn Obtains Good Fortune from Bad and Cleverly Wins the Election Battle; Chu YÜ-ying Makes Two Mistaken Moves and Loses Everything]. 1968. Tzu-chih, Ko-hsin 181, 1 May, 10.

HSIN-SHENG PAO [New Life Journal], 1967-1968.
"HSIN-YING KO-CHIA YIN-HANG, SHIH-YÜAN CH'AO-P'IAO HUAN-KUANG"
[Every Ten-Dollar Bill Held by Hsin-ying's Banks Withdrawn].
1968. Lien-ho Pao (Tainan local area edition), 21 January, 7.
HSU, FRANCIS L. K. 1970. Americans and Chinese. Garden City, N.Y.:
Doubleday Natural History Press, American Museum Science Books.
HSÜ CHO-YÜN. 1954. "The Changing Social Bases of Political Power
in the Western Han Dynasty, 206 B.C.-8 A.D." Unpublished paper
presented at the International Conference on Asian History, Uni-
versity of Hong Kong, 30 August-5 September..
"HSÜAN-CHÜ CHIEN-T'AO TSUO-T'AN-HUI" [Election Analysis Symposium].
1973. Ta-hsüeh Tsa-chih, 62, February, 11-33.
"HSÜAN-CHÜ KUNG-PAO" [Public Election Reports]. 1963, 1968.
Published for every election in each district by the district
Election Affairs Office (Hsüan-chü Shih-wu-suo).
HUANG FU-TAI. 1968. "'Shih Tzu-mei' Fei-hsüan Sheng I-hui"
[Sisterhood of Ten Songbirds Fly About the Provincial Assembly].
Liao-wang Chou-k'an, 44, 20 January, 13-15.
HUANG YÜ-FENG. 1968. "Lin Ting-shan Shih-pai Yüan-yin" [The Reason
Lin Ting-shan Lost]. Lien-ho Pao (Taichung local area edition),
23 April, 7.
HUNG CH'UN-MU. 1968. "Chung-hsien Hsüan-chü Te Shih Chien-t'ao"
[Reviewing the Successes and Failures of the Taichung County
Elections]. Lien-ho Pao (Taichung local area edition), 23 April,
7.
"I TE WEI HSIEN" [Put Morality First]. 1968. Lien-ho Pao, 9
February, 7.
"I-T'ANG CH'I K'O YUNG JIH-YÜ FA-YEN!" [How Can Japanese Be Used to
Speak in an Assembly Hall!]. 1967. Lien-ho Pao (Taipei City
edition), 20 May, 7.
IKE, NOBUTAKA. 1972. Japanese Politics: Patron-Client Democracy.
2d. ed. New York: Alfred A. Knopf.
ISAACS, HAROLD. 1967. "The New Awakening." The China Reader:
Republican China. ed. F. Schurmann and O. Schell. New York: Random
House, Vintage Books, 92-104.
ISRAEL, JOHN. 1964. "Politics on Formosa." Formosa Today. ed.
M. Mancall. New York: Frederick A. Praeger, 59-67.
JACOBS, J. BRUCE. 1971. "Recent Leadership and Political Trends
in Taiwan.: The China Quarterly, 45, January-March, 129-154.
_____. 1973. "Taiwan 1972: Political Season." Asian Survey,
XIII, 1, January, 102-112.
_____. 1974. "Taiwan 1973: Consolidation of the Succession."
Asian Survey, XIV, 1, January, 22-29.
_____. 1975. "Local Politics in Rural Taiwan: A Field Study of
Kuan-hsi, Face, and Faction in Matsu Township." Unpublished
Ph.D. dissertation, Columbia University.
_____. 1976. "The Cultural Bases of Factional Alignment and
281

Division in a Rural Taiwanese Township." The Journal of Asian
Studies, XXXVI, 1, November, 79-97.
JOHNSON, CHALMERS A. 1962. Peasant Nationalism and Communist
Power. Stanford, Calif.: Stanford University Press.
JORDAN, DAVID K. 1972. Gods, Ghosts, and Ancestors: The Folk
Religion of a Taiwanese Village. Berkeley: University of California
Press.
KAO CHUN. 1975. "T'ai-wan Ch'üan-li Mao-tun chi Ch'i Chieh-chüeh-
chih Tao" [Taiwan's Power Contradiction and the Method for Its
Resolution]. Ming-pao Yüeh-k'an, 109, January, 78-83.
"KAO-HSIUNG HSIEN-CHANG T'I-MING, HUNG PAI LIANG-P'AI LIANG HU
HSIANG-CHENG" [Kao-hsiung's Red and White Factions Struggle Like
Two Tigers for the County Mayor Nomination]. 1967. Tzu-chih,
170, 1 November, 8.
KAUTSKY, JOHN H. 1972. The Political Consequences of Modernization.
New York: John Wiley and Sons.
KERR, GEORGE H. 1965. Formosa Betrayed. Boston: Houghton Mifflin
Company.
KU I-CH'ÜN. 1971. Ts'ung Tui Shih-chü-te Kuan-ch'a Lai Chien-
t'ao Chung-hua Wen-hua Ching-shen [Analyzing the Spirit of China's
Culture in View of the Current World Situation]. Taipei: Chiao-yü-
pu Wen-hua-chü.
"KUNG SHANG PAO-MU, CH'EN HSIN-FA" [Nursemaid of Labor and Commerce,
Ch'en Hsin-fa]. 1963. Ti-fang Tzu-chih, 60-61, 19 April, 30.
KUNG-SUN CH'OU. 1967. "Ch'ao-ling Hsien-shih-chang Lien-meng
Fan-tui Mu-ch'ien Mu-hou" [Report from on Stage and behind the
Scenes as Overage County and City Mayors Unite in Opposition].
Tzu-chih, 163, 20 June, 3.
"KUNG-YEH CHÜ-TZU, LI CH'ING-YÜN" [Industrial Giant, Li Ch'ing-
yün]. 1963. Ti-fang Tzu-chih, 60-61, 19 April, 30.
KUO TZU-MING. 1968. "Hsin-chu Chu Yü-ying Ts'an-pai, Yu Hsieh
Ts'uo-shih Hsü Chien-t'ao" [The Disastrous Defeat of Chu Yü-ying
in Hsin-chu, Some Tactics in Need of Examination]. Lien-ho Pao
(Hsin-chu local area edition), 23 April, 7.
"KUO YÜ-HSIN WEI I-LAN TSAI-MIN CHIU-CHI CH'ING-MING, PAO PING PEN-
TSOU" [Kuo Yü-hsin, Although Sick, Rushes About, Seeks Relief for
I-lan's Disaster Victims]. 1967. Tzu-chih, 170, 1 November,
10.
KUO-KUANG HUA-K'AN [National Glory Pictorial], 1968.
LANDÉ, CARL H. 1973. "Networks and Groups in Southeast Asia:
Some Observations on the Group Theory of Politics." The American
Political Science Review, LXVII, 1, March, 103-127.
LERMAN, ARTHUR J. 1972. "Political, Traditional, and Modern
Economic Groups, and the Taiwan Provincial Assembly." Unpublished
Ph.D. dissertation, Princeton University.
_____. 1976. "The Kuomintang as Mediator between Taiwan's
Local-level Political Factions." Asian Forum, VIII, 3, Summer,

282

122-137.

_____. 1977. "National Elite and Local Politician in Taiwan." The American Political Science Review, LXXI, 4, December, 1406-1422.

LEVY, MARION J., JR. 1949. The Family Revolution in Modern China. Cambridge, Mass.: Harvard University Press.

_____. 1952. The Structure of Society. Princeton: Princeton University Press.

_____. 1953. "Contrasting Factors in the Modernization of China and Japan." Economic Development and Cultural Change, II, 161-197.

_____. 1966. Modernization and the Structure of Societies. 2 vols. Princeton: Princeton University Press.

LIAO-WANG CHOU-K'AN [Newsweek], 1967-1968.

LIEN-HO PAO [United Daily News], 1967-1968.

LIN HENG-DAO. 1966. T'ai-wan-te Li-shih yü Min-su [The History and Folkways of Taiwan]. trans. Feng Tsao-min. Taipei: Ch'ing-wen Ch'u-pan-she.

LIU YEN-FU. 1964. Ti-fang Tzu-chih Lun-chi [Collected Essays concerning Local Self-Government]. Taipei: Min-chien Chih-shih-she.

LO KUAN-CHUNG. 1924. San Kuo Yen-i [Romance of the Three Kingdoms]. Shanghai: Ya-tung T'u-shu-kuan.

LOCKARD, DUANE. 1963. The Politics of State and Local Government. New York: The Macmillan Company.

LOCKWOOD, WILLIAM W. 1956. "Japan's Response to the West: The Contrast with China." World Politics, IX, 1, October, 37-54.

LONG, HOWARD R. 1960. The People of Mushan: Life in a Taiwanese Village. Columbia: University of Missouri Press.

LU, F. C. 1966. "Hero of the Revolution." Free China Review, XVI, 4, April, 9-14.

LU HSÜN. 1968. "Li-hun" [Divorce]. Lu Hsün Hsiao-shuo Hsüan [Selected Novels of Lu Hsün]. Hsiang Kang: Hsin I Ch'u-pan-she, 280-293.

"MAN-T'AN CHENG-CHIH YÜ TAO-TE" [Speaking of Politics and Morality]. 1968. Min-sheng Jih-pao, 24 January, 2.

MANCALL, MARK. 1964. "Introduction: Taiwan, Island of Resignation and Despair." Formosa Today. ed. M. Mancall. New York: Frederick A. Praeger, 1-42.

MATHEWS, R. H. 1963. Mathews' Chinese-English Dictionary. rev. American ed. Cambridge, Mass.: Harvard University Press.

MATTHEWS, DONALD R. 1960. U.S. Senators and Their World. New York: Random House, Vintage Books.

MEISNER, MAURICE. 1964. "The Development of Formosan Nationalism." Formosa Today. ed. M. Mancall. New York: Frederick A. Praeger, 147-162.

MENDEL, DOUGLAS H., JR. 1970. The Politics of Formosan Nationalism. Berkeley: University of California Press.

283

_____. 1974. "The Formosan Nationalist Movement in Crisis."
Taiwan's Future? ed. Y. H. Jo. Hong Kong: Union Research Institute
for the Center for Asian Studies-Arizona State University, 144-
157.
MESKILL, JOHANNA MENZEL. 1970. "The Lins of Wufeng: The Rise of
a Taiwanese Gentry Family." Taiwan: Studies in Chinese Local
History. ed. L. H. D. Gordon. New York: Columbia University Press,
6-22.
"MESSAGE OF CHIANG KAI-SHEK." 1950. In Riggs, Fred W. 1952.
Formosa under Chinese Nationalist Rule. New York: The Macmillan
Company, 153-156.
METZGER, THOMAS A. 1972. "On Chinese Political Culture." The
Journal of Asian Studies, XXXII, 1, November, 101-105.
MEYER, ALFRED G. 1965. The Soviet Political System: An Interpre-
tation. New York: Random House.
MIN-SHENG JIH-PAO [People's Voice Daily], 1968.
MING-PAO YÜEH-K'AN [Ming Pao Monthly], 1973-1975.
"THE MONTH IN FREE CHINA." 1966. Free China Review, XVI, 4, April,
3-4.
MOTE, F. W. 1972. "China's Past in the Study of China Today--
Some Comments on the Recent Work of Richard Solomon." The Journal
of Asian Studies, XXXII, 1, November, 107-120.
MU JUNG-TS'UI. 1967a. "Chi-wei Sheng I-yüan Hsiang Tang Hsien
T'ai-yeh" [Some Provincial Assemblymen Set Hopes on Becoming
"His Honor the Mayor"]. Liao-wang Chou-k'an, 33, 28 October, 14-16.
_____. 1967b. "Sheng I-yüan-te Szu Sheng-huo" [The Private
Lives of Provincial Assemblymen]. Liao-wang Chou-k'an, 25, 2
September, 7-9.
_____. 1967c. "T'ai-sheng I-hui Tzu-hui Li-ch'ang" [Taiwan
Provincial Assembly Undercuts Its Own Standpoint]. Liao-wang
Chou-k'an, 42, 30 December, 18-19.
NATHAN, ANDREW J. 1973. "A Factionalism Model for CCP Politics."
The China Quarterly, 53, January-March, 34-66.
"NATIONALIST AIDE ASKS FIRST ELECTIONS ON TAIWAN." 1971. The New
York Times, 10 January, 12.
THE NEW YORK TIMES, 1969-1974.
NEWSWEEK, 1969-1970.
"NIANG-TZU CHÜN CH'U-TUNG WEI CHU-HSÜAN TSENG-SE" [Amazon Army
Moves into Action, Adds Color to Election Campaigning]. 1968.
Lien-ho Pao (Taichung local area edition), 12 January, 7.
NICHOLAS, RALPH W. 1965. "Factions: A Comparative Analysis."
Political Systems and the Distribution of Power. ed. M. Banton.
A.S.A. Monographs, no. 2. London: Tavistock Publications. New
York: Frederick A. Praeger, 21-61.
NING K'O. 1963. "Pu Pu Kao Sheng" [Step By Step Rising High].
Ti-fang Tzu-chih, 60-61, 19 April, 19.
OKA, TAKASHI. 1971. "Rift inside Taiwan as Wide as the one between

the Two Chinas." The New York Times, 26 September, 20.

OSBORN, DAVID L. 1970. "Going to the Fair? How to Understand the Japanese." The New York Times Magazine, 22 February, 23.

PAI CHÜN. 1963. "Je-hsin Fu-wu Ti-fang-te Lai Sen-lin" [Ardent Servant of the Locality, Lai Sen-lin]. Ti-fang Tzu-chih, 60-61, 19 April, 25.

PALOCZI-HORVATH, GEORGE. 1963. Mao Tse-tung, Emperor of the Blue Ants. Garden City, N.Y.: Doubleday and Company.

PAO CH'ING-CHIU. 1964. T'ai-wan Sheng I-hui [The Taiwan Provincial Assembly]. Mu-shan: Kuo-li Cheng-chih Ta-hsüeh Kung-kung Hsing-cheng Ch'i-yeh Kuan-li Chung-hsin.

PASTERNAK, BURTON. 1969. "The Role of the Frontier in Chinese Lineage Development." The Journal of Asian Studies, XXVIII, 3, May, 551-561.

_____. 1972. Kinship & Community in Two Chinese Villages. Stanford, Calif.: Stanford University Press.

"PEI-HSIEN I-HUI PIAO-SHIH FAN-TUI, CHÜEH CH'ING CHUNG-YANG, CHI YÜ CHIH-CHIH" [Taipei County Assembly Expresses Opposition, Decides to Request Central Government Immediately to Issue Enjoinment Order]. 1967. Lien-ho Pao (Taipei County local area edition), 8 November, 7.

"PEI-HSIEN SHENG I-YÜAN HSÜAN-CHÜ MING-LANG, KUO-MIN-TANG T'I-MING HOU-HSÜAN-YÜAN, CHIANG YU PA-WO TSUO-SAN WANG-SZU" [Taipei County Provincial Assemblymen Electoral Situation Clarified, Kuomintang Nominees in Position to Win Three Seats and Hope for a Fourth]. 1968. Lien-ho Pao (Taipei County local area edition), 1 April, 7.

"PU TS'UO YÜAN-TZU T'ANG, CHEN FANG-CH'I CHING-HSÜAN" [Not Making Dumpling Soup, Really Withdrawing from the Election]. 1968. Lien-ho Pao (Taichung local area edition), 20 January, 7.

PYE, LUCIAN W. 1968. The Spirit of Chinese Politics. Cambridge, Mass.: The M.I.T. Press.

REISCHAUER, EDWIN O. 1965. The United States and Japan. Cambridge, Mass.: Harvard University Press; New York: Viking Compass Edition.

REISCHAUER, EDWIN O., and FAIRBANK, JOHN KING. 1958. East Asia: The Great Tradition. Boston: Houghton Mifflin Company.

ROHSENOW, HILL GATES. 1974. Review of Kinship & Community in Two Chinese Villages, by Burton Pasternak. The Journal of Asian Studies, XXXIII, 3, May 476-478.

SCHURMANN, FRANZ. 1968. Ideology and Organization in Communist China. 2d ed. Berkeley: University of California Press.

SCHWARTZ, BENJAMIN. 1961. Chinese Communism and the Rise of Mao. Cambridge, Mass.: Harvard University Press.

_____. 1964. In Search of Wealth and Power. Cambridge, Mass.: Harvard University Press, Belknap Press.

SCOTT, JAMES C. 1969. "Corruption, Machine Politics, and Political Change." The American Political Science Review, LXIII, 4,

December, 1142-1158.

_____. 1972. "Patron-Client Politics and Political Change in Southeast Asia." The American Political Science Review, LXVI, 1 March, 91-110.

SHAPIRO, DONALD H. 1972. "Taiwan's Election Campaign Is Lively and Loud." The New York Times, 23 December, 7.

"SHENG I-T'AN LAO-CHIANG LI CHIEN-HO, CH'U CH'IEN YU CH'U LI CHIEN-SHE T'AI-PEI HSIEN" [Provincial Legislative Veteran Li Chien-ho Contributes Money and Contributes Effort to Build Taipei County]. 1968. Cheng Lun. I, 1, 16 April, 3.

"SHENG I-YÜAN HOU-HSÜAN-YÜAN CH'ÜN-HSIANG" [Group Potrait of Provincial Assembly Candidates]. 1968. Lien-ho Pao (Taipei County local area edition), 29 March, 7.

"SHENG I-YÜAN PAI SHIH-WEI" [Provincial Assemblyman Pai Shih-wei]. 1968. Kuo-kuang Hua-k'an, 8 April, 1.

"SHENG I-YÜAN TS'U SHENG FU HSIA CHUNG-YANG, CHIANG-TI SHENG-CH'AN TAI-K'UAN LI-HSI" [Provincial Assemblymen Urge Provincial Government to Confer with Central Government, Lower Interest on Production Loans]. 1967. Lien-ho Pao, 27 May, 2.

SHIH T'U. 1967. "Hung T'iao Chüan T'u Ch'ung Lai Hu-shih Chang-hua" [Surveying Changhua County with a Tiger's Covetous Eyes, Hung T'iao Rides Forth in a Cloud of Dust, Staging a Comeback]. Tzu-chih, 162, 5 June, 7.

SHIH-TZU LUN-T'AN [Crusade Tribune], 1966.

SOLOMON, RICHARD H. 1969. "Mao's Effort to Reintegrate the Chinese Polity: Problems of Authority and Conflict in Chinese Social Processes." Chinese Communist Politics in Action. ed. A. D. Barnett. Seattle: University of Washington Press, 271-351.

_____. 1971. Mao's Revolution and the Chinese Political Culture. Berkeley: University of California Press.

SUN CHIA-CH'I 1961. Chiang Ching-kuo Ch'ieh Kuo Nei-mu [Behind-the-Scenes Report on How Chiang Ching-kuo Stole the Country]. Hsiang Kang: Tzu-li Ch'u-pan-she.

SUN I-CH'I. 1967. "Chung-Kuo Kuo-ming-tang T'ai-wan Sheng Tang-pu Wei-yüan Hsüan-chü Mu-hou" [Behind-the-Scenes Report on the Elections for the Taiwan Provincial Committee of the Chinese Nationalist Party]. Liao-wang Chou-k'an, 20, 29 July, 5-7.

SUN YAT-SEN. 1965. San Min Chu I [The Three Principles of the People]. Taipei: Ta Chung-kuo T'u-shu Yu-hsien Kung-szu.

TA-HSÜEH TSA-CHIH [The Intellectual], 1973.

"T'AI-CHUNG HSIEN-CHANG HSÜAN-CHÜ, CH'EN LIN LIANG-P'AI HSIANG-CHENG" [Taichung's Ch'en and Lin Factions Struggle over the County Mayor Election]. 1968. Tzu-chih, 175, 1 February, 9.

"T'AI-CHUNG HSIEN-CHANG T'I-MING, LAO-P'AI HSIN-P'AI KO HSIEN SHEN-T'UNG" [Taichung's "Old Faction" and "New Faction" Each Reveals Its Magical Powers in the Competition for the County Mayor Nomination]. 1967. Tzu-chih, 170, 1 November, 12.

"T'AI-CHUNG SHIH TANG-PU, TSUO FA-CH'U CHUNG-KAO" [Taichung City
Party Committee, Yesterday Issued Benevolent Warning]. 1968.
Lien-ho Pao (Taichung local area edition), 28 March, 7.
"T'AI-CHUNG SHIH-CHANG LIN TENG-CH'IU HUO-TE SZU TA CHU-LI, LIN
TING-SHAN HUI T'IEN FA LI" [Taichung City Mayor Lin Teng-ch'iu
Obtains Four Big Helping Hands, Lin Ting-shan Lacks Strength to
Propitiate Heaven]. 1968. Tzu-chih, Ko-hsin 181, 1 May, 5.
T'AI-PEI HSIEN TI-SZU-CHIEH SHENG I-YÜAN HSUAN-CHÜ KUNG-PAO [Taipei
County Fourth-Term Provincial Assemblymen Public Election Report].
1968. Taipei: T'ai-pei Hsien Ti-szu-chieh Sheng I-yüan chi Ti-liu-
chieh Hsien Chang Hsüan-chü Shih-wu-suo.
"T'AI-SHENG I-HUI, CH'ING CHIANG-TI CH'I-CH'E HAO-P'AI FEI" [Taiwan
Provincial Assembly Requests Lowering of Automobile License Plate
Fee]. 1967. Hsin-sheng Pao, 23 February, 4.
"TAIWAN WARNS CANDIDATES ON MUDSLINGING." 1972. The New York Times,
20 December, 4.
"T'AI-WAN CHING-HSÜAN-TE MI-MI WEN-CHIEN" [Secret Taiwan Election
Campaign Document]. 1974. Ming-pao Yüeh-k'an, 99, March, 95-
98.
T'AI-WAN KUANG-FU ERH-SHIH-NIEN [Two Decades of Taiwan's Restoration].
1966. ed. T'ai-wan Sheng Hsin-wen-ch'u [Taiwan Provincial
Department of Information]. Taipei: Chung-hua Ta-tien Pien-yin-hui.
"T'AI-WAN SHENG FANG-HAI HSÜAN-CHÜ PA-MIEN CH'Ü-TI PAN-FA" [Taiwan
Province Regulations for the Extirpation of Harmful Election
Practices through the Dismissal of Offenders from Office]. 1967.
T'ai-wan Sheng Ti-fang Tzu-chih Fa-kuei. Chung-hsing Hsin-ts'un:
T'ai-wan Sheng Cheng-fu Min-cheng-t'ing, 137-150.
T'AI-WAN SHENG HSIN-CHU HSIEN SHENG I-HUI I-YÜAN HSÜAN-CHÜ KUNG-
PAO [Taiwan Province, Hsin-chu County, Provincial Assemblymen
Public Election Report]. 1963. Hsin-chu: T'ai-wan Sheng Hsin-
chu Hsien Sheng I-yüan Hsüan-chü Shih-wu-suo.
T'AI-WAN SHENG I-HUI TI-SAN-CHIEH TI-PA-TZ'U TA-HUI I-YÜAN CHIH-
HSÜN YÜ PEN FU TA-AN HUI-PIEN [Records of the Taiwan Provincial
Assembly, Third Term, Eighth Plenary Session, Assemblymen's Inter-
pellations and This Government's Answers]. 1967. Chung-hsing
Hsin-ts'un: T'ai-wan Sheng Cheng-fu Mi-shu-ch'u.
"T'AI-WAN SHENG I-HUI TSU-CHIH KUEI-CH'ENG" [Taiwan Provincial
Assembly Organizational Regulations]. 1967. T'ai-wan Sheng
Ti-fang Tzu-chih Fa-kuei. Chung-hsing Hsin-ts'un: T'ai-wan Sheng
Cheng-fu Min-cheng-t'ing, 1-7.
"T'AI-WAN SHENG KO HSIEN HSIANG CHEN HSIEN-HSIA SHIH MIN TAI-
PIAO HUI TSU-CHIH KUEI-CH'ENG" [Taiwan Provincial Organizational
Regulations for People's Representative Assemblies in Each County's
Rural Districts, Townships, and County Subordinate Cities]. 1967.
T'ai-wan Sheng Ti-fang Tzu-chih Fa-kuei. Chung-hsing Hsin-ts'un:
T'ai-wan Sheng Cheng-fu Min-cheng-t'ing, 75-83.
"T'AI-WAN SHENG KO HSIEN SHIH SHIH-SHIH TI-FANG TZU-CHIH KANG-YAO"

287

[Essentials for the Implementation of Local Self-Government in Each County and City of Taiwan Province]. 1967. T'ai-wan Sheng Ti-fang Tzu-chih Fa-kuei. Chung-hsing Hsin-ts'un: T'ai-wan Sheng Cheng-fu Min-cheng-t'ing, 50-63.

"T'AI-WAN SHENG KO HSIEN SHIH TS'UN LI MIN TA-HUI SHIH-SHIH PAN-FA" [Implementation Regulations for Rural Village and Urban Precinct People's Assemblies in Each County and City of Taiwan Province]. 1967. T'ai-wan Sheng Ti-fang Tzu-chih Fa-kuei. Chung-hsing Hsin-ts'un: T'ai-wan Sheng Cheng-fu Min-cheng-t'ing, 152-164.

"T'AI-WAN SHENG SAN-CHIEH SHENG I-YÜAN HSÜAN-CHÜ HOU-HSÜAN-YÜAN TIEN-CHIANG-LU" [Roll Call of Election Candidates for Third-Term Taiwan Provincial Assemblymen]. 1963. Ti-fang Tzu-chih, 60-61, 19 April, 14-24.

T'AI-WAN SHENG T'AI-PEI SHIH TI-SAN-CHIEH SHENG I-HUI I-YÜAN HSÜAN-CHÜ KUNG-PAO [Taiwan Province, Taipei City, Third-Term Provincial Assemblymen Public Election Report]. 1963. Taipei: T'ai-wan Sheng T'ai-pei Shih Sheng I-yüan Hsüan-chü Shih-wu-suo.

T'AI-WAN SHENG TI-FANG TZU-CHIH CHIH-YAO [An Introduction to Local Self-Government in the Province of Taiwan]. 1965. ed. Hou Ch'ang. Taipei: T'ai-wan Sheng Ti-fang Tzu-chih Chih-yao Pien-chi Wei-yüan-hui/Chung-hua Ta-tien Pien-yin-hui.

T'AI-WAN SHENG TI-FANG TZU-CHIH FA-KUEI [Local Self-Government Statutes of Taiwan Province]. 1967. Chung-hsing Hsin-ts'un: T'ai-wan Sheng Cheng-fu Min-cheng-t'ing.

T'AI-WAN SHENG, YÜN-LIN HSIEN, TI-SAN-CHIEH SHENG I-YÜAN HSÜAN-CHÜ KUNG-PAO [Taiwan Province, Yün-lin County, Third-Term Provincial Assemblymen Public Election Report]. 1963. Tou-liu: T'ai-wan Sheng Yün-lin Hsien Sheng I-yüan Hsüan-chü Shih-wu-suo.

TAN, CHESTER C. 1971. Chinese Political Thought in the Twentieth Century. Garden City, N.Y.: Doubleday and Company, Anchor Books.

T'ANG YING-YÜ. 1968. "Chia-i Hsien-chang Hsüan-ch'ing-te Hsin Hsing-shih" [New Trends in the Chia-i County Mayoral Election Situation]. Lien-ho Pao (Chia-i County local area edition), 29 March, 7.

"T'AO-HSIEN FU-I-CHANG HSÜAN-CHÜ, CHING-CHENG CHI CHI-LIEH" [T'ao-yüan County Deputy Speaker Election Competition Extremely Heated]. 1968. Lien-ho Pao (T'ao-yüan local area edition), 22 February, 7.

"T'AO-HSIEN HSIA-CHIEH CHENG-FU-I-CHANG HSÜAN-CHÜ, CHAN HUANG-SHUN K'O SHUN-LI TANG-HSÜAN, HSÜ SAN-T'UNG HSÜ CH'ÜAN-LI FU-TAO" [Elections for Next Term's T'ao-yüan County Speaker and Deputy Speaker, Chan Huang-shun Can Easily Be Elected, Hsü San-t'ung Needs All the Help He Can Get]. 1968. Lien-ho Pao (T'ao-yüan local area edition), 16 February, 7.

T'AO-YÜAN HSIEN I-HUI TI-LIU-CHIEH TI-CH'I-TZ'U TA-HUI CHI TI-CHIU, SHIH-TZ'U LIN-SHIH TA-HUI I-SHIH-LU [T'ao-yüan County Assembly, Plenary Meeting Records for the Sixth Term, Seventh Session, and Ninth and Tenth Special Sessions]. 1967. T'ao-

288

yüan: T'ao-yüan Hsien I-hui Mi-shu-ch'u.

TARDIO, FELIX, 1966. Mr. Tardio Sees Taiwan. Taiwan: Felix Tardio.

TI-FANG TZU-CHIH [Local Self-Government], 1963, 1968.

TIEN HUNG-MAO. 1975. "Taiwan in Transition: Prospects for Socio-Political Change." The China Quarterly, 64, December, 615-644.

TOWNSEND, JAMES R. 1967. Political Participation in Communist China. Berkeley: University of California Press.

TS'AO MIN. 1971. Lun Fu-hsing Chung-hua Wen-hua Chi-ko Szu Shih Erh Fei-te Kuan-nien Chi Ch'i Fu-hsing-chih Tao [Discussing Some Concepts that Appear Correct But Are Mistaken in Regard to China's Cultural Renaissance and Discussing the Method of China's Cultural Renaissance]. Taipei: Chiao-yü-pu Wen-hua-chü.

"TS'U-CH'ING CHENG-FU LI-TING, PAO-HU NUNG-YEH CHENG-TS'E [Urge Government to Establish Policy to Protect Agriculture]. 1967. Chung-yang Jih-pao, 17 February, 2.

TSUNG HSIN et al. 1968. "Fa-shih Mei Ts'uo Yüan-tzu T'ang, Teng T'ai Tzu Ch'eng Lao-yu-t'iao" [Swears to Not Having Made Dumpling Soup, Mounts Rostrum and Calls Self Sly Old Fox]. Lien-ho Pao (Taichung local area edition), 17 January, 7.

"TS'UNG 'LUO-PEN' NAO-CHÜ LUN TZU-YU YÜ CHIH-HSÜ" [In View of the "Streaking" Farce, a Discussion of Freedom and Discipline]. 1974. Chung-yang Jih-pao, 11 March, 2.

TUAN-MU HSI. 1968. "T'ao-se Chiu-fen K'un-jao Sheng I-yüan" [Conflicts of Love and Sex Disturb Provincial Assemblymen]. Liao-wang Chou-k'an, 43, 13 January, 14-15.

"TUO-SHAO JEN 'YÜ T'UI PU TE'?" [How Many People "Want to Retire But Cannot"?]. 1967. Lien-ho Pao, 19 May, 7.

TZU-CHIH [Self-Government], 1967-1968.

VAN GULIK, ROBERT. 1960. The Chinese Lake Murders. New York: Harper & Brothers; New York: Avon Books.

"VETERANS ADJUST TO TAIWAN LIFE." 1969. The New York Times, 20 July, 11.

WAHLKE, J. C.; EULAU, H.; BUCHANAN, W.; and FERGUSON, C. L. 1962. The Legislative System. New York: John Wiley and Sons.

WANG CHIEN-CHIH. 1968. "Huang Ch'en Sen Huo Chih-ch'ih Ch'u-ma, T'ai-hsi Kung-szu Li-ch'ang Wei Pien" [Huang Ch'en Sen Obtains Support to Enter the Race, the Position of the T'ai-hsi Company Remains Unchanged]. Lien-ho Pao (Yün-lin County local area edition), 15 March, 7.

WANG KUO-YÜAN. 1973. "Lun Hsien-hsing T'ui-hsiu Chih-tu" [Discussing the Current Retirement System]. Chung-kuo Jen-shih Hsing-cheng, VI, 12, 15 December, 4-6.

"WANG SUNG CH'IUNG-YING, K'ANG JIH CHU KUNG-HSÜN, CHIEN T'AI TSAI CH'U-LI" [Wang Sung Ch'iung-ying Contributed Meritorious Service in the Battle against Japan, Now in Building Taiwan She Again Contributes Effort]. 1968. Cheng Lun, 16 April, 3.

WANG YA-TUNG. 1968. "Cheng-tuo Cheng-fu I-chang T'i-ming. T'ou

Ch'ing-kuo Chieh Hsiung Hsin Po Po" [Battling for Speaker and
Deputy Speaker Nominations, Nan-t'ou County's Vegetable and Fruit
Interests Intensely Ambitious]. Lien-ho Pao (Nan-t'ou County
local area edition), 10 February, 7.
WEI YUNG. 1974. "A Methodological Critique of Current Studies
on Chinese Political Culture." Unpublished paper prepared for
delivery at the XXVI Annual Meeting of the Association for Asian
Studies, Boston, 1-3 April.
WEINER, MYRON. 1965. "India: Two Political Cultures." Political
Culture and Political Development. ed. L. W. Pye. and S. Verba.
Princeton: Princeton University Press, 199-244.
WILSON, RICHARD W. 1970. Learning to Be Chinese: The Political
Socialization of Children in Taiwan. Cambridge, Mass: The M.I.T.
Press.
WOLF, ERIC R. 1966a. "Kinship, Friendship, and Patron-Client
Relations in Complex Societies." The Social Anthropology of Complex
Societies. ed. M. Banton. A.S.A. Monographs, no. 4. London:
Tavistock Publications, 1-22.
_____. 1966b. Peasants. Englewood Cliffs, N.J.: Prentice-Hall.
WOLF, MARGERY. 1968. The House of Lim. New York: Appleton-Century-
Crofts.
WU-TI. 1963. "Ku-ko Chih-shih" [Jottings of Ku-ko]. Ti-fang
Tzu-chih, 60-61, 19 April, 16.
YANG, C. K. 1959. A Chinese Village in Early Communist Transi-
tion. Cambridge, Mass.: The M.I.T. Press.
_____. 1961. Religion in Chinese Society. Berkeley: University
of California Press.
"YANG CHIN-HU CH'U-CH'I CHIH-SHENG CH'EN WU-CHANG" [Yang Chin-hu
with Novel Tactics Defeats Ch'en Wu-chang]. 1968. Tzu-chih,
Ko-hsin 181, 1 May, 4.
YANG I-FENG. 1962, Chung-kuo Ti-fang Tzu-chih Hsin-lun [New
Discussion of China's Local Self-Government]. Taipei: Cheng-chung
Shu-chü.
YANG LIEN-SHENG. 1956. "Great Families of Eastern Han." Chinese
Social History. ed. E-tu Zen Sun and J. De Francis. Washington,
D.C.: American Council of Learned Societies, 103-134.
YANG, MARTIN M. C. 1970. Socio-Economic Results of Land Reform
in Taiwan. Honolulu: East-West Center Press.
YEN CHANG-HSÜN. 1967a. "Cheng-shou Chiao-yü Chüan Wen-t'i, Tsai
I-hui Chung Tou Ch'üan-tzu" [Levying Educational Tax, Assembly
Continues Circling Problem without Directly Confronting It].
Lien-ho Pao (Taipei County local area edition), 18 May, 7.
_____. 1967b. "Su Ch'ing-po Ch'i Kao I-chao" [Su Ch'ing-po
Is One Move Ahead]. Lien-ho Pao (Taipei County local area edition),
24 July, 7.
YING CHEN-KUO. 1967. "Hsiu-hui Chiao-she-te Mu-hou" [Report from
behind the Scenes concerning the Recess in Order to Negotiate

Strategy]. <u>Lien-ho Pao</u>, 2 June, 7.

YÜ JEN. 1963. "T'ieh-mien Wu-szu, Min-chung Hou-she--Huang Chan-an" [Principles of Iron, the People's Voice--Huang Chan-an]. <u>Ti-fang Tzu-chih</u>, 60-61, 19 April, 27.

YÜ YING-CHIH. 1968. "I P'iao Chi K'o Tang-hsüan, Le-te Tzu-tsai Yu-hsien" [Needs Only One Vote to be Elected, Happily Carefree and Leisurely]. <u>Lien-ho Pao</u> (Taichung local area edition), 12 January, 7.

YÜN I. 1963. "Wu K'uei Yü Hsüan-min-te Wang Kuo-hsiu" [No Reason for Shame before Her Constituents, Wang Kuo-hsiu]. <u>Ti-fang Tzu-chih</u>, 60-61, 19 April, 26.

YÜN-LIN HSIEN, TI-SAN-CHIEH SHENG I-YÜAN HSÜAN-CHÜ CHIEH-KUO PIAO [Yün-lin County, Third-Term Provincial Assemblymen Election Results Chart]. 1963. Tou-liu: Yün-lin Hsien Cheng-fu.

INDEX

aborigines, 1, 5, 119, 223, 231, 267
aggression, emotional, 39-46
Agriculture and Forestry Committee, 4-5, 224-225
anthropological approach, 7, 38, 97, 181, 237-238
association-assemblymen, 221-222, 224, 228
associational interest groups, 198-203, 209, 212, 230
authority figures, 39, 42-50, 104-105, 108-109, 143-144, 149, 163, 202, 209, 230, 245
authority structures, 191-192
bribery, 111, 128, 136, 206
brotherhoods. See ceremonial brotherhoods
budget, assembly influence on, 3, 26, 58, 63-65, 89, 91-92, 129, 186, 225-226
Bureau of Inspection, 37, 67, 184-185
business, 3, 5, 119, 181, 189, 193-194, 197, 200-202, 206-207, 212, 220-223, 227-229, 231
    people dependent on a, 190-193, 198, 200, 209, 214
business association-assemblymen, 226, 229
businessmen, Taiwanese, 12, 15
businessmen-assemblymen, 2, 31, 34, 72-73, 130, 181-193, 197-198, 222, 224, 227-229, 234
businessmen-politicians, 55-56, 87, 107
ceremonial brotherhoods, 6-7, 166-172, 197, 200-203
Chiang Ching-kuo, 13, 17, 85
Chiang K'ai-shek, 17-18, 77, 84, 95

ch'in-ch'i, 140-142. Also see in-laws; relatives
China Democratic Socialist Party (Min She Tang), 32, 87
Ch'ing Nien Tang (Young China Party), 87, 90
Chu Wan-ch'eng, 224-226
Churchill, Winston, 183
clans, 6, 143-148, 167, 200-203. Also see surnames
clients, 102, 105, 108, 112, 157, 161, 170, 193, 200-201
coal mine owners, 114, 119, 130, 191, 223, 225, 234
coal miners, 191
Communist China, 1, 8, 12
Communists, 18, 20, 22-23, 25, 60, 74, 77-78, 80, 213
compromise, 47, 61, 95, 218-219
conflicts of interest, 184-186, 219, 229
confrontation approach, 7, 181, 237
consensus, 101, 218-219
constitution, 19-20, 23-24, 26, 28, 54
contractual relationships, 102, 104, 108
Control Yuan, 20-22, 83
co-optation, 33, 50-51
corruption, 111-113, 124-128, 136, 158, 171, 206, 242-244
cross-class relationships, 202-203, 243
cross-kin associations, 143-145, 149-153, 159-160, 181
De Tocqueville, Alexis, 210-211
democracy and science, 60-64, 239
dependency relationships, 104, 202-203, 163, 209, 230, 242
displacement, psychological, 40
distinguishing traits, 102-105, 138-139, 144, 148, 153, 159-

167, 172, 181, 202, 209, 241
Liu Chin-yüeh, 224, 226
liu-mangs, 170-171
lobbying, 5, 7, 181, 185, 189,
    195-198, 204-205, 212, 220-
    221, 229-230
  by provincial government
    personnel, 57-59, 205
  "reluctant," 197, 204
Mah-jongg, political, 4, 206
Mandarin, 3, 70, 225
mainlanders, types of, 11-17,
    32-33
mediation, 38, 44-45, 47-51
Minnan, 1, 160-161
modernization, 44, 142, 148,
    152, 159, 181, 191, 193,
    195, 198-203, 209, 212, 243
money and politics, 68, 86-
    87, 107, 112, 125-126, 128-
    129, 134, 136, 139-140, 171,
    174, 177, 186-187, 191, 204,
    242
mountain people, 11. Also see
    mainlanders
National Assembly, 19, 21-22,
    82, 119
Nationalist Party. See KMT
newspapers, 3, 5, 8, 30-32,
    78, 89, 93-94, 99-100, 188,
    206, 232
noncooperation, right of, 215,
    219-220
nonelite electoral politicians,
    54, 63-65, 67, 97, 100-101,
    113-114, 196, 238, 241-245
nonfaction electoral poli-
    ticians, 86-87, 89-90
non-KMT electoral politicians,
    22, 30-35, 53, 55, 76, 86-
    90, 94-96, 124, 217-218
non-Western governing elites,
    60-64, 66, 239-245,
obligation, 108-109, 113.
    Also see jen-ch'ing
obstruction, right, of, 215,
    219-220

opposition. See governing elite's
    opposition
particularism, 102-104, 198, 202-
    203, 242-244
patron-client relationships. See
    clients; patrons
patrons, 102, 105, 108, 161, 170,
    192-193, 200-203, 241, 243
patronage, 49, 51, 77, 106, 113,
    127-131, 192, 202
peer (status-equal) relationships,
    42-45, 48, 168-170, 198,
    201-203, 209, 229, 230, 242
people's associations, 119, 181,
    197-200, 203, 209, 212-214,
    217, 220-231
personalization, 108, 163. Also
    see legitimization of support-
    ive-exchange dyads
pharmacists, 107, 184, 223, 234
"ping-pong" diplomacy, 8, 84
platform statements, political,
    54, 228, 233, 270, 272
political bossism, 113-114
political parties, 183, 195-196,
    221
prestige, 123-126, 128-129, 131,
    174, 217, 241-242
pride, 60, 123, 125, 130, 239
projection, psychological, 40-41
Provincial Assembly
    committee chairmen, 67-68, 268
    committees, 3-5, 91, 123,
    183-184, 189, 224-225, 268
    deputy speaker, 2, 5, 36, 67-
    68, 161, 174-178, 190
    factions. See faction(s)
    interpellation, 26, 58-59, 63,
    88-93, 118, 120, 122, 189, 228,
    233, 269, 272
    KMT Party Group Executive
    Committee, 67
    KMT party leadership, 2, 5,
    9, 37, 67
    leadership, 2, 5, 67-68, 72
    legislative power of, 90-91
    professionalization of, 91

quorum, 89
resolutions, 3, 91-93, 118-120, 122, 177-178, 189, 228, 233, 267-268, 270, 272
roll call votes, 89
speaker, 2, 5, 36, 67-68, 161, 177-178, 190, 226
provincial assemblymen
aborigine, 1, 5, 231, 267
competence of, 63-66, 69-70, 81, 91-93, 177-178, 238-239,
broker-role orientation of, 193
Hakka, 1, 4, 268
half-mainlander, 1, 5, 71-73, 268
half-mountain, 1, 5, 71-73, 268
independent KMT, 2, 5, 79
as interest-group agents, 7, 181-184, 188-190, 197-198, 200, 204, 221, 230
of Japanese background, 1, 5, 86
KMT, 2, 5, 79, 86-89
mainlander, 1, 16-17, 69-73, 79, 268
non-KMT, 2, 5, 73-74, 78-79, 85-93, 218, 268
old age, 4-5
poor, 2, 114, 186
protecting personal interests, 181-192, 219-221, 234
subject-matter experts, 2, 5, 269
Taiwanese, 70
Taiwanese KMT, 72-73, 78
young, 4, 5, 268
provincial assemblywomen, 2, 5, 232, 234, 268
Provincial Senate, 176
Provisional Provincial Assembly, 176
psychological approach, 38, 77, 181, 237
psychological defense mecha-

nism, 40-42, 45
public associations. See people's associations
relatives, 3, 5, 46, 72, 112, 123, 140-143, 149, 157, 164-166, 188, 200-201, 203. Also see ch'in-ch'i; in-laws
repression, psychological, 40-42, 45
resolutions. See Provincial Assembly
retirement, 12-13
role differentiation, 183, 195-198, 221, 230
rule-making, 183, 196-197, 221
scarce resources, 59, 173, 177-178, 201, 203, 229
science and democracy, 60-64, 239
secret police, 4-6, 28-30, 54, 66, 84
security system, 104-109, 116, 130, 133, 136-137, 141-143, 148-149, 162, 176, 181, 191-193, 200-203, 209, 219, 229-230, 241-243,
shaming, 39, 41, 45-46
shared traits, 102-105, 138, 144-155, 158-160, 164-167, 175, 198
Shieh Tung-min. See Hsieh Tung-min
social disorder, 39-44, 48, 61-62
social status, 126, 165, 169-171
socialization, 39, 60, 62, 80, 105, 107, 201-202, 238-239
Sun Yat-sen, 17-19
supportive-exchange dyads, 102-105, 109, 111, 113, 137-138, 144, 147-149, 153-155, 157-160, 163-167, 172-173, 175
Surnames, 6, 47, 102, 143-151, 153-154, 157, 164-166, 172, 175. Also see clans
sworn brotherhoods. See ceremonial brotherhoods

About the Author

Arthur J. Lerman is an assistant professor of political science at Baruch College, City University of New York. He has
taught at a number of other universities,
including the University of Missouri-Colum-
bia and Yeshiva University. He received a
B.A. from Hobart College in 1963, an M.A.
from Princeton University in 1966, and a
Ph.D. from Princeton University in 1972.

Between 1966 and 1968, while a student at the Inter-University Program for
Chinese Language Studies in Taiwan, the
author did much of the research for this
book. He revisited Taiwan in 1974.